Navajo-English Dictionary

Navajo-English Dictionary

Leon Wall
and
William Morgan

HIPPOCRENE BOOKS, INC.
New York

Originally compiled in 1958 by Leon Wall and William Morgan of the Bureau of Indian Affairs, Division of Education, United States Department of Interior.

Hippocrene paperback edition, 1994

Thirteenth printing, 2016.

Cover photograph: Navajo blanket; copyright © National Museum of the American Indian.

For information, address:
HIPPOCRENE BOOKS, INC.
171 Madison Avenue
New York, NY 10016I
www.hippocrenebooks.com

ISBN-10: 0-7818-0247-4
ISBN-13: 978-0-7818-0247-5

CONTENTS

Preface
7

The Sound System of Navajo
11

Navajo-English Dictionary
15

PREFACE

This Navajo-English dictionary is presented with the hope that the vocabulary may be of aid to Navajos who are learning English as well as to non-Navajos who are interested in acquiring some knowledge of the Navajo language. The authors have listed Navajo vocabulary and have attempted to provide definitions in simple, easily understood English.

Grateful acknowledgment is made to all the people who contributed their knowledge and time to the development of this dictionary.

Navajo-English Dictionary

The Sound System of Navajo

VOWELS:

The vowels have continental values. They are as follows, the first example being a Navajo word, the second the closest approximation to that sound in English. Example:

a gad (juniper) father
e 'e'e'aah (west) met
i sis (belt) sit
o hosh (cactus) note

Vowels may be either long or short in duration, the long duration vowel being indicated by a doubling of the letter. This never affects the quality of the vowel, except that the long duration i is always pronounced as in the English word **see**. Examples:

sis (belt) the vowel is short.
siziiz (my belt) the second vowel sound is of long duration.

Vowels with a hook (ǫ) beneath the letters are nasalized. This means that some of the breath passes through the nose when sound is produced. All vowels following **n** are nasalized though not marked. Examples:

bizęęs (his, her wart)
'áshįįh (salt)
tsinaabąąs (wagon)
bįįh (deer)

A little mark above the letter (ó), indicates that the voice rises on that letter. Examples:

ni (you) ——ní (he says)

'azee' (medicine)   ———'azéé' (mouth)
nilį̃ (he is)   ———nilí (you are)
doo (not)   ———dóó (and)

When only the first element of a long vowel has a mark above it the tone falls. If only the last element is marked the tone rises. Examples:

a   (short, low) as a in father.
ą́   (short, high)
ą   (short, low, nasal)
ą́   (short, high, nasal)

aa   (long, low)
áá   (long, high)   áa (falling) aá (rising)
ąą   (long, low, nasal)
ą́ą́   (long, high, nasal)   ą́ą (falling) ąą́ (rising)

e   (short, low) as e in met.
é   (short, high)
ę   (short, low, nasal)
ę́   (short, high, nasal)

ee   (long, low)
éé   (long, high)   ée (falling) eé (rising)
ęę   (long, low, nasal)
ę́ę́   (long, high, nasal)   ę́ę (falling) ęę́ (rising)

i   (short, low) as i in sit.
í   (short, high)
į   (short, low, nasal)
į́   (short, high, nasal)

ii   (long, low) as ee of English word see.
íí   (long, high)   íi (falling) ií (rising)
įį   (long, low, nasal)
į́į́   (long, high, nasal)   į́į (falling) įį́ (rising)

o   (short, low) as o in note.
ó   (short, high)
ǫ   (short, low, nasal)
ǫ́   (short, high, nasal)

oo (long, low)
óó (long, high)   óo (falling) oó (rising)
ǫǫ (long, low, nasal)   ǫ́ǫ (falling) ǫǫ́ (rising)
ǫ́ǫ́ (long, high, nasal)   ǫ́ǫ (falling) ǫǫ́ (rising)

DIPHTHONGS:
The diphthongs are as follows:

ai   hai   (winter)
aai   shínaaí   (my elder brother)

ao   daolyé   (they are called)
aoo   'aoo'   (yes)

ei   'ei   (that one)
eii   'ádaat'éii   (that which are)

oi   deesdoi   (it is warm, weather)
ooi   Tséhootsooí   (Ft. Defiance, Arizona)

CONSONANTS:
(') this is the most common consonantal sound in Navajo, and is called a glottal stop. It sounds like the hiatus between the two elements of the English exclamation oh! oh! and hunh unh. In actual speech the difference between **Johnnie yearns** and **Johnnie earns,** is that the latter has a glottal closure between the two words. More examples:

ha'a'aah   (east)
'a'áán   (a hole in the ground)
'abe'   (milk)
yá'át'ééh   (it is good)
b   bááh   (bread) — like **p** in spot

ch   chizh   (firewood(— like **ch** in church
ch'   ch'ah   (hat. cap)

d   dibé   (sheep) — like **t** in stop
dl   dlǫ́ǫ́'   (prairie dog) — something like **gl** in
                                              glow
dz   dził   (mountains)

g   gah   (rabbit) — like **k** in sky
gh   'aghaa'   (wool)

h   háadi   (where?) *

hw   hwíídéeltǫ'   (slippery place) — like **wh** in
when

j   jádí   (antelope) — like **j** in jug

k   ké   (shoes) — like **k** in kitten

k'   k'aa'   (arrow)

kw   kw'é   (right here) — like **qu** in quick

l   lájish   (gloves) — like **l** in late

ł   łid (smoke) — like **th** in athlete

m   mósí   (cat) — like **m** in most

n   naadą́ą́'   (corn) — like **n** in new

s   sin   (song) — like **s** in song

sh   shash   (bear) — like **sh** in she

t   tin   (ice)

t'   t'eesh   (charcoal)

tł   tłah   (salve, ointment)

tł'   tł'ízí   (goat)

ts   tsah   (needle) — like **ts** in hats

ts'   ts'ah   (sagebrush)

w   Wááshindoon   (Washington) — like **w** in
Washington

x   yiyiisxį   (he killed him)

y   yá   (sky) — like **y** in yellow

z   zas   (snow) — like **z** in zeora

zh   bízhi'   (his name) — like **s** in pleasure

* h — represents the sound of **ch** in German **ich,**
as well as that of **h** in English word **have.** Ordinarily,
both of the sounds are written **h,** but when **h** follows **s**
it is necessary to distinguish the resulting **sh** sequence
from the digraph **sh.** This is accomplished by sub-
stitution of **x** for the **h.** Thus: **yiyiisxį** (he killed him)
for **yiyiishį.** X is also employed to distinguish between
such forms as **łitso** and **łitsxo,** the latter being more
strongly aspirated than the former.

- A -

'aa', well. (anticipation, as when a person approaches one as though to speak, but says nothing.)

'aa'adiniih, veneral disease.

'aa 'ádoolnííł, it will be opened.

'aa 'áhályáanii, body guard.

'aa'q'ii, magpie.

'aa 'ályaa, it was opened.

'aa 'ályaa, bich'į', it was opened to them; they were invited.

'a'áán, hole in the ground; tunnel; cave; burrow.

'aa 'át'é, it is open.

'aa 'át'éego, since it was open.

'á'ádaat'éhígíí, the fundamentals, elements.

'áádahojoost'įįd, they quit, backed out, desisted, surrendered.

'áádahoost'įįd, t'óó, they gave up, surrendered.

'aa dahwiinít'įįį', into court (a place where justice is judicially administered.)

'áádéé', from there (a remote place).

'aadéé', from there.

'aa deet'á, transfer (of property, or ownership).

'áádeisįįd, they discontinued, stopped, or ended it.

'aadi, there.

'áadi, there, over there (a remote place).

'áádįįł, it is progressively dwindling away; disappearing.

'áadiish, there? thereat?

'aa díneest'á, they increased, multiplied. ('aa has the meaning of extension or spread.)

'aadóó, from there.

'áádóó, from there on; and then; and; from that point on; from there. **Shash yiyiisxį 'áádóó shi níseł'ah.** He killed the bear and I skinned it.

'áádóó bik'iji', after that.

'áádoolzjįł, it will be discontinued.

'áádeessįįł, I shall discontinue it.

'aahasti', care; respect; care or respect toward a fragile object; fragility.

'aqh 'azlá, pawn.

'aqh dahaz'á, illness, sickness, an ailment.

'aqh dah dzisnilgo, they were also included; since they also were included.

'aqh dahoyooł'aałii, disease.

'aqh dah sitáni, license plate.

'aqh háá'á, debt.

'aqh ha'ajeeh tó da'diisoołígíí, chicken pox.

'aqh háát'i, fringes (saddle).

'aqh naaznilée, the pawns.

'aqh nahóókaad, disappointment.

'aqh ni'it'aah, cast (plaster).

'aa hojoobá'i, poor.

'aahoolzhíish, to be one's turn.

'aqh sita', cervical.

'á'áhwiinít'į, kindness.

'aa hwiinít'į, trial (at law), molestation.

'aa hwiinít'į bá hooghan, courthouse.

'aahwiinít'įįgo, during the court session.

'aa hwiinít'įįhígíí, the court session that is to come up.

'ą́ą́hyiłk'as, body chill.

'áaji', as far as that point; up to there; toward there; to that point and no farther.

'áají, in that direction; on that side.

'aak'ee, fall, autumn.

'aak'eedą́ą́', last fall, last autumn.

'aak'eego, in, or during the fall or autumn months.

'aak'eejį', near or close to the fall season.

'aa kwáánííł, it is expanding; it is getting bigger.

'áá̧ł dabidii'ni, we (pl.) mean by that.

'áá̧ł deiłni, they mean by that.

'aa'na' (ee'na'), yah, he crawled in (an enclosure, as a hole, house, etc.).
'aaniigóó, t'áá, the truth.
'aaniinii, that which is true.
'aanii, t'áá, it is true; truly; really; verily.
'aanii, t'áásh, is it so; is it true?
'áánitigii, that which is occurring; the happening; the event.
'a'át'e', sin; injustice; meanness.
'áát'įįdée, what he did; his aforementioned act.
'aa yílyáii, donation.
'abąąh náát'i', border strand (of the warp of a rug).
'abaní, buckskin.
'abe', milk, teat, dug, pap.
'abe' 'astse', udder, mammary gland.
'abe'é, ch'il, milkweed.
'abéézh, there is boiling.
'abid, stomach.
'abida'diisdzil, they were forced to.........
'abid dijooli, duodenum.
'ábi'diilyaa, he was made to be.........
'ábidiiniid, I said to him.
'ábidini, you say thus to him.
'ábidini, ha'át'ii shą', what do you mean?
'abi'doogi, he was hauled away.
'abi'dool'a', he was sent; he was commanded to go.
'ábi'dool'įįdii, t'áá 'aanii bee, that with which he was really harmed.
'abi'doolt'e'igii, yah, the fact that he was imprisoned.
'abi'doolt'e', yah, he was jailed, confined (as within an enclosure), imprisoned.
'ábidooldįįt, it will annihilate them. 'ábidooldįįtgo, since it will annihilate.
'ábidoo'niidée, what he was told; what he had been told.
'ábiilaa, it made him.
'ábiłni, he says to him.
'abini, morning.
'abinidóó, from the morning on.........
'abinigo, in the morning.
'ábi'niidįįd, it started to dwindle; it began to run out.

'ábisdįįdii, that which caused them to disappear, or become extinct.
'ábizhdiiniid, he said to him.
'abizhí, paternal uncle or aunt.
'ábizh'niilaa, he started to make it.
'ach'á, hunger for meat.
'ách'ą́ąh, in front of.
'ach'ą́ąh na'adá, protection.
'ách'ą́ąh neilyéii, that which he protects himself by.
'achaan 'aghádaana'igii, diarrhea.
'achaan yítł'is, piles (hemorrhoids).
'achą́'áshk'azhí, kidney.
'achą́'áshk'azhí dideeshchii', nephritis.
'ach'áhayah, armpit.
'achą́ hwiidéeni, addiction.
'acháshjish, diaphragm (in anatomy).
'ach'é'é, daughter, niece (daughter of one's sister) (female speaking).
'ach'é'édą́ą́', one's yard, or dooryard.
'acheii ('achaii), maternal grandfather.
'achí, the act of giving birth.
'ách'į', toward oneself.
'ach'ii', intestine.
'ach'ii' bits'áni'nisą́, appendix (a growth from the intestines).
'ach'íídíil, large intestine.
'ach'ii' dootł'izhí, small intestine.
'áchįįh, nose, snout.
'áchįįshtah, nostril, sinus.
'áchįshtah 'az'ą́, adenoid.
'áchįįshtah 'aztį, adenoid.
'áchįįshtah dóó 'adáyi' hashch'íí', catarrh.
'achįįshtah nahasdzání, sinus.
'achįįshtah nahasdzání nanichaad, sinus trouble.
'ach'į' nahwii'ná, to have trouble; to have difficulty; to suffer.
'ach'į' na'ilyé, payment; to receive pension.
'ach'į' niná'ilyá, repayment.
'acho', genitalia (male).
'achó, maternal great-grandfather.
'acho' biyęęzhii, testicle.
'acho' bizis, prepuce.
'ach'ooni, comrade, partner.
'ach'oozhlaa', elbow.

'ach'ozh, calf of the leg.

'achxoshtł'óól, cinch, surcingle; girdle for a horse.

'ada', nephew (son of one's sister) (male speaking).

'ádá, for self (myself, yourself, etc.).

'ádaa, to, about-self, concerning, to oneself. 'ádaa 'áhojilyá, he takes care of himself; he is on the alert.

'adaa', lip.

'adą́ą́dą́ą́', yesterday.

'ádaadahalni'go, when they tell about themselves.

'ádaadįįh, they are disappearing, about to disappear.

'ádaadin, there are none of them; 'they are non-existent; they are absent.

'ádaadinigíí, the ones that are gone; absentees; decedents.

'adą́ą́dit'áhí, stopper, lid, cap.

'ádaadzaa, they did. 'ádaadzaa yę́ęgi 'át'éego, like they did. 'ádaadzaaigi 'át'éego, like they did.

'ádąąh, upon oneself. 'ádąąh ádahast'ą́, he committed a crime; made a serious mistake. 'ádąąh dahosist'ą́, I committed a crime.

'ádąąh dah hast'áanii, the defendant, law breaker.

'áda'ahisdįįd, they annihilated one another.

'ádaahłe', you (pl.) make them; build them; construct them.

'ádaaht'į, you (pl.) are; you are doing.

'ádaal'į, they are made; they are being manufactured.

'ádaal'iinii, the things that are made.

'ádaal'inigíí, their making it; those that are made.

'ádaalyaa, they were made. 'ádaalyáá dóó bik'iji', after they were made.

'ada'ałgo'ii, tó ko'í yiká, the oil drillers.

'ádaałts'íísí, they are small; they are little.

'ádaałts'íísígíí, those that are small, short.

'ádaałts'óózí, they are long, slender. 'ádaałts'óózigo, since they are long, slender. 'áłts'óózí, it is long, slender.

'ádaa nahasni', he told all about himself.

'ádaaní, they say thus; they say; they are mewing, croaking, oinking, mooing, etc.

'ádaaniidí, they are new.

'ádaaniigo, they are saying thus.

'ádaanii łeh, they (customarily) say thus.

'ádaaníiłgóó, t'áá, whatever they do.

'ádaa ntséskees, I am thinking about myself.

'ádaa ntsídaakees, they think, or are thinking about themselves.

'ádaasdįįd, they went out of existence, become extinct, vanished, faded away.

'ádaasdįįdę́ęgóó, to where they had disappeared, vanished.

'ádaasdįįdgo, when they became extinct.

'ádaasdįįdigíí, those that disappeared, vanished.

'ádaashłaa, I made them.

'ádaaszóólí, they are light (in weight).

'ádaat'é, they are thus.

'ádaat'é, 'ayóó, they are enormous, huge, remarkable.

'ádaat'ée, they are.........

'ádaat'eegi, their characteristics; their dispositions; their qualities.

'ádaat'éhę́ęgi 'át'éego, since they are like they used to be.

'ádaat'éhígíí, those that are.........

'ádaat'éhígíí, 'ał'qq, those that are different; the fact that they are different.

'ádaat'éii, such as.

'ádaat'į, they do, did; they are; they are doing. Díí 'ádaat'į béeso bá hooghandóó béeso deineez'įį'. They are the ones who robbed the bank.

'ádaat'įį, doo—da, they did not do it.

'ádáát'įįd, they acted, did something.

'ádáát'įįdígíí, what they did.

'ádáát'įįdii, those that did it; those that acted.

'ádáát'įįd, yá, they acted for them.

'ádaat'įįłgóó, what they are in the process of doing?

'ádaat'ínígí 'át'éego, acting or doing likewise; doing like them.

'ádaat'ínígíí, what they do, did.

'ádaaz'áago, they are sticking into (the air or earth).

'adaazbaa', they went off to war.

'adabidíneesh'ah, I will lure them; I will trick them (into——).

'ádabi'dool'įįd, ch'ééh, the attempts on them were futile.

'adabiiztiin, their trails extend.

'ádadéshłáá', I became exasperated with it; I got tired of it.

'áda'diilyaa, they made themselves——.

'ada'díiníildiingo, while we throw light on it.

'ádadíninih, hadą́ą́' shą', when did you hurt yourself?

'ádadoodįįł, they will disappear.

'ádadoolnííł, they will be made.

'adadziiłdongo, while they are shooting their guns.

'adághaa', mustache, whiskers.

'adahaashzhee'go, since, or when they have gone hunting.

'adahaaskai, they went off one after another.

'adahaaswodgo, yóó, since, or when, they ran off.

'adahaazbaa'go, since, or when, they went to war.

'adahaaz'éél, they float away.

'adahajááh, they are usually carried to——, one after another.

'adahajáhígíí, those that are carried to——, one after another.

'ádahale', they are making. **Kwii wóláchíí' bighan 'ádahale',** The red ants are making their homes right here.

'ádahalyáni, t'áadoo, without their knowing.

'ádahalyá, yaa, they take care of them.

'ádahasdįįdígíí, bąąh, surviving relatives; properties left by decease of the owner.

'adahasdzá, there are holes on the surface.

'adahayóí, t'óó, they are many.

'adahayóíyí, t'áadoo t'óó nihił, do not be afraid; do not be flabbergasted (you, plural)!

'adahineest'įį', they slipped away one after the other.

'adahineezhchą́'ą́ą, those that escaped from captivity, or escaped from danger.

'adahineezhchą́ą́', they escaped; they fled.

'adahineezhchą́ą́', yóó, they ran away, escaped one after the other; they fled one after another.

'adahizhdoojih, yóó, they will carry them off one after the other.

'adahizh'niigą́ą́', there will be fights.

'ádahnánídaahii, chairman.

'ádahodeedlá, weariness (a feeling of), boredom, monotony, laziness.

'adaho'diiłk'ą́ą́h, they are usually burnt up.

'adaho'diiltł'iid, they are usually thrown into.

'adahodi'niilkaad, they (people) are usually herded into——.

'ádahodoolnííł, they (areas) will be made into——.

'ádahojiilaa, they made them (areas).

'ádahojilyą́, baa, they take care of it; they care for it.

'ádahonízini, t'áadoo, without their thinking about it; before they became aware of it.

'ádahoolyaa, they (areas) were made.

'ádahoołts'íísigo, since they were small (areas). **'áhoołts'íísí,** it (area) is small.

'ádahooniitii, things that are happening.

'ádahooniłígíí, the current events.

'ádahoot'éegi, the characteristics of the places.

'ádahoot'éego, bił 'ayói, since they are partial or fanatical about it.

'ádahoot'éhę́ę́gi 'áhoot'éa da, doo, things are not like they used to be.

'ádahóót'įįd, they occurred.

'ádahóót'įįdę́ę, things that happened.

'ádahóót'į̜dígíí, past events; those things that happened.

'ádahóót'įįdii, those things that happened.

'ádahóóyóí, t'óó bił, they stood aghast; they were terror stricken.

'ádah sitá, top crossbeam of the loom.

'ádahwiilyą́ągo, baa, if we are careful with it; when we (three or more) took care of them.

'adahwiis'áádéé', from everywhere (distant places).

'adahwiis'áágóó, everywhere (distant places).

'adá'i, maternal uncle (mother's brother).

'ádajiilaa, he made them; they made it.

'adajiiljooł, they carry them in one after another (as fluffy matter, wool, etc.).

'adajiiniił, they placed them (one after another.).

'ádajił'į, they usually make it.

'ádajił'į, bits'áádóó, they obtain it from—.

'ádajił'íí ńt'éé', they used to make it.

'ádajił'inígíí, the things they make.

'ádajił'inígóó, doo, when they have nothing to do.

'adajiłkał, one drives them in (like spikes, pegs, etc.).

'ádajiniigo, they say; according to them.

'ada'jiztsih, he stuck something up here and there.

'adá;éó;h, epiglottis.

'ádajósin, they keep it, them. Bi'éé' chin baąh 'ádingo 'ádayósin. They keep their clothes clean.

'ádá ndahat'áago, they have control of their own affairs, self-government.

'adaneezhchą́ą́', yóó, they fled; they escaped.

'ádanihi'niiłdįįd, they are annihilating us.

'ádá nihodiił'aah, resolve, fixed determination, etc.

'ada'niiyą́ą́', they have started to eat; they are going to eat.

'ada'niiyą́ą́', bił, they are going to eat with him.

'ádaníldííl, 'ayóó, they are large (animate objects); they are big.

'ádaníłdáás, they are heavy (in comparison with something named or unnamed).

'ádaníłnééz, they are tall; they are long (in comparison with, or in proportion to something else).

'ádaníłneezgo, since they are long or tall.

'ádaníłtéél, they are wide (in comparison with something else).

'ádaníłtéelgo, since they are wide.

'ádaníłtsogo, since they are large (houses, trucks, etc.).

'ádanoolin, 'ał'qq, they looked different; they all have different appearances.

'adaólzin, they are kept.

'adáyi', throat (inside).

'adáyi' dáhodínícha', diphtheria.

'ádayiilaa, he made them; they made it.

'ádayiilaago, since they have made it.

'adayiishóósh, they shove them into (usually).

'adayiisxan, they threw it down (or in).

'adáyi' nanildzidí, gargle (noun).

'ádayósin, they keep. Bighan hózhónígo ádayósin. They keep their house nice and clean.

'ádazhdííniid, they said thus.

'ádázhdi'níłbaal, he enclosed himself by draping the entrance.

'adazh'niiyą́ą́', it is time to eat.

'adáziz, glottis.

'adee', gourd, dipper, spoon, horn.

'ádee 'ajeeshghaal, I threw myself down.

'ádeehadadoodzii', yee, they promised, vowed it.

'ádeehadahideesdzíí'éé, yee, that which they promised one after another.

'ádeehadahizhdeesdzíí', bee, they promised it one after another.

'ádeehadoodzii', promised; he pledged.

'ádeehadoodzii, yee, he promised; he vowed it.

'ádeeńdeineest'ą́ągo, they having raised an excess.

'adeesbąs, to go, make a trip (by auto or wagon).

'adeesdee', a group (of people) are about to go, are about to leave for..............
Wááshindoongóó 'adeesdee'. They are going to Washington.

'adeesdee'ígíí the fact that they are going.

'adeesdǫǫh, a shot (gunfire). 'Adeesdǫǫh yiists'ą́ą́'. I heard a shot.

'adeesdǫǫhéé, bił, the one that was shot.

'adeesdǫǫh, hoł, he shot him.

'adeesdǫǫh, yił, he shot him.

'adees'óél, sailing (or about to sail).

'adées'eez, one pace or foot (in measurement).

'adeeshch'il, thunderbolt, thunderclap.

'adeeshchííł, to give birth, have a baby.

'adeeshchííł, to defecate.

'adeeshjííł, I will eat; I will have a meal.

'adeeshjííł, nits'ą́ą́', I will have a meal off of you; I will eat with you (at your expense).

'adeeshjoł, I will carry it (in); I will put it in (an enclosure) (loose matter, as hay, wool, a handful of weeds, etc.).

'ádeeshłííł, I shall make it.

'ádeeshnííł, I shall do it; I will act.

'adeesht'ííł, I shall get rich.

'adeeshwoł, I shall run.

'adeeshwoł, níká, I will help you.

'adeeshwoł, yóó, I will run away.

'adéest'íí', lookout, observation point.

'adéest'íí', bee, binocular, telescope.

'a'deet'á, permission, permit.

'adeez'á, yaa, it is mid-afternoon.

'adeez'éél, shił, I am sailing.

'adeezhi, she is the younger sister.

'adeezná, they are to move (with their belongings).

'adeeznáago, the fact that they are moving (with their belongings).

'adeideez'ą́ą́ da, doo yóó, they do not want to give it up.

'adeididoo'ą́ą́ł, yóó', they will abstain, cease, desist, from it.

'ádeidiit'á, he took it off (from himself).

'ádeidoolííł, they will make, build it. Kwii yíkaigo hooghan shá **'ádeidoolííł.** When they arrive they will build a hogan for me.

'ádeidooliiłgo, since they will make them.

'áde'iao, t'áá, just about to; nearly.

'ádeiil'í, we make it.

'ádeiilyaa, we made it.

'adeiiníilzin, we keep. Hooghan góne' honeezdogo **'ádeiiníilzin.** We keep our hogan warm.

'adeiinóhsin, you (pl.) keep.

'ádeiit'įįd, we did; we acted, strove. Ch'ééh biká **'ádeit'įįd.** We searched in vain for it (or for them).

'áde'i'jiil'įįhgo, when one overburdened himself with something—.

'ádeile', they usually make it.

'ádeile'go, when they make them. Látsíní **'ádeile'go naalyéhé bá hooghanjį' nayiiłniih.** He sells the bracelets to the trading post when he makes them.

'ádeil'íinii, what we make.

'ádeiłdįįh, they destroy it.

'ádeił'í, they usually make it.

'ádeił'íí ńt'éé', they used to make it.

'ádeił'įįgo, they are making it.

'ádeił'inigíí, that which they make.

'adeiłmas, hoł, they usually roll it with (accompanied by) him.

'ádeisdįįd, they destroyed it.

'ádeishłaa, I made them.

'ádí, sister, (elder).

'ádich'id, he is scratching himself (to relieve itching).

'ádidahodiyiilt'ééh, they get into trouble.

'adidees'ą́ą́ł, yáá, I will give it up, quit it, desist from it.

'ádideeshch'il, I will scratch myself (to relieve itching).

'adideeshdǫǫ́ł, nił, I will shoot you.

'ádideiidzííł, they struggle along. (as to struggle against odds).

'adidloh, roping.

'adidoolch'il, to lighten.

'adidoo'dǫǫ́ł, bił, he will be shot.

'adidooldǫǫ́łígíí, the fact that there will be shooting, gunfire.

'adigąsh, witchcraft; to perform magic; to bewitch; enchantment.

'adíí'ą́, doo yóó—da, I do not want to lose it; I do not want to give it up.

'adii'ą́, yóó, I gave it up, quit it.

'adii'éél, nihił dah, we sailed off; we set out (by boat).

'ádįįhgo, when it disappears.

'adiijah, bíká, we will help him.

'adiijah, nihíká, we will all help you (pl.).

'adiik'ą́ą́', it burned up completely.

'adiildee', dah, they started off (group of people).

'adiilgááh, sterilize.

'adiilkǫǫh, smoothness.

'adiiłkǫǫ', dah, he swam off; he started off (swimming).

'adiiná, dah, he, they, started off (migrating), moving with belongings.

'ádíiniidę́ę, what I (or he) had said.

'ádíiniidgi, t'áá, just as he said.

'adiitaa', disintegration.

'adiitłah, hysteria.

'adiits'a'í, one who hears, interpreter.

'adiits'a'ii, interpreter. 'Adiits'a'ii Sání, Old Interpreter, Chee Dodge.

'adiiyįįł, you will eat; you will have a meal. Sits'ą́ą́' 'adiiyįįł, you will eat a meal off of me; you will eat with me (at my expense).

'ádíjį', t'áá, at its termination; the end. T'áá 'ádíjį' 'iłįį ńt'éé'. It seemed (to them) that this was the end.

'adik'ą́hą́ądą́ą́', t'ahdoo, before it was completely destroyed by fire.

'ádíláah, mischief.

'adilohii, the one that lassoes.

'adilyé, adultery.

'ádił, to oneself; in company with oneself.

'ádił yáłti', he is talking to himself.

'adiłgashii, witch.

'ádił hadzoodzol, to sigh.

'adiłhash, it bites.

'adiłt'oh, he shoots (with reference to an arrow).

'ádin, there is nothing, none; he is absent; zero; deceased; extinct. Dibé nihee 'ádin. We have no sheep.

'ádin, bee, he has none of it; he doesn't have it.

'ádinda'jidlo', they are fooling, deceiving themselves.

'adinées'qad, yaa, the level went down (and stayed down) (as reference to the level of the water at low tide).

'ádineeshtįįł, bee, I am teaching myself with it.

'adinéesna', fatigue.

'ádingo, there being none.

'adi'ní, it thunders.

'adinidiin, light. 'Ooljéé' bee 'adinidiin. There is moonlight.

'adiniiłtła, convulsion.

'adiniiłt'íísh, to wet.

'ádinootįįł, yee, he is teaching himself with it.

'adishdił, to play the stick dice game.

'ádíshni, I say (thus).

'ádistsiin, stirring stick.

'ádiyoolyééł, to kill oneself, commit suicide.

'adláanii drunkard.

'adlizh, urination, to urinate.

'adó'eeł, shił, that I might set out (in a boat).

'adoh, muscle.

'adoh bits'id, tendon, ligament.

'adoh dah diik'qqd, cramp.

'adókeedí, beggar.

'adoobishii, bee, something in which boiling will be done.

'adooch'ih, to stop blowing (as a breeze, etc.).

'adoolch'ił, a rolling thunderstorm.

'adoochííł, to stop snowing (i.e. to move out of sight—the storm).

'ádoodįįł, it, he will disappear, dwindle out, become extinct; it will become exhausted.

'adoodįłigii, bił, something which will be added to the meal. Łóó' bił 'íiyą́ą́', I had fish for dinner.

'ádoohnííł, you (pl.) will do it.

'adoojah, 'ahiłká, they will help one another. shíká 'adoojah, they will help me.

'ádooji', he named himself; he announced his name.

'adóola, gruel.

'adooleeł, bą́ąh, it will cost; it will be worth..........

'ádoolnííł, it will be made, done. bee 'ádoolníłii, with which it will be made.

'ádoolniiłgi, what to do with. 'Ádoolniiłgi yaa nídadóot'įįł. What to do with it will be discussed.

'adoolwołii, 'áká, a helper; one who will help.

'adoolwoł, yah, he will run in. Łééchąą'í bighan góne' yah 'adoolwoł. The dog will run into his house.

'adoołchííł, she will give birth; she will bring forth an offspring.

'adoołchosh, to graze.

'ádóone'é, clan. Haadóone'é nílį́? To what clan do you belong?

'ádoonííłígíí, what will take place; what it will do.

'adoo'oł, shił, I will make a voyage. Shił 'adoo'ołgóó, toward where I shall sail.

'adoot'įįł, he will get rich.

'ádzaa, he did; it happened.

'ádzaa, bił yaa, it bent down with him.

'ádzaagóó, t'áá, just for fun; not seriously; aimlessly.

'ádzaa, łahgo, it, he, changed.

'adzíítááł, he let fly a kick.

'agąąłóó', lower arm, ulna.

'agąąłóó' bąąh ni 'áhi, radius (bone).

'agaan, arm (anatomy).

'agaan bita' sitáni, humerus.

'agąąstsiin, shoulder blade (scapula).

'agąąziz, sleeve.

'aghá, utmost, best.

'aghaa', fur, wool, fleece.

'aghaa' binda'anishdi, woolen mills.

'agháadi most, extreme, favorite. díí 'agháadi shinát'oh. This is my favorite tobacco. 'agháadi 'át'éii, fine things; the best things.

'agháadi yá'át'ééh, excellent.

'agháadi yá'át'éhígíí, best

'agháál, rattle.

'agháál nímazígíí, gourd rattle.

'agháda' dildlaadí, to examine or diagnose with X-ray.

'aghá'deeldlaad, X-ray.

'agha'deet'aah, persuasion.

'agha'diit'aahii, defense attorney, lawyer.

'agháhwiizídí, laxative, purgative, purge.

'agháhwiizídí 'ak'ahígíí, castor oil.

'agha'ilyé, robbery.

'aghá'neeldóhí, bee, diathermy apparatus.

'aghá'neeldóóh, diathermy treatment.

'aghas naha'ná, indigestion (dyspepsia).

'agizii, rheumatism.

'agiziitsoh, chronic rheumatism.

'agod, knee. shigod, my knee.

'agod dist'ání, knee cap.

'ahaa' da'iildéhígíí, (people) coming together, meet; joined by marriage; etc.

'áhą́ą́digo, t'áá, close together.

'aha'ádzaago, since, or when, they came together (a multitude).

'aháádzogo, it is divided. Díí kéyah díígóó 'ahaadzo. This land is divided into four parts.

'ahąąh, abreast; side by side. siláago díí 'ahąą naazįįgó yikah łeh. Soldiers usually march four abreast.

'ahąąh naaznil, they are lying side by side. (inanimate objects).

'ahąąh njiníł, to compare them; putting them side by side; to match them.

'ahą́ą́h, t'áá, simultaneously.

'ahą́ą́h, t'áá, frequently; often.

'ahááldládigíí, that which has been torn apart, or separated, by drawing a line through it.

'ahaa nda'ayiilniihgo, since, or when, we carry on trade with one another.

'ahaa nda'iilniih, they carry on trade with one another; commerce.

'ahaa nda'iilniihígíí, those who carry on trade with one another.

'ahaa ndajiilniih, they trade them to one another.

'ahaa ndajiilniihígíí, those things which they trade to one another.

'ahaa ndayiilniih, they trade them with one another.

'ahaa yit'áázh, they married; they came to live together.

'áháchį', anger.

'ahada'deest'ą́, they made an agreement.

'ahada'deest'ą́ągo, since they made an agreement.

'ahada'deest'áanii, those who made the agreement.

'ahada'deest'ánę́ędą́ą́', when they made an agreement.

'ahadadit'ą́ą́góó yaa yinít'íinii, arthritis.

'ahada'dit'áahgo, when they make an agreement with one another.

'ahadazh'deest'ánígíí, bee, that about which they made the agreement.

'ahadazhdi'doot'ááł, they will sign the treaty, or an agreement.

'ahadeesht'áázh, they ran a race with one another.

'aha'deet'aah, treaty; agreement.

'ahadésht'áázh, t'áadoo bił—da, I did not run a race with her (him).

'ahadidiit'ash, we two will run a race; let us run a race, we two.

'ahadit'áán, joints.

'ahaghał, withers (of horse).

'ahá'iigeh, matrimony, marriage.

'aháiniłdlááD, he, she, tore it in half.

'áhálchįįhgóó, doo yaa, without his suspecting it; catching him unawares.

'áhálnééh, it (area) is being made.

'áhálniih, 'ayóó, it is very tasty; it really tastes good.

'áhályáanii, yaa, those that, (he who), care for them, it.

'áhályą́, yaa, he, she, is taking care of it.

'ahanááda'deest'ą́, yił, they again made another agreement with them.

'ahanááda'didiit'ááł, we shall make another agreement.

'áhá'ní, it is said.

'áhání, near, nearby.

'ahanibidi'neelkaad, they were driven together, they were herded together.

'áhánídéę́', t'áá, from nearby.

'áhánígi, at a nearby place.

'áhánígóó, nearby.

'ahaniheeznáago, since they moved together (with their belongings).

'ahaniheeznánígíí, those who moved together (with their belongings).

'ahanihidínóolkał, they will be herded together; they will be driven together.

'ahaniijah, they usually gather at one place.

'áhániji', (to a) nearby (place).

'ahaninájahgo, they repeatedly run together at one place.

'áháshchįįh, baa, I am aware of it.

'áháshchįįhí, t'áadoo, without my being aware of it.

'áháshłééh, I am establishing, or building; I am (in the act of) making it (place, area). Naalyéhé báhooghan 'áháshłééh. I am building a trading post.

'ahásht'óózh, tree bark.

'áháshyą́, I am careful, alert, wary. Baa 'áháshyą́, I take care of it (him).

'áhát'iinii, doings, acts.

'áháyą́, baa, care is taken of it; it is cared for.

'áháyą́qgi, baa, the taking care of.

'áháyą́qgo, baa, taking care of it.

'ahayóídi, t'óó, many times.

'ahayói, t'óó, there are many, much, a lot of it.

'ahbíní ('abíní), morning.

'ahbínigo ('abínigo), in the morning.

'ahbínigo da'adánígíí, breakfast.

'ahédiłí, béésh, scissors.

'ahéédahodoolzįįł, they will know about one another.

'ahéédahólzin, yił, they are acquainted with one another.

'ahéédahooszįid, they got acquainted; they became known to each other.

'ahééda'iiłkeedgo, they make (so much) an hour.

'aheeda'nt'įįh, they usually steal from one another.

'aheedéetą́ą́', of equal thickness or depth.

'ahééh, appreciation, thankfulness, grateful.

'ahééhéhááh, t'áá — bik'eh, all the year around.

'ahééhéshįįh, where it is always summer.

'ahééh 'íłį, baa, it is appreciated.

'ahééhnízin, yaa, he gives thanks for it.

'ahééhoodzo, zone.

'ahéé'ilkid, hour(s) passed.

'aheejólyeedí, baseball game.

'aheelt'é, they are alike, similar, same; they are equal.

'aheelt'éego, since they are equal or similar.

'aheenéelt'e', they are in equal quantity, number.

'aheeníldííl, the same in size (as animals, people, logs, etc.).

'aheeníldáás, of equal weight.

'aheeníłnééz, of the same length.

'aheeníłtsááz, the diameter or thickness is the same.

'aheeníłtso, same in length or size.

'aheesgí, they were hauled away one after another, shipped. Béésh nít'i'góó dibé yázhí shá 'aheesgí. I had my lambs shipped to the railroad.

'aheeskai, they went; they followed one another out.

'aheeyol, yóó, it blew away one after the other.

'aheezhjéé', yóó, they ran away one after another.

'aheezná, they moved one after another.

'ahéhee', thank you.

'ahéníná'álki', hours pass.

'ahe'ol, yóó, they are floating away one after another.

'áhí, fog, mist.

'áhí bee chahałheeł, foggy.

'ahidaałt'éhígíí, those that are similar; the fact that they are similar.

'ahidaałt'é, they are alike; they are similar; they are of the same color.

'ahidaałt'é, yił, they are similar to one another.

'ahida'ats'ih, they fuss or quarrel with one another.

'ahidadii'nilęę, bił, those that were mixed, put with them.

'ahidahididoonéełgo, since they will move together (with their belongings).

'ahidahoołt'éego, being alike (referring to an area); being evenly matched, (as in a contest, competition, battle, etc.).

'ahidajiyiinilgo, since, or when, they collected them, brought them together.

'ahidaneesdin, they became accustomed to one another; they got used to each other.

'ahidanoolin, similar in appearance.

'ahídaółtą'go, all of them together; total; sum.

'ahidayiistł'ǫ́, he tied them together.

'ahideełk'id, two hills run together.

'ahideezgohgo, when they (two) collided with one another.

'ahideidiinil, yił, they mixed them with them, put them together with them.

'ahidii̢'áázh, yił, he met him.

'ahí'diiljeeh, to weld.

'ahidiiłjéé', I welded them together.

'ahidiniilcháá', dah, they (two) started off running.

'ahidi'níilchééł, nihiká, we (two) will help you (plural).

'ahidi'níisą, adhesion (two surfaces become stuck to each other; the process of adhering or uniting of two surfaces or parts as in a wound).

'ahidiniłnáago, they pass by each other going in opposite directions. Kǫ'na'ałbąąsii 'ahidiniłnáago 'ahąąh sizí. The trains are standing side by side facing opposite directions.

'ahidziskéii, spouse; married couple.

'ahigá, combat.

'ahihé'o', I pulled out one after another (fish); I caught them.

'ahiikaigo, since, or when, they met, or held meetings.

'ahii'nilgo, having brought them together.

'ahíiyi̧, it (water) extends inward (as in reference to a bay or inlet).

'ahiłghan, to throw one object.

'ahił, with each other; in each other's company; with one another; to one another (in sense of accompaniment). 'Ahił neii'-né, we are playing together; we're playmates.

'ahił hani', conversation.

'ahił hojilni'go, they are carrying on a conversation.

'ahił hojoolni'go, when they (two) talked with one another.

'**ahiłká**, for (sake of) each other, one another. **ahiłká 'ańdaajah.** They usually help one another.

'**ahiłká 'aná'áłwo'**, cooperation.

'**ahił neli'né**, we are playing together.

'**ahił nidahasni'**, they told each other (of what they knew , informed one another.

'**ahinahaalyéii**, weapon, arms.

'**ahindayiilyéhigíí**, their weapons.

'**ahineel'ą́**, they are equal to each other.

'**ahineelchą́ą́'**, **yaa**, they (two) went running to them.

'**ahinéikah**, they (customarily) come together, usually meet, hold meetings.

'**ahinidééh**, **bá**, they usually get (as money of an appropriation). (Equivalent to English "they realize a profit.")

'**ahi'niiłgo**, putting them in (customarily).

'**ahinoolchéłę́ę**, those two who were running along.

'**ahinoolin**, similar (in appearance).

'**ahióóltą'go**, all together; counting all. **Hastiin bitsi' naaki, biyé' 'éí táá', 'áko t'áá 'ałtso 'ahióóltą'go ba'áłchíní 'ashdla'.** The man has two daughters and two sons, so all together he has five children.

'**ahisheegizh**, **k'aasdá 'áts'iistah**, blood poisoning, septicemia, toxemia, pyemia.

'**ahishk'ash**, sprain.

'**ahishniłigíí**, **yóó**, the things I toss away; my garbage.

'**ahizhdi'níigo**, saying thus to one another.

'**ahizhneezdee'**, to fall in one after another.

'**áhodéeszéé'**, it is calm, still, quiet.

'**áho'diilyaa**, they (people) were made into something else, formed, transformed, etc.

'**áhodiilzee'**, it became calm.

'**áhodííníszéé'**, **t'óó**, I kept quiet; I remained still.

'**áhodiniiltłóóh**, relax.

'**ahodi'niiłtłid**, it (an area) began to shake, quake, tremble.

'**ahodi'noolkaad**, they were driven to a point (in reference to people or prisoners of war, etc.).

'**ahodool'a'**, he was sent, commanded. **Na'nízhoozhígóó 'iit'a'.** I sent him to Gallup.

'**áhodoolnííł**, it will be done, made.

'**aho'doolt'e'**, he or she was placed.

'**áhodooniiłii**, something that would happen.

'**áhodooniłígíí**, the things that will happen.

'**áhodooníił**, it will happen.

'**áhojilchįįhí**, **t'aadoo**, before he realized what was up; without his being aware; taking him by surprise.

'**áhojilyą́ągo**, **baa**, one caring for it.

'**áhojilyą́**, **baa**, he takes care of it.

'**aho'niiłtą́**, **bee**, it began to rain on him.

'**áhoniłt'éelgo**, **haashjį́**, being wide to an undetermined extent, very wide, for much distance around; undetermined extent (an area).

'**áhoniłtso**, it (an area) is large, big (in a comparative sense).

'**áhoniłtsogo**, since it is big, large (an area).

'**ahoodzą́**, hole, perforation, cavity.

'**áhoodzaa**, something that happened. **Hádą́ą́' 'áhoodzaa?** When did it happen?

'**ahoodzą́**, **baa**, there is a hole in it.

'**áhoodzaago**, when it happened.

'**áhoodzaa**, **łahgo**, things changed; there was a change in the weather.

'**áhóodziil**, energy.

'**ahool'á**, it (area) extends endlessly.

'**áhoolaa**, he made it (area).

'**áhoolyaa**, it (area) was made.

'**áhoolyaaigíí**, that (an area) which was made.

'**áhoolyé**, the place is called.

'**ahoolzhiizh**, time passed. **Nízaadgóó 'ahoolzhiizh**, a long time passed.

'**áhoołdįįł**, it is destroying them; it is annihilating them.

'**áhoołts'íísígo**, since it (an area) is small.

'**áhoołts'óózí**, it is a small place, or area; the area is narrow and long.

'**áhooniiłgóó**, **t'áá**, as things happen.

'**áhoot'é**, it (area, space, things, conditions) is. '**áhoot'éhigíí**, the things, places that are.

'áhoot'éhé, doo — da, nothing unusual about the (place, weather, etc.).

'ahóót'i', it extends, stretches (with regard to a place or area).

'áhóót'iid, it happened; it occurred.

'áhóót'iidęęgi 'át'éego, like it happened.

'áhóót'iidgo, when or after it happened.

'áhóót'iidígíí, that which has happened.

'áhóót'iidii, occurrence.

'ahóóyói, it became much; they became many.

'ahóóyói dooleel ńt'éé', t'óó shįį, there would have been many.

'áhwiilyá, baa, we (two) take care of it.

'a'ilyé, loan.

'a'i'nil, the loan was made of (them); they were loaned out.

'a'i'nilii, those were loaned.

'ajaa', ear.

'ajáád, leg.

'ajáád bita' sitání, femur, thigh bone.

'ajáád shizhah, to be bowlegged.

'ajáágiizh, crotch (between legs).

'ajaat'áástą́ą́n, mastoid process.

'ajaat'áástą́ą́n dideeshchii', mastoiditis.

'ajaat'ah niichaad, mumps.

'ajaayi', inner (or interior of) ear.

'ajaayi' dáádiníbaalí, eardrum.

'ajaayi' hodiniih, earache.

'ajádígíí, the leg.

'ajánil, fringe (of a shawl, etc.).

'ajástis, shin bone, tibia.

'ajéé', axle grease.

'ajééht'iizh, ear wax.

'ajéí, pleural organs, heart.

'ajéídishjool, heart.

'ajéí nahalingo heets'óóz, heart shaped.

'ajéí nidiníbaalí bits'óóz, phrenic nerve.

'ajéíts'iin, thorax (trunk of body).

'ajéí yilzólii, lung.

'ajéí yilzolii baa 'ahoodzá silį́į́', lung cavity.

'ajéí yilzólii biih yiłk'aaz, pneumonia.

'ajéí yilzólii bik'ésti'ígíí, pleura.

'ajéí yilzólii bik'ésti'ígíí nááltsaii, dry pleurisy.

'ajéí yilzólii bik'ésti'ígíí tázil silį́į́', pleurisy (pleuritis).

'ájidin, he is deceased.

'ájidingo, when he, she, died.

'ajíí'áázh, biká, they two went for (after) him; they two went to get him.

'ájiilaa, he made it.

'ájiilaa, bá, he, she, made it for him, or her. Yoostsah bá 'ájiilaa ńt'éé' doo bííghah da. He made a ring for her but it wasn't the right size.

'ajíílizh, he urinated.

'ajiiłhaazh, he slept; he went to sleep.

'ájiił'įid, ch'ééh, he tried in vain; he acted on it in vain.

'ájiił'įjh, one makes.

'ajiił'įjhgo, when one makes (something).

'ajiiłta', he went to school, had an education.

'ájiił'įjdę́ę, what he did.

'ajííyá, he went away; he went in.

'ajííyą́ą', he ate; he dined.

'ajilchii', anus, rectum.

'ájilééh, to create; he is (in the act of) making it.

'ájiléehgo, while he is making it.

'ajilizh, to urinate.

'ajiłhosh, he is asleep; he is sleeping.

'ájił'į, he makes it (customarily).

'ájíní, one says.

'aji'oł, one will float, or wash, away.

'ajisiihgo, when one makes a mistake.

'ájit'i, he does; he is; he did it.

'ájit'įjgo, he is doing, having done. t'áá 'aanii 'ájit'įjgo, he being guilty.

'ajiyą́, he is eating.

'ajiyą́ągo, eating.

'ajółta', he, she is going to school, attending school.

'ajółta'go, since she, he, is attending school.

'ajoo'į, he, she, can see.

'ajóózh, vagina.

'áká, for (after) someone, something.

'ak'á, to grind. (as: to grind corn, etc.).

'akáá' diitł'iizh, cyanosis.

'ak'áán, flour.

'ak'áán dich'izhi, cream of wheat (cereal); cornmeal.

'akáá' ni'níkéé̱z, rash.

'ak'aashjaa', pelvis.

'akáá' yihé̱é̱s, itch, pruritis.

'akáá' yiikiizh, rash.

'akááz, tonsil, gland.

'akááz dideeschii', tonsilitis.

'áká 'azhdoojah, they will all help.

'akááz jéí 'ádjih silį́į́', tubercular gland.

'áká 'é'élnééh, order.

'áká 'e'elyeed, succor.

'akágí, hide, pelt, skin.

'akágí 'ánóolingi, complexion.

'ak'ahko', oil; kerosene; oil lamp; candle; vaseline; mineral oil.

'ak'ah 'agháhwiizídí, castor oil.

'ak'ah diltłi'í, candle.

'ak'ahkǫ', oil; kerosene; oil lamp; candle.

'ak'ahkǫ' biih yít'i'í, lamp wick.

'akai', pelvis bone; hip.

'akáisdáhí, milky way.

'akał, leather.

'akał 'agháál, hide rattle.

'akał bee 'ak'aashí, strop.

'akał bistłee'ii, cowpuncher, or cowboy.

'akáshtł'o, body hair.

'akaz, cane (as sugarcane).

'ákaz łikani, sugar cane.

'ak'e'alchi, to write.

'ak'eda'alchíhígíí, writing. 'ak'eda'alchíhígi 'át'éego, it being similar to their writing.

'ak'e'deeshchííł, to write (on something).

'akédinibiní, toes.

'akéé', behind. 'akée'di, at the rear, afterward, in the tracks. 'akée'di tsé'naa niikai, they (pl.) came across last.

'akee', one's foot or feet.

'ak'ee'qq 'ahééhonit'i', detour.

'akéédé̱'ígíí, the one in the rear, the one which is last.

'akéedi yé̱e̱dą́ą́', the last (time).

'ákéé' hanéi'nil, he takes them up after him.

'ak'e'elchí, one writes.

'ak'e'elchíhígíí, bee, with which it is written.

'ak'e'elchíigi, writing; about writing; how to write.

'ak'e'eshchį̱, he wrote; it was written; an inscription; scripture.

'ak'e'eshchí, I write; I am writing.

'ak'eh dadeesdlį́'ígíí, the conquerors.

'ak'eh dadeesdlį́į'go, when they won (in a fight), overcome.

'ak'eh dadidlį̱į̱go, they defeated.

'ak'eh hodeesdlį́', the battle is won; conquest.

'ak'eh hodeesdlį́'ígíí, since the battle was won.

'ak'eh hól'į, obedience.

'ak'éí, kin, relatives.

'akénį́į', arch (of the foot).

'ak'eń'jiłchííh, he writes.

'akéshgaan, toenail, hoof, claw.

'akéshgaan 'agháál, hoof, rattle.

'akétal, calcaneous, heel bone.

'akétł'ááh, sole (of foot).

'akétł'óól, root, shoe lace.

'akéts'iil, small particles of foot (small bones).

'akétsiin, ankle.

'akéts'iin, tarsus, ankle joint.

'akéwos, bunion.

'akézhoozh, toes, phalanges of the foot.

'akézhoozh bii'noot'ii', paronychia, felon.

'ak'i, on top.

'ak'ida'ashchį, they wrote.

'ak'idadidisi, bandages, friction tape, etc.

'ák'idadoodlaał, they will help themselves, support themselves.

'ak'idahi'nilí, saddle blanket.

'ák'idajidláhą́ą, bee, the things with which they were supporting themselves.

'ak'ida'iiłchį, they write; one writes; writing. 'ak"da'iiłchíhę̱ę, what they (pl) wrote.

'ák'idazneeskaad, they drove them off.

'ak'i'diitjih, comprehension, understanding.

'ak'ihodiit'á, accusation.

'ák'iididis, he is winding it on himself; he is coiling it on himself.

'ak'i'iilchį, nightmare.

'ak'inaalzhoodí, harrow.

'ak'inaazt'i', harness.

'ák'inálchįįh, masturbation.

'ák'indaaldzil, they are self-sustaining, self-supporting.

'ak'inda'a'nilí, bee, camera.

'ak'inizdidlaad, luster.

'ak'is, friend, sibling, or maternal cousin (all of the same sex).

'ák'izhdoodlaalii, bee, that with which he will be self-supporting.

'áko, so then.

'ákó, bił t'áá, it meets with his approval; it is agreeable to him.

'ákódaaní, they say thus. t'áá 'ákódaanii ńt'ęę́', they used to say that way.

'ákódaat'éhígíí, the things that are thus; those that are thus.

'ákódaat'éego, since they are that way.

'ákódadooniił, that is what they will do.

'ákódadziidzaa, they did likewise.

'ákódadziidzaíí, those that did likewise.

'ákóda'hool'įįd, they did thus to one another.

'ákódahooniłígíí, in cases like those; when things like those happen.

'akódahoot'éégóó, places like those; things like those.

'ákódajíít'įįd, they did thus.

'ákódanidooliił, that is what they will do to you.

'ákódaniit'éégóó, doo, since we were in a despondent mood; since we were not feeling well.

'ákódayiilaa, they did likewise to it, them.

'ákódayiilaago, since they did thus to it.

'akodei, up there. 'ákódei ha'atiin. The road goes up there.

'ákódigo, t'áá, enough, that is all, that being all.

'ákódíílííł you will do thus to it; this is what you will do.

'ákódzaa, it happened thus; that is the way it happened.

'ákohgo, so, consequently, therefore, then.

'ákohgo 'índa, when, then, until. Chizh ła' 'ahididíítkał 'ákohgo 'índa nich'į' ni'deeshłeeł. When you chop some wood I will pay you.

'ákohgo, ts'ídá, at that moment; right then.

'ákóhodiil'įįh, this is what happens to one.

'ákóhóót'įįd, it occurred, happened thus.

'áko 'índida, then. Altso k'i'diiláago 'áko indida hooghan 'ádeeshłííł. When I have finished planting then I'll build a home.

'ákólyaa, há, it has been done for him thus.

'akon, see, I told you so.

'ákónaa, across there.

'ákónáádayiil'įįh, they usually do that way again.

'ákónáánát'é, it is again thus; it also is thus; it also is this way.

'ákónáánéelą́ą́', there is that much again; there is again a like amount.

'ákónát'įįh, he does that.

'ákó ndi, nevertheless, however, but, yet, notwithstanding.

'ákóńdoo'niił, it will change back to be like it was.

'ákóne', there inside (an enclosure); in there.

'ákónéehee, t'áá, essential, necessary.

'akonee, jó, see now; now you see.

'ákónéelą́ą'go, there is so much; a great amount.

'akǫ́ǫ́, toward there; that way; thereabout; to there; thither; there.

'ak'ǫ́ǫ́', seed.

'akóó, get out of the way; make way; look out. (warning).

'ákǫ́ǫ́ ndeizh'eezh, they lead them to there.

'akóó niláahdi nanich'įįdii, go on; scram; get away from here.

'ak'os, neck.

'ak'os doolwółi, atlas bone.

'ákoshį́į́, then probably.

'áko, t'áá, right then; that is all right.

'ákót'é, it is thus; **Doo bił 'ákót'ée da,** he disapproves.

'akót'é, it is right, correct.

'ákót'ée, doo — da, it is not right; it is not correct.

'ákót'éegi, in such cases; in that case.

'ákót'éego, it is thus; correct; in this way; in the right way.

'ákót'éego 'iinánígíí, that particular way of life.

'ákóyaa, down there. **'ákóyaa to nílí,** down there a river flows.

'ákóyííł'įįd, he did thus to it.

'ákózhdooniił, he will do thus; it will happen thus to him; etc.

'ákózhnéeláá', there are that many.

'ákwe'é, there, right there (at a closely circumscribed point). **'ákwe'é tóháálí,** there is a spring there.

'ákwii, there (at a more general and less definite place); thereabout. **'ákwii shiba',** wait for me there.

'ákwíí, that many.

'ákwii da'ółta'ígíí, those that go to school there.

'ákwiidooliił, he will do thus (or likewise) to it, him, her, them.

'ákwii jį́, t'áá, everyday.

'ákwiinízin, he thinks thus.

'ákwíí, t'áá, every; each; it is still the same (in amount).

'ákwiyiilaa, he did thus to it.

'ákwiyiilaa, t'áá, he made it correctly.

'al'á, order.

'óla', hands.

'aláah, bigger, more, greater.

'óla' 'aháąh dadé'áhígíí, knuckles.

'aláah 'ánízáád, fartherest.

'aláahdi, fartherest, furthermost, most, greatest, superlatively.

'aláahji, on the farther side. **'Aláahji naa'ołí k'idiílá.** I planted beans on the farther side.

'aláąjį', foremost, ahead, first of a series.

'aláąjį' dah sidáhígíí, one who is the chairman, or president.

'aláąjį' dah sidáii, the chairman, the president.

'aláąjį' naazị, they are leaders.

'aláąjį' naaziinii, the leaders; the officers; the executives.

'aláąjį' ndaakai, they are the leaders; they are older.

'aláąjį' sizį́ịgo, since he is the leader.

'aláąjį' sizíinii, the leader, the master, the captain.

'alah, sibling or maternal cousin (of the opposite sex).

'álák'ee, in the hand.

'álashgaan, fingernails.

'áláóstsii', seeds, grain, for seeds.

'álátah, tip, extremity.

'álátł'ááh, palm (of hand).

'álátsíín, wrist.

'álátsịịts'in, wrist bones.

'álátsoh, thumb.

'é'ázhoozh, fingers, phalanges of the hand.

'aldzéehgi, a tannery.

'ál'į da, doo, it is not usually done; it is not usually made.

'ál'įigi, the technique of making; how it is made; how to make; the making of.

'ál'įigo, it is usually made.

'ályííł, slight of hand; legerdemain; magic; supernatural power.

'alizh bikááz, prostate gland.

'aljił, flirtation.

'álnééh, it is being made, done.

'álnééhgi, the making of; the creating of.

'álnééhgo, when it is in the process of being made; while it is being made.

'álnéhę́ę, that which was being made.

'álnéhígíí, that which is being made.

'alohk'e', pancreas, sweet bread.

'alóós, rice.

'ályaa, it was made.

'ályaago, when it was made; since it was made.

'ályaa yígíí, the one that was made, built.

'alzhish, he dances or is dancing.

'ał'qq, separate, each, individual, different, distinct, apart, divide, varies.

'ał'qq 'ádaat'éii, different kinds; different colors.

'ał'qq 'ánildíilgo, since they (animate objects) are of different sizes.

'ał'qq 'át'é, distinct.

'ał'qq, t'áá, each, separately, different, there is a variety of.

'ał'qa dine'é, (different) tribes.

'ał'qq, t'áá, each; separately; different; distinct.

'áłah, together.

'áłah 'ádayiilaa, they gathered them; they brought them together; they assembled them.

'áłah 'ádoolníił, they will be gathered; they will be brought together.

'áłah 'aleeh, conference, convention, meeting, assembly.

'áłah 'ánáánályaago, when they were brought together again.

'áłah 'áyiilaa, he gathered it.

'áłah 'áyiilaago, when he brought them together; when he gathered them.

'áłch 'azlįį', people assembled; people gathered.

'áłah daazlįį', they gathered together; they held a meeting.

'áłah da'azlįį'góó, where people assembled; where people got together.

'áłah daazlįį'ii, those who gathered together; those who assembled.

'áłah 'iłįįgo, when there were many people present.

'áłahjį', at all times.

'áłahjį', t'áá, all the time; constantly; frequently; always.

'áłah náá'ásdlįį, there was another meeting.

'áłah náá'ásdlįį'go, when people got together again.

'áłah ná'ádleehígi, at the next meeting.

'áłah nádleeh, they gather together.

'áłah ńda'adleeh, meetings are held.

'áłah nida'adleehígíí, the meetings, conferences.

'áłah siidlįįgo, when we assembled.

'áłah silįį', they gathered; they held a meeting.

'áłah, t'áá, both of them.

'ałch'į', toward each other; together.

'áłch'įdi, insufficient.

'áłch'ídigo, t'áá, just a few; just a little.

'áłch'įįdí, it is small in amount; few; little; insufficient. **Shibéeso 'áłch'įįdí.** I just have a little money. I have not much money.

'áłch'įįdígo, a small amount; just a little bit.

'atchin, wild.

'áłchíní, children.

'áłchíní da'ółta'i, school children; pupil.

'atchiní, łįį', wild horse.

'atchiní, tł'izi, wild goat.

'áłchíní yaa 'áhályání, one who takes care of children; matron; advisor.

'áłchíní yázhí, small children; tots.

'áłchíní yii' danijahi, children's dormitory (or dormitories).

'áłch'ishdéé', from both sides; from either side.

'atch'ishii, on both sides; or either side; on the opposite side.

'atchozh, he grazes, eats leafy things.

'áłdįį, t'áá, at hand; in readiness. **T'áá 'áłdįį hoołt'éego 'áshłaa,** I have everything in readiness.

'ałdó', also, too.

'ałdzéhé, tanner, one who tans hide.

'aleehé, t'áadoo yee lá, before he accepts it.

'athaa, to each other, to one another.

'athąą', he is snoring.

athááda'ii'niilgo, when they exchange gifts with one another.

'athqqh, side by side; in juxtaposition (also **'ahqqh**).

'athaa nda'iilniihígií, the trade that they carry on with one another; their commerce.

'athosh, he is sleeping.

'atjitnii, whore, prostitute.

'atk'ą́ą́h dahalyeed, they collide head-on.

'atkéé', following each other; consecutive; in each other's tracks; behind each other.

'atk'eedadi'niihígií, those who dislike one another.

'atk'éédeijah, they usually attack one another.

'atk'éédeijahdą́ą́', when they used to attack one another; when they were at war with one another.

'atk'éé'iijah, battle.

'atk'éí, relatives one of the other; mutually related (as kin).

'atk'éí nidlíígo, since they are related

'atk'ésdisí. candy.

'atk'ésgiz, it is twisted.

'atk'idą́ą́', long ago; formerly.

'atk'ídooltas, it will be twisted.

'atk'iijéé', they attacked one another.

'atk'iilwod, yit, he started to fight with him.

'atk'iishjéé', bit —, I started to fight with them.

'atk'iishwod, bit, I started to fight with him.

'atk'iji', on top of each other.

'atk'iji' 'anidéehgo, they are falling on one another; they are falling on top of one another.

'atk'iijiiéé', there was an attack.

'atk'ináánéijéé', they again attacked one another.

'atk'inaazkaad, they are spread one upon the other.

'atk'inéijah, they usually attack, fight one another.

'atk'iniilaizh, jerked meat (jerky).

'atk'is, mutual friends; mutual siblings (of the same sex).

'atnáá'á'ot, bit, he voyages back and forth; he sails back and forth.

'atnáádaajah, they run back and forth; travel back and forth (on foot).

'atnáádaakah, they travel back and forth.

'atná'ádaat'jjgo, when they move back and forth.

'atná'áhát'i, traffic.

'atnáá'iyooldah, to take turns.

'atnánádááh, he goes back and forth.

'atnáánihi'ish, he leads us back and forth; he chaperons us on our trips.

'atnáánit'ash, shit, you go back and forth with me.

'atnáá'ooldee'go, when changes (of personnel) have taken place.

'atná'át'jj nt'éé', they used to move back and forth.

'atnáháádláád, oblique fracture.

'atnáájidááh, he goes back and forth.

'atnánáshdááh, I go back and forth.

'atnánásht'ash, bit, I go back and forth with him; I accompany him on his trips (back and forth).

'atnánéigééh, he hauls it back and forth.

'atnánéiikah, bit, we accompany them back and forth.

'atné'é'ááh, it becomes noon.

'atné'é'áahgo, at noon; during noon hour.

'atnjj', center, middle, midway.

'atní'ídóó, t'áá, from half; just a half; only part of it.

'atnjj'gi, at the middle; in the center.

'atnjj'ji, as far as the middle; midway.

'atni'ni'ą, it became noon; it is noon; midday.

'atni'ni'ą́ą́dóó bik'iji', after-noon.

'atta', between each other.

'átt'qq, in spite of their wishes; to their dismay.

'altaadaokai, they went among one another.

'ált'áá'i, thin, shallow, flat. tó 'á:t'áá'i the water is shallow.

'ált'áá'igo it is thin; it is flat. Nahasdzáán 'ált'áá'igo dah sikaad. The earth is flat.

'altaas'éí, assorted, various, varied.

'altádahiniilgéésh, they usually cut them open.

'altah, among one another; mixed.

'attah 'áát'eelii, mixture.

'altah 'át'éego, since they are mixed; since they are of different kinds.

'ált'á'i, shallow.

'alta'vi'nil, alteration.

'altįį', bow: she'eltįį', my bow.

'altįįtł'óól, bow string.

'alts'áá', away from each other; in opposite directions; divergently.

'alts'áá' deeníní, pick (tool).

'alts'áádóó, from each other.

'alts'ááhji, on either side; on both sides; bilaterally; on each side.

'alts'ádadi'dii'nil, we will divide them up among ourselves; we will share them among us.

'alts'ádahaazná, they moved apart; they migrated apart.

'alts'ádaho'diiłts'ood, their bodies are pulled apart.

'alts'á'ii'níií, division.

'álts'áznaago, when they moved apart.

'áltsé, first; before. (also, 'áltséédand 'átsé).

'áltséédáá', before; formerly; originally; previously.

'áltsé t'áá 'ákǫǫ naniná, stay around (you).

'álts'iísí, he, it, is little, short.

'álts'iísigo, because it was small, or little.

'altso, all completed; finished. Kin t'ahdoo 'altso 'áshłeeh da. I have not finished building my house yet.

'altso da'iiłta'go, when they have finished school; when they graduated from school.

'altsogóó, t'áá, everywhere.

'altso hadidzaa, it is complete; it is put together.

'altsoji', to the finish; until it is finished.

'altsoji', t'áá, in every way.

'altso la' hoodzaago, when everything is completed; when the goal has been reached.

'altsoni, t'áá everything.

'áłts'óózí, it is narrow, slim, slender.

'eltso, t'áá, all of them.

'áłts'ózi, it is narrow. (opposed to niteel)

'amá, mother; maternal aunt. (shimá, my mother).

'amá sání, maternal grandmother. (shimá sání, my grandmother.)

'amá yázhí, niece (daughter of one's sister) (male speaking); or aunt (maternal).

'anaa', war, enmity, discord.

'anáá', eye, seed.

'anáá'át'aah, sun setting again; day passing again.

'anaa' baa na'aldechgo, during the war; during the hostilities.

'ánáábidish'ni. I again said thus to him.

'anáá' bik'i'niiséhígíí, pterygium, growth over cornea.

'ánáábi-h'niidlaa, he started to make it again; he started making another.

'ánáádaa'yaa, they were made again; others were made.

'ánáádaalyaaígíí, those that were made again.

'ánáádaat'é, 'ał'aa, they are again different, contrary, unlike, distinct.

'ánáádaat'éego, łahgo, because they, too, are different.

'ánáádabi'niilyaago, when they started to be made again by them.

'ánáádabizh'niidlaa, he started to make them again; he started to make some more of them; they started to make it again (to make some more).

'ánáádadi'niigo, they say again.

'ánáádadi'nii łeh, they again habitually say thus.

'ánááda' doodlííł, they will write another letter.

'anáádahakáahgo, they start off (one after another) again.

'anááda'iiniilta', the schools are back in session.

'ánáádao'ne'gi da, t'áadoo, there was again nothing that we could do.

'ánáádeeshdlííł, I will make it again; I will make another.

'ánáádeiidzaa, łahgo, we again changed our tactics.

'ánáádi'ní, he again says (thus).

'anáádoot'ał, to present it again; to file again. (as to file a complaint).

'anáádzá, he again went away; he went back.

'anáádzá, yah, he went back in.

'anáádzíłhaałí, t'áadoo tó 'aadéé', before the water could rush back.

'anáágo', it again flowed away; it again fell away.

'ánááhodoolnííł, it (an area) will again be made to —.

'anááhodoolzhish, time will pass.

'ánááhoodzaa, łahgo, the weather changed again.

'ánááhoo'niiłgo, łahgo, because of weather changes.

'ánááhoo'nííłgíí, łahgo, the fact that it (the weather, world, conditions) changes again.

'ánááhoot'é, it is again.

'anaa' hwiiniidzįį', declaration of war.

'ánaaí, elder brother. shínaaí, my elder brother.

'anáájéé', t'áá', they ran back; retired; retreated.

'anáájidáahgo, when one goes back again.

'anáájiidlaa, he again made it; he made another.

'ánáájiil'įįh, one makes (it) again.

'anáájookai, they went again.

'anáákai, they went back, returned.

'áná'álnééh, reconstruction; being repaired.

'ánáálnííł, it can be made over.

'aná'álwo', bíká, she, he, receives aid; she, he gets relief.

'onáá'wodgo, since he ran back.

'ánáá!wod, yah, he ran in (an enclosure, as a hole, house, etc.).

'anaałání, Sioux or Comanche.

'anáá'ná, they migrated back.

'ánáánádjįhgo, when it, (supplies, etc.) is gone again.

'ánáánádzaago, when he did it again.

'ánáánát'éego, łahgo, there is still another way it can be done.

'ánáá'nííł, łahgo, it is changing.

'ánáá'nilgo, bikék'ehji', to replace (several).

'oná'á'nilgo, yah, putting them into.

anaanish, business. shinaanish, my business.

'anáá'oot'á, the sun set again.

'anaasází, ancient people; enemy ancestors.

'anaashashi, Santa Clara Pueblo (New Mexico).

'anááshiyííłhan, it again threw me.

'anááshwod, yah, I ran in again.

'aná'át'ááh, the sun sets.

'ánááyiidlaa, he made it again; he made another.

'anáá' yilch'ozh, sty.

'ánaazį, they are leaders.

'anábidi'noolkaad, they were herded, driven back.

'anábin, neutralizer.

'anádabineeskaad, t'áá', they drove them back, or forced them back (as in struggle for ground gains).

'anadanidzin, warlike, belligerent, bellicose, hostile.

'anadanidzin yéé, those who were for war.

'anádiz, eyelash.

'anádloh, he is laughing; he is having a laugh.

'ánádzaago, 'ał'ąą, when they changed back.

'anágaii, white of the eye. binágaii, white of his eyes.

'anáhaazhjéé', yóó', they escaped one after another.

'anáhálghą́ą́h, it is customarily thrown.

'anáhálghą́ą́h ńt'ę́ę́', it used to be thrown.

'anáhálzhishgo, when time passes again.

'anáhálzhish, nízaadgóó, long periods of time pass; there are long periods (when, during which).

'anáhá'niiłgo, bich'ą́ą́hji', when they were replaced by.........

'anáhá'niłígíí, bich'ą́ą́hji', they were replaced by.........

'anáháshgééh, yah, I pack them in one after another; I haul them in.

'anáháta', flash.

'anáhinidééh, they replace them; they automatically fall in place.

'ánáhodoo'nííł, łahgo, it (weather, world) is changing.

'anáhoolzhiizhgo, time having completed a cycle back to a point.

'ánáhoo'niłígíí, łahgo, the changing of the weather; the changing of the world.

'ánáhoot'jih, it happens (that).

'ana'í, enemy, foreigner, alien, stranger, outsider.

'aná'íí'eezh, he returned leading; he lead his party back.

'anák'ee, eye socket; ocular area.

'análi, paternal grandfather; paternal grandmother. shináli, my paternal grandfather or grandmother.

'ánál'jihgo, when it is reconstructed.

'ánálnééh, it is being made over; it is being repaired.

'análwo', yah, he runs in (an enclosure, as a hole, house, etc.).

'ánályaa, it was made again; another was made.

'ananáánínídzin, you are again in favor of war; you are again bellicose.

'ánaní'a', os pubis; lower portion of pelvic bone.

'anáníídee', they fell back in.

'anánishka', I herd them back (in or away).

'anáshdloh, I am laughing.

'anáshiyiiłhan, t'ą́ą́', it threw me back.

'anát'éézh, eyebrow.

'ánát'jihgo, 'áłah, when they (three or more) meet.

'anáts'iin, eyebrow, supraorbital.

'anáyíí'eezh, he led them back.

'anáyííjaa', he took them back (separable objects).

'ánáyiil'jih, they usually make them.

'anáyiis'nil, he, or she, put them back (one after another).

'anázhiin, pupil (of the eye).

'anázhiin yiiba', cataract.

'anázis, eyelid.

'anázis bii' diwozhí, trachoma.

'áńdaadjjhgo, when they (supplies) are exhausted.

'áńdaahdle', you repair them.

'áńda'ahildjjhgo, when they nearly annihilated one another.

'áńdaajah, they usually run.

'áńdaal'inigii, those which are repaired.

'áńdaalni', reparable.

'áńdaalnééh, they are being repaired, or being made over.

'áńdaalno'go, when they dive.

'áńdaasdjid, they reverted to a state of non-existence.

'áńdadoolnííł, they will be repaired.

'áńdahaaskai, they (many) have gone back (to their homes, or back to where they came from).

'áńdahaas'ná, they moved back one after the other.

'áńdahaazhjéé', yóó', they escaped one after the other.

'áńdaha'nil, naaltsoos, voting (by paper ballots).

'áńdahidoo'nééł, they (many) will move back (with their belongings, etc.).

'áńdchineezhchą́ą́', yóó', they escaped one after the other.

'áńda'iiz'ééł, bił, they sailed back (several boats).

'áńdayiidlaa, they rebuilt it. Tse'naa na'-nízhoozh 'áńdayiidlaa. They rebuilt the bridge.

'ándayiil'įįh, they usually make it.

'ándayiil'įįhgo, when they make them.

'andazneeskaad, yah, they drove or herded them back in. **Dibé nááyídooltah biniiy! yah 'andazneeskaad.** They drove the sheep back in to be recounted.

'andazneeskaad, t'ąą', they drove them back, as an attacking force.

'andazneeskaad, yóó, they drove them off, herded them off.

'andéehgo, because they are falling.

'andeiniiskaad, they all herded them, drove them back. **Dzilgóó bibéégashii 'andeiniiskaad.** They all herded their cattle back into the mountains.

'anditjoh, yóó', we will escape.

'andinóolkał, t'ąą', they will be driven back, be repulsed.

'andinóolkał, yah, they shall (or will) be driven back in.

'andinóolkał, yóó, they shall be driven off.

'andoojah, nihaa yóó', we will make them go back; we will drive them away.

'ándoolnííł, it will be repaired, fixed, rebuilt.

'ándoolníiłgo, to be fixed, repaired, rebuilt.

'ándoolwołgo, yóó, he will run back, escape.

'aneel'á, extension.

'ánéelą́ą́', it extends; there is (comparatively) much, many.

'áneelą́ą́', doo jóołta', innumerable.

'áneelt'e', number.

'áneelt'e'é 'áneelt'e', t'áá, it remains the same amount.

'áneelt'e'gi, the same amount.

'áneelt'e'igii, the amount; that is the number.

'ané'éshtił, snot, nasal mucus.

'aneest'įį', theft, burglary.

'Ane'étséyi', Canon del Muerto.

'aneeyą́, maturation.

'anéijahgo, 'áká, since we all helped.

'ání, he says.

'ání'áii, stem; the main beam (horizontal).

'aníchą́ą́', he fled.

'aníchxooshtł'ah, the corner of the eye.

'ánidaadįįhgo, bits'ą́ą́', when they exhaust their supplies.

'anidaadloh, they are laughing.

'anida'ajihgo, because they planted seeds.

'ánidaha'áii, governing body.

'anidahazt'i', the problems.

'ánida'iil'įįh, they write letters, notices, etc.

'anidajijahgóó, to where they run (roam).

'anidayii'nííł, they put them back in one after another.

'ani'ééł, bił, he arrived by boat; he sailed.

'ani'ééł, nihił, we arrived by boat.

'ani'eezh, he arrived leading.

'anigeed, I dug a ditch; I ran a ditch

'ánihiilaaígíí, the one who made us, our Creator.

'ánihwii'aahii, judge.

'ánihwii'aahii binant'a'í, the chief judge.

'áníí', nares, nostrils.

'anii', waist.

'anii', face.

'aniichą́ą́', yah — dooleeł ńt'ę́ę́', he would have been chased in.

'ániid, a short time ago; recently. **'Ániid nayiisnii' t'ah 'áníidigo.** He bought it recently when it was still new.

'áníid dah nááneesdáhígíí, one who took office recently.

'áníidí, it is new, fresh.

'áníidigo, t'áá, just recently.

'áníidí yę́ędą́ą́', when it was new.

'áníidlah, t'áá, we two; both of us. **T'áá 'áníidlah nihi'niidlí.** We are both cold (freezing).

'áníid naaghá, it is young.

'áníid naashá, I am young.

'ániigo, he says.

'aní'įį', thievery, larceny, robbery.

'ani'įįhii. thief, burglar.

'aniik'éédít'áhí, halter.

'aniik'idé'ání, halter.

'áníiltso, t'áá, (also, t'áá 'áníit'é), all of us.

'aniishjaa', cheek bone.

'aniitsi', cheek (flesh).

'áníldiil, 'ayói, large; big (animate objects only, but this could be used for "big log") **Tł'iish 'ayói 'áníldiil łéí yi'nah.** There's a big snake crawling along.

'ánildiilgo, since it is big (animate).

'anili, rags.

'aniłdjid, I survived for a certain length of time.

'aniłk'ah, fattening.

'aniłkǫ́ǫ́', he swam away; he swam along.

'ániłnééz, it is longer; he is taller (comparatively). Díí gad yáázh shilááh 'ániłnééz. This young juniper is taller than I am.

'ániłtéél, 'ayói, it is very wide. Be'ek'id 'ayói 'ániłtéél. The lake is very wide.

'ániłtéelgo, 'ayói, since it is very wide.

'ániłtsááz, it is thick. Nástáán 'ashdladi 'adées'eez dóó bi'ǫǫgi 'ániłtsááz. The log is more than five feet thick.

'ániłtso, 'ayói, very large, or too large. Kin 'ayói 'ániłtso. The house is very large.

'ániłtsogo, since it was large, or big.

'ániłtsooí 'ániłtsogo, t'áá, it remains the same in size. 'Ooljéé' t'áá 'ániłtsooí 'ániłtsogo k'ad táá' yiská. The moon has been the same size in the last three nights.

'aniná, they (group of people) arrived (with their belongings, or equipment); also they (people) moved along (with their goods, etc.).

'ánínę́ę, those who arrived (with their equipment).

'anísdáás, I am heavier. Nilááh 'anísdáás sha'shin. Maybe I am heavier than you.

'ánisht'é, I am. Doo Shitah hats'íidgóó 'ánisht'é. I am not feeling well.

'anisnééz, I am tall (in comparative sense).

'anists'iisí, I am small, short.

'onit'i', fence.

'ánit'i, you are; you did it.

'anit'i' bił 'adaałkaałí, staples (for fence posts)

'aníyá, he arrived leading (or served as a leader ——)

'ánizáád, 'ayoi, it is distant, far. Tóógóó 'ayói 'ánizáád. It is far to the waterhole.

'ánizáádę́ę́', from a considerable distance 'Ashdladiindi tsin sitá bilááh 'ánizaodę́ę́' łįį' shił yíldloozh. I rode my horse from more than fifty miles away.

'ánizáadi, bilááh, at a place farther than it.

'ánizah, distance.

'añjíjahgo, biká, since they helped him or them.

'añjíjah, yah, they (people) go in, run in

'ánółtso, t'áá, all of you. T'áá 'ánółtso danihiyooch'iid! You are all lying!

'ánoolinígíí, features, or characteristics (of a person).

'anoolzhee'go, there were (parallel) streaks, lines to a common point. Dził tát'ahjį' niłtsą́ 'anoolzhee'go hodíína'. There were streaks of rain on the side of the mountains for awhile.

'unoołchéłę́ę, the one that was chasing him; the one that was chasing (the other).

'anoołkał, he, she, is herding along.

'anooséél, adolescence.

'ant'ą́ą́góó, doo bikáá', since nothing would grow on it; unproductive; barren.

'áńt'įįh, poison (native).

'aoo', yes.

'as, an expression used to denote surprise.

'ásaa', pot; dish; bowl; or pan. 'ásaa' bee 'adoobishii, a pot to be used for boiling.

'ásaa' bá si'áni, dish cupboard.

'ásaa' bee yiłtązhi, drumstick.

'ásaa' dádeestł'ónígíí, pot drum.

'ásaa' ditáni, dutch oven.

'ásaa' tó bee naakáhi, pail, bucket.

'ásaats'iil, potshard.

'as'ah, a long time. Doo 'as'ah sédáa da, I can't sit long. Gáagii 'ayóǫ 'as'ah neaghá. The crow has a long life span.

'as'ahgóó, for a long time.

'asdá, sitting. Kóne' 'asdá bá haz'ą́. This is the sitting room.

'asdáhi, bikáá' dah, chair, bench.

'ásdįįd, it is all gone; it disappeared; it vanished; it faded away; it dwindled out; it ran out; it became exhausted; it became extinct. shibee'eldǫǫh bik'a' 'ásdįįdgo, when I ran out of bullets; when my supply of bullets became exhausted.

'ásdįįdgo, when it became extinct, disappeared.

'asdiz, I am spinning.

'ásdzaa, I did; I acted.

'asdzáá-n, elderly woman.

'asdzáni, women.

'asdzáni bahastiin daaztsánigii, widow.

'asdzáni da'iigisigii, laundress, washerwoman.

'asdzoh, inch (a mark on the ruler).

'aseezį, gossip.

'aseezį nisdzin, I like to gossip, exaggerate.

'asésiih, I missed; I made a mistake.

'asgą, pelt, hide. ,

'asháni, t'áadoo, without (my) eating. Abinidą́ą́' t'áadoo 'asháni hooghandę́ę́' dah diiyá. I left home this morning without eating.

'ashch'ąh, fit, hysteria.

'ashchį, she gave birth.

'ashchiinii, parents. bishchiinii, his parents.

'ashchin, I can smell.

'ashdla', five. 'ashdladi, five times.

'ashdla'áadah, fifteen. 'ashdla'áadahįį, up to fifteen.

'ashdla'ajį nda'anish, Friday.

'ashdla' 'asdzohgo, as much as five inches.

'ashdladi 'adées'eez, five feet.

'ashdladiin fifty. 'ashdladiindi, fifty times.

'ashdladiingo, fifty of them. Dibé 'ashdladiingo shaa nahaaznii'. I sold fifty head of sheep.

'ashdladi mííl, five thousand.

'ashdladi neeznádiin, five hundred.

'ashdla'go, five of them.

'ashdla'igíí, the number five.

'ashgish, incision.

'áshi'dólzin, I was kept.

'áshi'doo'niidę́ę́góó, what I was told; in line with what I was told.

'áshįįh, salt; Salt Lake, New Mexico.

'áshįįhigíí, that which is salt.

'áshįįh likan, sugar.

'áshįįh niłt'izí, crude salt, unrefined salt.

'ashiiké, boys.

'ashiikéjí, on the boys' side.

'ashíił'a', he sent me (to —). Shizhé'é naalyéhé bá hooghangóó 'ashíił'a'. My father sent me to the trading post.

'ashiyiiłhanigii, the one that threw me; that which threw me.

'ashja'eł'iinii, opportunity; opportunity maker.

'ashjada'ale'go, as opportunities present themselves.

'ashje'iilaa, the opportunity came.

'áshjiish, opportunity.

'ashkii, boy; lad.

'ashkiistł'inii, freckled boy.

'ashkǫ́ǫ́h, dah, I kept swimming (toward a point); I am treading water.

'áshłaa, I made it (something). Dáádilkał áshłaa. I made the door.

'áshłééh, I am making it; I am building it. 'likááh 'áshłééh. I am making a sandpainting.

'ashtéézh, sexual intercourse.

'asht'e'jiilaa, he, she, got things ready.

'asht'į, I am rich, well-to-do.

'ásht'į, I am; I did it; I have done it.

'ásht'įį, doo — da, I did not do it.

'ásht'į, shi, I did it; I have done it; it is I.

'ásht'į, t'óó, I am just fooling around; I'm not doing anything in particular.

'ásht'į, tsxįįł, I am doing it as fast as I can.

'ashzhish, I am dancing.

'ásité, crossbeam (lower) on a Navajo loom.

'ásizį, representative; a leader; a headman.

'ásizínę́ę, the one who was chief, leader, or headman.

'asłįį'go, he made something come into existence.

'asłįį'go, yee łą́, when he accepted it; when he agreed to it.

'asłįį', łą́, he, or she agreed, or consented.

'asnááhii, or 'asnéanii, captor.

'asohodéébéézhgóó, doo, extremely; exceedingly; insupportably. Doo 'asohodéébéézhgóó shi'niidlí. I am very cold (freezing).

'astsid, doo — da, I am not a silversmith.
'ászólí, it is light (in weight).
'at'a', wing. Tsidii bit'a' k'é'éltǫ' lá. The bird has a broken wing.
'ata', between. 'Ata'gi sizínigíí shizhé'é 'át'j.. The man between the other two is my father.
'at'qq, leaf, or leaves. Díí chéchil bit'qq' 'át'é. This is an oak-leaf.
'ataa', father.
'átáá', forehead. Shítáá' hadzííyá. I have a bump on my forehead.
'ataadaakaaígíí, those that go among.
'ataadaakai, they go among.
'ataaghéego, when he was walking among.
'at'aał, mastication.
'ataashá, I am walking among.
'atah, among. bitah, among them. 'Atah chił ni'deedéél. I was among those that were captured.
'át'ah, after a while; later; soon; wait, 'Át'ah shaa nóádiídaał. Come back and see me later.
'át'ahádóó, later on.
'ata' halni', he, she is interpreting.
'ata' halni'í, interpreter, translator.
'ata' halni'go, when he was translating, interpreting.
'atahazhosh, muscle under femur.
'atah ch'idabi'dit'ááh, they are among those being mentioned.
'atah danikinii, those which belong to, members.
'atah danilínigíí, those which are members.
'atah 'ídlį, membership.
'atah 'ídzá, entry.
'át'ahígo, in a little while; soon; later.
'atah 'ihooł'aah, he, she, is one of those who is learning, taking training.
'atah náádeesdzá, he, she, is one of those who is going again.
'atah naaltsoos 'adayiiniił, they are voters.
'atah naazbaa', he, she, is one of those who went on raids, to battle.
'atah nahaztseed, he is anesthetized.

'atahodiisnáá', nervous.
'átahodiniiltłóóh, relax.
'atah tázhdiłłiishgo, he served in an official capacity among them.
'atah yá'ádahoot'éehii, bee, something that keeps a person healthy, vitamins, etc.
'atah yaa yinist'įįd, he, or she took part in the discussion; took part in the action.
'átásiil, perspiration.
'át'é, it is; could. Díí tó 'át'é. This is water.
'át'é, 'at'qq, they are different. Ha'át'éegi shą' bee 'at'qq 'át'é? What makes the difference?
'até'át'iinii, that which is harmful.
'at'ééd, girl, maiden.
'át'éegi, characteristic of.
'át'éego, for being. T'áá bíhí 'át'éego k'ad 'awáalya sidá. He has himself to blame for being in jail.
'át'éego, 'ayóó, remarkable extraordinary. 'Ayóó 'át'éego yaa tsídeezkééz. He thought them remarkable.
'át'éégóó, being such. Doo ha'át'íhii da yáátis wóya' 'át'éégóó 'áyiilaa. He made it so strong that nothing could get over it.
'át'éégóó, t'áá doo, foolish, stupid.
'at'ééké, girls (pl. of 'at'ééd).
'atééł, ventral area.
'atééł siłtsoozí, apron.
'até'éł'į, it is harmful.
'até'éł'įį, doo — da, it is harmless.
'atéét'įįd, yaa, he did all he could for it; he really put in a lot of effort.
'át'éhégóó, t'áadoo, without any trouble; nothing unusual about it.
'át'éhígi, similar in appearance or characteristics; same.
'át'éii, that which is.........
'át'eii, 'agháadi, the best; handsomest; supreme.
'át'éii, łahgo, that which is different; otherwise.
'atéłí, spleen.
'atéł'įįgo, because he was being mistreated, harmed.

'át'é, t'áá, all of it; all of them; in its (their) entirety. Nibéeso t'áá 'át'é shaa níníił. Give me all of your money.

'át'į, he is, does, did.

'at'į, he is rich.

'atíbi'diilyaa, he was mistreated, harmed.

'atíbi'diilyaaigií, those who were mistreated.

'atíbi'dool'įįd, they were mistreated, harmed.

'atíbiilaa, it harmed him; he mistreated him.

'atída'ahiilyaii, those that harmed one another.

'atída'ahiilyaii, yee, that with which they harmed one another.

'atída'ahil'inéędą́ą́', at the time when they were mistreating one another.

'atída'ahil'inígií, those that harmed one another.

'atídaalyaa, they were harmed, mistreated.

'atídabi'dil'įįgo, because they were being mistreated.

'atídabi'dool'įįd, they were harmed.

'atídabidooliiłii, that which will harm them.

'atídabííł'įįdéę, the harm that they did to them.

'atídabił'inígií, those who do harm to them.

'atídahijiilyaaigií, the harm they did to one another.

'atídahijool'įįdéę, the fact that they harmed one another.

'atídahóół'įįd, they did them harm.

'atídazhdiilyaa, they were wounded; they were hurt.

'atídeił'įįgo, because they harm them, or it.

'atídeił'inígií, those (animate objects) that they harmed or mistreated.

'atídiilyaa, he, she was injured, wounded, hurt.

'atí'doolííł, it will do harm.

'atídoolnííł, he will be harmed.

'atí'doolnííł, to do harm (all he thinks of is—).

'atího'diilyaago, since they were mistreated, harmed.

'atí hodoolííł, it will harm him; it is likely to harm him.

'át'įįgo, since he did.

'at'įįgo, since he is rich.

'át'įįgo, t'óó, he is just pretending, just doing so.

'atííł'į, he harms it.

'atííł'įįgo, because he mistreats them.

'atiin, road, trail.

'atiin baghgóó, along the side of the road; near the road. 'Atiin baghgóó dibé naakai. There is a herd of sheep near the road.

'atiinidę́ę́', from the road. 'Atiinidę́ę́' t'áá ni' nánísdzá. I walked home from the road.

'atiinigií, that which is the road.

'át'iinii, the doer.

'atijiilaa, he did harm to him.

'át'ínéę, the one who did it; the one who committed it.

'át'inígií, his doings; what he did.

'atíniishłaa, I injured you; I hurt you. Doo 'atiniishłaa da. I did not hurt you.

'atíshiilaa, it injured me; he hurt me.

'atíyiilaa, he harmed him. yits'ą́ą́' 'atíyiilaago, he having damaged them for him (i.e. away from him).

'atíyiił'įįh, he does harm to it.

'atízhdiilyaa, he is harmed, injured.

'atízhdoolííł, he will harm him. T'áá'iidą́ą́' 'atízhdoolííł shą'shin nisin. I know he will harm him.

'atł'aa', rump, buttock.

'atł'eeyah dah sinili, singletree.

'atł'eeyah dah sinili bá ni'áhigií, doubletree.

'atł'eeyah dah sinili bił 'íí'áhigií, wagon hammer (queen bolt).

'atł'eh, crotch (of the legs).

'atł'izh, bile, gall.

'atł'izhtsé, gall stone.

'atł'ó, to weave.

'atł'ótsin, upper and lower loom poles.

'at'oh, nest (birds).

'at'ohigií, that which is the nest.

'at'oig, clavicle, collarbone.

'atoo', soup; juice; stew; gravy.

'atsą, inside of the body.

'atsá, eagle.

'átsą́ą́', ribs.
'átsą́ą́' bita', intercostal.
'átsą́ą́' bita' góne' 'ats'oos naalgizh, intercostal neurectomy.
'átsą́ą́' naalgizh, therocoplasty.
'atsá bit'oh, eagle nest.
'Atsá Biyáázh, February.
'ats'ádeet'ą́, prohibition.
'atságah, side (of the body).
'atsáhą́ą, that eagle.
'atsą́ ha'íí'óól, abortion or miscarriage.
'ats'áhá'niił, they are being taken away from the group.
'atsáhígíí, the eagle.
'atsą́'ízh'díłnééhgo, when preparing food for oneself.
'atsą́ na'alyol, flatulence.
'ats'éoz'a', limbs (of man or of a tree); bough; branches.
'ats'éoz'a' k'égéésh, amputation.
'atsą́stiin, fetus.
'atsáts'id, tendon back and above the heel.
'atsá yáázh, eaglet.
'átsé first (also 'áłtsé).
'átsé choo'įįhii, first aid.
'ats'éé', navel, umbilicus.
'atsee', tail, coccyx.
'atseeltsoii, western red tail hawk.
'atsék'ee, lap.
'atséziil, lumbar.
'atsi', daughter (of the man) or niece (daughter of the man's brother). Baa nánít'ínígíí 'atsi' nilį́. The one you have reference to is the daughter.
'atsį', meat, flesh.
'atsį' bii' ni'ílts'id, tumor.
'ats'id, sinew, tendon, ligament.
'atsį' diitł'iizh, gangrene.
'atsidi, bee, hammer.
'atsiditsoh, bee, sledge hammer.
'atsii' hair (on the head).
'atsiigha', mane.
'atsiighąą', brain.
'atsiighąą' bii' hasdił, brain concussion.
'atsiighąą' bik'ésti'ígíí, meninges, membranes that cover the brain.

'atsiighąą' bik'ésti'ígíí didooshchii, meningitis.
'atsį'ígíí, the flesh.
'atsiin, stem (see 'éní'áii).
'ats'iis, body.
'ats'iis bitoo', body fluid.
'ats'iis doo hináanii, corpse, carcass.
'ats'iis naalnish, metabolism.
'ats'iistah 'áshįįh łikon nanit'ą' silį́į', diabetes.
'ats'iists'in, skeleton.
'ats'iis yiganigíí, mummification.
'atsiit'ą́ą́d, crown (of the head).
'atsiit'ą́ą́d tó 'áłnééh, baptism.
'atsiits'iin, head, craneum.
'atsiiyah, back of head, occiput.
'atsili, the younger brother. Baa holne'ígíí 'atsili nilį́. The one you are talking about is the younger brother of the two.
'ats'in, bone(s). (also, ts'in).
'atsiniłtł'ish, lightning, electricity.
'atsiniłtł'ish bee da'diłtłi'ígíí, electric light.
'atsiniiłtł'ish bee 'adinidiin, electric light.
'atsói, grandchild.
'atsoo', tongue (organ).
'ats'oos, blood vessel(s); nerve.
'ats'oos dahyiiye' varicose (veins).
'ats'oos dootł'izhigíí, vein.
'ats'oos dootł'izhigíí bii'alt'ood, intravenous injection.
'atsoosk'id, front of femur.
'ats'oos łichi'ígíí, artery.
'ats'oos naalgizh, neurectomy.
'ats'oostsoh dootł'izhigíí, vein.
'ats'oosts'óóz, capillary, or capillaries.
'ats'oos yita', pulse.
'ats'oos yita'gi, pulsation of —.
'ats'óóz, nerves.
'ats'óóz naaztseed, local anesthesia (nerves in one part of the body are made numb or anesthetized).
'ats'os, down, downy feathers.
'awáalya, jail.
'awáalya hótsaai, penitentiary.
'awáalyaai, prisoner, convict.
'awáalya yaa 'áhályáni, jailer.

'awéé', baby, papoose.

'awee' 'atsá haalteeh, cesarean operation.

'awéé' bibeeldléi, oaby blanket.

'awéé' binichxǫ'í, baby things

'awéé' biyaałái, placenta, or after-birth.

'awéé' doo hináágóó yizhchí, still birth.

'awéé' hanoodzá, premature birth.

'awéé' hayiidzįįsii, midwife.

'awééshchíín, doll.

'awééts'áál, cradle, cliff rose.

'awéé' yaa 'áhályáni, baby-sitter.

'awéé' yii' nitéhí, crib.

'awóchaan, tartar (on teeth).

'awók'iz bee na'atsii, toothpick(s).

'awoi, marrow.

'awołí, t'áá — bee, as fast as (he) could; at full speed; your utmost.

'awoo', teeth, tooth.

'awoo' bee yich'iishí, toothbrush.

'awoo' diniih, toothache.

'awoo' yinaalnishi, dentist.

'awos, shoulder.

'awosh, sleep.

'awótsiín, gums (of teeth).

'awózhah, eyetooth.

'ayá, ouch.

'áyaa, under one's self.

'áyaa 'ayoo'nil, he put them under subjugation; he put them under himself.

'ayaadi daa'é'ígíí, underclothes.

'ayaadi 'éé', underclothes.

'áyaańda, no wonder. 'áyaańda yídloh. No wonder you're laughing.

'ayaats'iin, chin, jaw, mandible.

'ayaayááh, throat (outside).

'ayaayááh dah 'iiye', goiter.

'ayaayááh niichaad, mumps.

'ayáázh, young green corn; son.

'ayadahojooligo, baa, because they are suspicious of it.

'ayadahooli, yaa, they are suspicious about it.

'ayadahoosni'ę́ę, baa, the suspects; those of whom people were suspicious.

'ayahdidi'nił, incense.

'Ayahkinii, Hopi.

'ayahooli, he is suspicious.

'ayahooli, yaa, he is suspicious of them; distrustful of them.

'ayahoolni, suspicion.

'ayáni, bison, buffalo.

'Ayáni Bito', Iyanbito, New Mexico.

'aye', son.

'ayęęzhii, egg; testicle. biyęęzhii, his testicle. be'ayęęzhii, his (hen's) eggs.

'ayęęzhii bits'iil, egg shell.

'ayid, chest, sternum, breast.

'ayi'dę́ę́' dił, hemorrhage.

'ayih, breath.

'ayi' hodilid, heartburn.

'áyiilaa, he made it.

'áyiilaago, when he made it.

'áyiilaaígíí, the one who made it; or the one which he made.

'áyiilaa yę́ę, that which he or she has made. Shimá diyogi 'áyiilaa yę́ę kǫ́ǫ́ 'atah sił tsooz. Here is the rug that mother made.

'ayííł'a', he sent him to —.

'ayííł'éél, he sailed it away.

'áyííł'įįd, ch'ééh, he acted in vain, failed. ch'ééh 'áyííł'įįdgo, he having failed in it.

'áyííł'įįh, he makes it.

'ayiiłkǫ́ǫgo, 'áajį', when that day comes.

'ayíiłna', he swallowed it; he gulped it.

'ayíímal, to bolt food (as a coyote or dog).

'ayíínil, he put them in.

'ayiishóód, yah, he dragged it in (an enclosure, as a hole, house, etc.).

'ayiistł'iid, he threw them down.

'ayiistł'iid, naa, he pushed them down (like posts, etc.).

'ayiistł'iid, yił yah, he threw them in (an enclosure) to him or them.

'ayiistł'iid, yóó, he threw them away.

'ayiitsih, he stuck it in; he set it up (as with reference to a stake).

'áyi'niiłdįįd, he began to destroy it.

'ayói, very, exceedingly, extraordinarily, remarkably.

'ayóigo, exceedingly, remarkably, very.

'ayói 'ó'ó'ni, love.

'ayóo, very; extremely (also 'ayóó or'ayóo-go). 'Ayóo deesk'aaz. It (weather) is very cold.

'ayóo bizhąda'íłį, they are very stubborn.

'ayóo da 'át'éé léi', a big one.

'ayóogo, really; remarkably; strongly; extremely; exceedingly. 'ayóogo niłchxon. It smells very bad, stinks terribly.

'áyooliił, he has been making them right along.

'ayóo yíní si'ą, irascibility.

'áyósin. he keeps it; he maintains it.

'azáát'i'í, bridle.

'azaatł'óól, rein.

'aza'azis, pocket.

'azági, esophagus, gullet.

'azahat'ági, palate.

'azák'í dii'níih, strangulation.

'azanátsihi, clinical thermometer.

'azázi, ancestor.

'azéé', mouth.

'azee', medicine; drug.

'azee' qqh 'ádaal'į bá náhoot'aah, a clinic.

'azee'aditidi łizhinigii, iodine.

'azee'á!'į, hospital.

'azee'ál'įįdóó, from the hospital.

'azee'ál'įį góne', in the hospital.

'azee'ál'įįjį', to the hospital.

'azee'ál'inídi, at the hospital.

'azee'ál'inigii, that which is a hospital.

'azee' bááhádzidii, poison (drug).

'azee'.bá hooghan, drug store.

'azee' bee 'iilgháshi, ether.

'azee' bich'į' 'adánígíí, tonic.

'azee' bił baa 'ada'atsi, shots of medicines; injections.

'azee' bił na'ané, ambulant clinic.

'azéédéenili, hames (of harness).

'azéé'deest'ą, conspiracy.

'azéédéetáni, collar (harness).

'azeedi, cousin (daughter of one's paternal aunt, or of one's ·maternal uncle). shizeedí, my cousin.

'azeedich'ii', chili pepper.

'azeediilch'iłii, blue flowered lupine.

'azee'étłohí, liniment.

'azéé' hahatłeeh, trench mouth.

'azéé' hazłįį', deceased.

'azee'igii, that which is medicine.

'azee'iiłchíhigii, mercurochrome.

'azee'iił'íní, doctor, physician.

'azee'iił'íní 'achí ye'aniihii, obstetrician.

'azee'iił'íní na'ałgizhigii, surgeon.

'azee' łikoní, alcohol (for medicinal use).

'azee' naa'niih góne', dispensary.

'azee' nayiiłniihi, druggist.

'azeeniłchin, peppermint plant.

'azéé' si'áni, bit (on the bridle).

'azee'tł'ohii, blue-eyed grass.

'azhą́ — ndi, even then; even though; although. 'Azhą́ hasistih ndi ayóo 'eesh'í. Even though I am old I see well.

'azháenee', even though; in spite of the fact that; despite the fact that.

'azhdeesdǫǫh, bił, he shot him.

'azhdees'éél, he (they) sailed along; he is on his way (by boat). Bíighahgi 'azhdees'éél, He (they) sailed along past it.

'azhdii'ą, yóó', he gave it up; he desisted from it; he quit it.

'azhdii'eezh, dah, he started off in the lead; he started off leading; he took charge.

'azhdisoł, bee, to sputter (to throw out solid or fluid particles in a succession of explosions from the mouth, etc.).

'azhdisoł, hazhéé' bee, to splutter.

'azhdoo'ał, he will throw it. Bich'į' 'azhdoo'ał, He will throw it at him, deliver it to him.

'ázhdooliił, he will make it. Bitsiiziz 'ázhdooliił, He will scalp him.

'azhéé', saliva (also shéé').

'azhé'é, father. Shizhé'é naalnish. My father is working.

'azhi', torso, body.

'azhí, voice (also 'iinéé').

'azhiih, cedar bast.

'azhǫǫh, domestication.

'azid, liver.

'azis, bag, sack. 'azisígíí, the bag.

'azis, naaltsoos, paper sack or bag.

'azis, tł'oh, gunnysack.

'aziz, penis.

'azlį̜'ę̜ędą́ą́', at the time of the happening of an event. Késhmish 'azlį̜'ę̜ędą́ą́' hooghandi náníshdzá. I returned home last Christmas.

'azlį̜į̜', it became; it was thought; it occured. T'áá 'iiyisíí dooda lá 'azlį̜į̜'. Things became hopeless.

'azlį̜'gi, bą́ą́h, at the value; the value; how much it is worth.

'azlį̜į̜'go, bee lą́, when it was agreed upon, approved.

'aznízin, doo — da, he wants nothing; he has no appetite. Shiłééchąą'í doo 'anízin da. My dog has no appetite.

'azóól, corn or wheat tassle.

'azool, trachea, windpipe.

'azool biih yiłk'aaz, bronchitis.

'azǫ́ǫ́z, stinger.

– B –

bá, in his favor; in favor of him; for him, her, it (for his sake). **Bá yá'át'ééh,** It is good for him. **Bá 'ádeeshłííł,** I will make it for him.

baa, about or to, him, her, it, them. **Baa dajoodlohígíí,** The fact that they laugh cbout it. **Baa ní'ą́,** I gave it to him. **Baa hashni',** I am telling about it. **Baa ntséskees,** I am thinking about it. Before initial **yi-** of a following verb, **baa** and **yi-** merge by assimilation to **beei-,** thus **Baa yishdloh** becomes **beeishdloh,** I am laughing at him. This assimilation is not written.

bąą, on account of (see **biniinaa**).

baa', heroine (component of many feminine personal names).

ba'ąą, in addition to it, excess of. (also **ba'aan**).

baa 'ada'a'nilgo, when they drill into it.

baa 'ádahojilyą́ągo, since they took care of it; since they were cautious of it.

baa 'áháshchįįh, to be aware of it.

baa 'áháyą́ągi, taking care of; watching.

baa 'áháyą́ą ndi, although it is being cared for, watched.

ba'aan, in addition to it. (see **ba'ąą**).

baa 'ayahoolni, it, he, she, is dangerous, doubtful, questionable; to be suspicious of.

baa ch'ídahodziz'ą́, something was said about it. (news about it came).

baa ch'íhoot'ą́, something was said about it.

baa dáádahodidooldoh, they will be left behind, retarded.

baadaaní, his, her, son-in-law; stepfather.

báádahadzidii, those things which are awful, tabu.

baa daha'niihgo, because they are praised.

baa dahonohsą́ągo, act with caution; be very careful of it; be wise to it; take steps with caution.

baa dahóóni', they were brought about (as news about them) etc.

bą́ą'déé'ééł, the covering was washed away.

bááh, bread. (also **łees'áán**).

bąqh, beside it; on; on it; alongside it; up on it, upon it. **'Atiin bąqhgi tsin 'íí'á,** The tree stands beside the road. **Dził bąqh yas,** There is snow on the mountain.

bąqh 'ádoolníiłji, that which to put on; to apply; to treat with.

bááhádzid, it is fearful; threatening; awful; tabu; injurious to health (like contaminated water, etc.). (also **báhádzid**). seriously; badly; very. **Tł'éédą́ą́' t'óó báhádzidgo deesk'aaz.** It was very cold last night.

bááhádzidgo 'át'é, it is dangerous (as injurious to health); it is tabu.

bąqhági, immoral; wrong.

bąqhági 'áhát'į́, misbehavior.

bąqhági 'át'éii, sin.

bááh 'ál'į́įgi, bakery.

baa hani', story about it; news concerning him, her, it, them, (etc.).

baa ha'niih, commendation expressed; glorified.

baa ha'niihgo, being praised.

baa has'nih, got honorable mention, praised.

bááhádzidii, it is poison.

bááh bighan, outdoor oven.

bááh bił 'ál'íní, yeast. (also **diik'ǫsh**).

bááh bizéí, bread crumbs.

bąąh daah'íní, t'aadoo do not forbid him, her, them, or it, the use of, or service of, or forbid him to attend, etc.

bááh dá'áka'í, crackers.

bąąh dahaatł'ǫ, we tied it to it. **Łééchąą'í 'anít'i' bąąh dahaatł'ǫ.** We tied the dog to the fence.

bąąh dah dahoo'a'ígíí, the sick, the injured.

bąąh dah dahoyoo'aałii, those who became sick.

bąąh dah haz'ąągo, since he is in poor health; since he is sick.

bąąh dah naaztánígíí, those which are hanging (stiff objects) on it.

bąąh dah nahaz'ąągo, because they were sick.

bąąh dah nahaz'ą́ą́ lá, they are sick, (they are affected with disease, etc.); lack of health.

baah dah nahaz'aanii, invalids.

bąąh dah ndahaz'ánígíí, the sick, the injured.

bąąh dahoo'a'go, because he was hurt, injured, became sick, or disabled.

bą́ą́h da'ílį́, the cost, the value of them (many).

bąąhdę́ę́' off; down from it. **Tsin bąąhdę́ę́' bilasáana naalts'id.** An apple fell off the tree

Bááh Diilid, Fruitland, New Mexico.

bąąhgóó, alongside of; near it. **Be'ek'id bąąhgóó 'atiin.** The road runs along the side of the lake.

bąąh hááda' 'aldahígíí, stairway.

bąąh hadasooł'áago, since they owe you something; they are under obligation to you, as for money, goods, services, benefit, or help.

bąąh ha'íízhahí, cup.

bááh 'íłt'íní, baker.

bą́ą́h 'ílį́, it is worth; it is valuable.

bą́ą́h 'ílįįgo, because it is worth.

bááh łikaní, cake.

bááh łikaní daazganígíí, cookies.

bááh łikaní dah díníilghaazhígíí, doughnuts.

bááh łikaní náhineests'ee'ígíí, cinnamon rolls.

bááh nímazí, biscuit, buns (also **bááh yázhí**).

baa hóch'į', (an area) is reserved or restricted for a purpose.

baa hodeeshnih, I will tell about it; I will spread the news about it.

ba'ahódlí, dependability.

baa honeeni, it is fun; for fun; it is interesting.

baa honishchį', be stingy with an area (as land).

baa hwiiníst'įįd, it was discussed; he had been tried.

bá 'áhwiinít'į́, he is very generous, or charitable.

baa hwiinít'įįh, it will be discussed, or will be tried.

baa hwiinít'inígíí, one who is under discussion; one who is being tried.

bááh yázhí, buns (also **bááh nímazí**).

baa'ih, to be dirty, filthy.

baa'ih, t'óó, it is dirty, filthy. **T'óó baa'ihii,** That which is filthy.

ba'áłchíní, his, her, their, children, family.

ba'ałk'ee, at his place; at his home. **Tł'éédą́ą́' díí hastiin ba'ałk'ee shiiską́.** I stayed overnight at this man's place last night.

bááłk'iisjí, beside it; parallel to it.

baa na'aldeeh, doings, proceedings, etc. **Nighandi shą' ha'át'íí baa na'aldeeh?** What is going on at your house?

baa na'aldeehgi, at certain doings.

baa na'asdee', what took place; it took place (past tense of doings). **Tł'éédą́ą́' díí kin biyi' ha'át'íí baa na'asdee'?** What took place in this house last night?

baa nahonitł'a, hinder, hamper, impede.

baa ńdadiit'įįł, we will discuss it; we will take action toward it.

baa ńdahast'įįd, it was discussed; action has been taken, etc.

baa ńdchidit'aahii, that which was given back; forgiveness; remission.

baa nihideeshdááł, I will ambush them; to waylay.

baa ni'iiyeedzá, ambuscade.

baa nijighá, doing.

baa niná'áldah, it takes place. **Kwii na'a-hóóhai baa niná'áldah.** The rodeo takes place right here.

baanishchį', I am stingy with it.

baa ntsídadzikeesgo, what they think, or consider.

baa ntsínááhákeesgo, reconsidering it.

baásh náhásin, it is not funny.

bááshzhinii, jet (stone).

báá síníti'go, carefully.

ba'át'e', his, or their, faults; wickedness; evilness.

ba'át'e' 'ádin, it is faultless; he is harmless.

báátis, over it; high over it. **(sháátis,** over me).

baa yádááti', it was discussed; talks were made about it.

baa yádááti'ígíí, the subject which was discussed.

baa yádaati'ígíí, that which is being discussed; the subject under discussion.

baa yideeshbįįł, I will win it from him.

baazhnítá, he gave it (a stiff, slender object) to him; he brought it to him. **Habee'el-dǫǫh baazhnítá.** He gave him his gun.

bada'éłchíní, their offspring, descendents.

badahani', their stories, their tales.

badahastói, their elder men.

bádahooghan, naalyéhé, trading posts.

bada'iis'nil, they received gifts; they were loaned to them. **Béeso bada'iis'nil.** They received money as a loan.

bádá'ólta'í, the school teachers.

báda'ólta'ígíí, school teachers.

ba'deet'á, he received permission, consent.

ba'deet'ą́ągo, since he received permission or consent.

ba:doo'nił, a loan will be made to him. **Béeso ba'doo'niłgo yee kin 'iidoolííł.** He will get a sum of money as a loan and will build a house with it.

báhádzidgo, t'óó, seriously, badly, extremely, awfully. **Díí jį t'óó báhádzidgo dees-k'aaz.** It is awfully cold today.

báhádzidígi, t'óó — 'áł'éego, in a frightful manner; terrible. **T'óó báhádzidígi 'áł'ée-go nihee deeyol 'adą́ą́dą́ą́'.** We had a terrible windstorm yesterday.

báhádzidii, fearful thing.

bahaghałji', as far as its withers or shoulder. (with reference to the point above the shoulder of quadrupeds only).

báhá·yáahii absentee.

bahastiin, her husband.

bahastiin naakii, bigamist (i.e. one with two husbands).

bahat'aadí, t'áadoo, obviously, evidently, clearly, doubtlessly.

báhaz'ą́, bee, he has the right, privilege.

bá haz'ání góne', a place or space (for it). **Atsį' bá haz'ání góne' honeezk'az.** A place where the meat is kept is very cold.

báhodeeshchįįł, I will make him angry.

ba·hódlí, reliability.

báhóóchįįd, he is angry, disturbed.

bá hooghan, a house for it; a hogan for it. **Kóne' sodizin bá hooghan,** This is the church. (a house for worship)

bahoo'ih, t'óó, it (area) is ugly, filthy, useless, no good.

ba'it'ą́ągo, since it was loaned to him. **T'ááłá'í béeso ba'it'ą́ągo yee gohwééh nayiisnii'.** He borrowed a dollar (coin) with which he purchased some coffee.

bá nááhásdlįį'go, since it became available for him again. **Naanish bá nááhásdlįį'go 'ákǫǫ dah náádiidzá.** He has gone to work again since there was an opening.

bánáhásdzo, it (area) was marked off around for them; reserved.

bá nahaz'ą́, rooms or places for them; time set for them.

bánáhoo'aah, there is usually room for them; time is usually set for them. **báhwiidoo'aeł,** there will be room for them. **hani' báhwiidoo'aeł,** time will be set for a story.

bá nanideehgo, in existence for them; available to them.

bá nináádadoo'nił, they will be placed for them again; it will be made available for them, or for their use.

bá'ólta', he is the teacher; he teaches.

bá'ólta'í, teacher.

bá'oonishii, dependents of one; one who supervises the work; boss; foreman.

baozbá, he lost it (by gambling); it was won from him.

bá shódaozt'e'go, after they were acquired, or obtained from them; made available for them.

bá sohodoozin, a prayer was said for it, for him, for her, for them, etc.

bá yá'át'ééhii, that which is necessary.

Báyóodzin, Paiute. (Tribe of Indians).

be'ade', his gourd; his dipper; his spoon. **Díí shą' háíí be'ade'?** Whose spoons are these?

be'adee', his horns; his antlers (as referring to trophies, etc.).

be'ádiláah, mischievous, (he is —).

be'ak'id, lake, pond. (also **be'ek'id**).

Be'ak'id Baa 'Ahoodzáná, Pinon, Arizona.

Be'ak'id Halchíí', Red Lake, Arizona.

Be'ak'id Hóteelí, Mariano Lake, N. Mexico.

be'áłííl, his supernatural power.

be'aná'ázt'i'ígíí, that which is his fence.

be'áshįįh, his salt. **'áshįįh,** salt. **Díí na'aldloosh be'áshįįh 'ádaat'é.** This is salt for livestock.

be'ashiiké, their boys (**'ashiiké** is the plural of **'ashkii**).

be'astsį', his meat.

be'atiin, his road. **Nihe'atiin doo yá'áhoot'éeh da.** Our road is not so good.

be'azee'al'j, their hospital. **Háadi shą' Wááshindoon be'azee'ál'j?** Where is the government hospital?

beda'alyaa, the images of it; copies of (like photographs, statues, duplicates).

beda'alyaago, having made facsimiles or pictures of it.

bee, with; by means of it. **Wááshindoongóó góó chidí naat'aí bee déyá yiską́ą́go.** I am going to leave for Washington tomorrow by plane. (airplane)

bee 'ąąh 'ii'nihí, wringer.

bee 'aandítjhí, key.

bee 'aanídítjhí bá 'ahoodzání, keyhole.

bee 'ach'j' 'ahood'í', the problems of — difficulties, etc.

bee 'ach'lishí, saw (tool), file (tool), rasp.

bee 'ádasdin, they (more than three) have none. **Dibé bee 'adaadin.** They have no sheep.

bee 'ádá nihodlit'aahii, resolution; determination.

bee 'adéest'įį', telescope, binocular, field glass.

bee 'adiltąshí, slingshot, bean shooter.

bee 'ádiłłahi, vaseline, ointment, salve.

bee 'aditł'jįh, sling (for hurling a stone).

bee 'ádit'oodí, towel.

bee 'adiyin, immunity.

bee 'adizí, distaff, spindle.

bee 'ádzaa, that which caused something.

bee 'adzooí, comb (for weaving).

bee 'agháda'a'nilí, drill, bit, auger.

bee 'aghá da'dildlaadí, X-ray apparatus.

bee 'aghádadzilne'é, center punch (tool).

bee 'aghá'neeldóhi, diathermy apparatus.

bee 'aghá'níldéhi, sieve.

bee 'ahida'diiljeehi, glue, mucilage, solder.

bee 'akałi, bat, club.

bee 'ak'e'alchíhi, pencil, chalk, steel stamp, pen.

bee 'ak'inda'a'nilí, camera, kodak.

bee 'ałch'j' didloh, buckle.

bee 'a'nizhí, tweezers.

bee 'át'é, due to it; because of it.

bee 'atídahóót'įįd, they did all they could with it.

bee 'atsidí, hammer, mallet.

bee 'atsidítsoh, sledge hammer.

bee 'atsxis, quirt, whip

bee 'azhdoojahgo, because they will help out with it.

bee 'azk'azí, refrigerator.

bee béédahodoozįįł, with which a study will be made; it will be observed to learn more about it.

bee béého'dílzin, for which he is well-known.

bee bide'áhoot'éii, what constitutes his needs.

bee bik'eda' ashchį, the mark by which identity is made.

bee bóhólníih, his responsibility, duty, or trust.

bee chaha'ohí, umbrella.

béédááhai, their ages (in years).

bééhdááhaiji', hastą́'áadah, up to sixteen years of age.

bee da'ahijigą́, by which fighting or war is waged.

béédaałniih, you (pl.) remember it.

béédaałniihgo, if you (pl.) remember.

bee da'diłti'igíi, electricity.

béédahadzid, they are feared.

béédahadzidii, things that are feared.

bee dahatáligíi, songs about (a holiday, circus, etc.).

bee dahazlįį', they acquired it.

béédahidídoochił, they will be released; they will go free.

béédahidídoohchił, you (pl.) will let them go free; release them one after another.

bee dah ní'diidlohi, scales (for weighing).

béédaho'dílzinę́ę, those who were known.

béédzhodoozįįł, it will be known about. **Nihił béédahodoozįįł,** We will know about it. **Shił bééhodoozįįł,** I shall know about it.

béédahodoozįįł, nihił, we will know about it.

bee dahóló, they have it; they possess it.

bee dahólǫǫgo, since they possess it.

béédahoozįįh, it is about to be known.

bééhadhoozįįh da, doo bił, they do not know about it.

béédahoozįįh da, t'ah doo nihił, we still do not know about it.

béédahoozin, knowledge of it was gained.

béédahoozin, bił, they have found out about it; come to know about it.

bééhdahoozingo, bił, when they have found out about it. **Shił bééhoozingo,** when I have found out about it.

béédahósin, they know all about him; they know him well.

béédahósin nt'ée'ii, those who used to know him well.

béédahózin, they are known, identified.

béédahózinígíi, the ones that are known.

béédahózinígíi, nihił, that which we (pl.) know about; those of us that know about it.

bee da'iináanii, livelihood.

béédazh'deetįįh, to solve; to decipher; to interpret; to guess.

bee dazhdiiłkǫǫh, to smooth it out with it.

béédazhdiiłt'ihgo, when they fasten it to it.

bee dazhneestsiz, they quench it by means of it.

béé'deeshdliił, I will copy it; I will do like him.

béé'deetą́, it was learned (by study); knowledge was acquired.

béédoochidgo, since he was set free; since he was turned loose.

béédoohah, naaki, he will spend two years.

bee doo 'ihodéélníinii, immunity.

béé'doolnih, they will be turned (in a direction as when one turns a flock of sheep).

bee 'ééhániih biniiyé 'ályaaigíí, monument; memorial.

bee 'ééhániihii, souvenir, memento.

bee 'ééhózinii, something serving as a guide; as a guide book; any device acting as an indicator, etc.

bee'eldǫǫh, gun. bee'eldǫǫhígíí, that which is a gun. bee'eldǫǫhtsoh, big gun, cannon.

bee'eldǫǫh bee 'anáháltahí, trigger (of a firearm).

bee'eldǫǫh biih nálka'í, shotgun.

bee'eldǫǫh bik'a', bullet, cartridge, ammunition.

bee'eldǫǫh bikǫ', gunpowder.

bee'eldǫǫh bikǫ' chidí naat'a'í bikáá'déé' bidah 'adaha'níligíí, bomb.

bee'eldǫǫh bitsiin, stock (gun).

bee'eldǫǫh bizis, gun holster, scabbard, or case.

bee'eldǫǫh nineezígíí, rifle, high-powered rifle.

bee'eldǫǫhtsoh, cannon.

bee'eldǫǫhts'ósí, rifle, (like .22 caliber).

bee'eldǫǫh yázhí, pistol, revolver.

beegashii, cow, cattle.

Béégashii Bito', Cow Springs, Arizona.

béégashii bitsį', beef.

béégashii bitsį' shibézhígíí, beef stew.

béégashii bitsį' sit'éhígíí, roasted beef.

béégashii cho'ádinii, steer.

béégashii yáázh, calf.

béégashii yáázhígíí, that which is a calf.

beego, by means of.

bee háádaʼaldahígíí, stairway.

bee ha'al'eelí, strainer.

bee haalzíídgo, by which it or he is being observed, or studied; to take notice by, etc.

bee hadadilyaago, that with which it is made.

bee hadah dah ni'diilwo'í, parachute.

bééhádzidgo, since it is feared.

bééhágod, hoe (garden hoe).

bee hahóóyá, the first number, or first event of any prearranged plan, or course of proceedings.

bee hchwiikaahí, scraper (farm implement).

Beehai, Jicarilla Apache, Eskimo.

bééháníih, bee, in memory of.

bee ha'nilchaadí, wool carders.

bee haz'ą́, allowab'e, permissible.

bee haz'ą́ą́ lá, it is permiss.b'e.

bee haz'áanii, law, regulation, rule.

beehaz'ánigíí, that which is the rule, regulation.

bee haz!įį', he acquired it; obtained it; procured it; etc.

bee hodoot'ihii, transportation.

bééhojísingo, since he knew about it or was acquainted with it.

bee hó'ǫ́, he has; he possesses.

bee hó!óonii, possessor.

bee hol ndahazne', they were told about it; they were instructed —.

bééhonisin, you (single) do know it; you are acquainted with.

bééhoosįįd, he, she, or it recognized him, her, or it.

bééhoozin, hol, he found out about it.

bééhoozin, shil, I found out about it.

bee hosél'ą́, my regulation; my system; my standard; etc.

bééhózin, it is known about; there is knowledge about it. **Bil bééhózin.** He knows it. **Doo shil bééhózin da.** I do not know about it. **T'áadoo bil bééhózini da.** There is no one who knows about it.

bééhózingo, obviously, clearly, evidently.

bééhózin, hol, he knows about it; he knows it.

bééhózínigo, understandable; also being beyond doubt.

bééhózínigo, t'áá, being understandable, in a comprehensible fashion.

bééhózinii, bil, the one who knows about it.

bee 'ida'diiljeehí dijé'ígíí, rubber cement, mucilage, glue.

bee 'ida'neel'ąąhí, measuring tape, ruler, yardstick.

bee 'i'diiljeehí, adhesive tape.

bee 'idílzoolí, whistle (instrument).

bee 'ihodiit'i'go, being troubled by; being concerned by; being bound by; etc.

bee 'ihojiił'aah, by which one is learning.

bee 'iikaałí, cold chisel.

bee 'ii' ná'álzoołí, tire pump.

bee 'ił 'ada'agizí, wrench.

bee 'ił 'ada'agizí tsin bigháąh dé'áhígíí, screwdriver.

bee 'ińdiidlohí, brake.

bee k'éé'álchxǫǫhí, eraser.

bee k'éé'áldǫǫhí, flatiron.

bee kééh ná'át'isí, shoe horn.

Be'ek'id Halgaii, Lake Valley, New Mexico. (also **Be'ak'id Halgaii**).

bee łą 'azłįį'dą́ą́' shįį, if it has been approved.

Be'eldíila Sinil, Albuquerque, New Mexico.

beeldléí, blanket (also **beeldíádí**).

be'elnééh, a picture is being taken of; a copy or image is being made.

be'elyaago, the image of it; copy of.

be'elyaaigíí, that which is the copy of, image of — etc.

heełt'é, similar; to match; go well with; pleasing combination. **T'áá beełt'ée łeh.** They are like them. **Díí zéédéet'i'í shi'éé' beełt'é.** This tie goes well with my shirt.

baełt'éii, something that is similar to it; something that will match with it.

bee na'adlo'í, steering wheel.

bee ná'ájeehí, grease gun.

bee na'al'eełí, oars.

bee ná'á;kadí, thread.

bee ná'á;kadí, tsah, sewing-needle.

bee na'anishí, tool, apparatus.

bee náás 'íldee', with which people have progressed, existed, survived, etc.

bee nahalzhoohí, broom (also **bé'ézhóó'**).

bee nahat'i'ii, transportation.

bee náhwiidzídí, rake.

be'ena'í, his enemy. **'ana'í,** enemy.

bee ná'nitałí, spurs.

bee na'nitin, with which instruction is carried out.

beenástł'ah, a corner; a nook; a recess.

bee ni'dildlaadí, flashlight, spotlight.

bee nihił béédchózin, we know it because.

bee nihił hashni', let me tell you (pl.) about it.

bee nihoołzhiizh, the last number, or last event of any prearranged plan, or course of proceedings.

bee nihoot'ą, it was decided upon; it was planned.

bee nihwiildlaadí, plow.

bee nikida'diildee', people began to go about by means of it. **Chidí naat'a'í 'aghá bee nikida'diildee'.** Airplanes became more common as a source of transportation.

bee nik'i'niłtłish, batten stick.

béénílniih, you remember it; do not forget it.

béénílniih, try to recall it; try to remember it.

bee 'ódleehí, trap, bird snare.

bee 'ótsa'í, pliers, tongs.

be'esdzą́ą́ 'ádinii, bachelor.

be'esdzáán, his wife, or wives. **Díí hastiin be'esdzáán naaki.** This man has two wives.

be'esdzą́ą́ naakii, bigamist (i.e. one with two wives).

be'esdzánę́ę, that which was his wife; his former wife.

béésh, flint, metal, iron, knife.

béésh 'ádaaszóóligíí, aluminum.

béésh 'adee', spoon (of metal).

béésh 'adee' ntsaaigíí, tablespoon; large spoon.

béésh 'adishahí, barbed wire. (also **béésh deeshzhaaí**).

béésh 'ahédiłí, scissors, snips.

béésh 'áłts'ózí, wire.

béésh 'ast'ogii, flint arrowhead.

béésh 'awéé' beehaha'niłigii, obstetrical forceps.

béésh bąąh dah naaz'éní, councilmen (Navajo).

béésh bee 'ak'e'elchíhí, typewriter.

béésh bee bighádá'a'nilí, drill, steel bit (for drilling metal).

béésh bee hani'í, telephone.

béésh bich'ahii, German soldiers.

béésh bii' kǫ'í, stove.

béésh bizis, knife sheath, or scabbard.

béésh da'ahólzha'í, chain.

béésh dah naats'ǫǫdigií, flat springs (in machinery).

béésh dit'óódigií, cast iron.

béésh dootł'izh, iron.

béésh haagééd, coppermine.

béésh haagéedgi, at the coppermine.

béésh hataałí, phonograph.

béésh kágí, tin.

béésh łichíí'ii, copper.

béésh łichíí'ii bee dahani'igií, telegraph.

béésh łigaii, silver.

béésh łigaii 'aniiłł'óól, silver bridle.

béésh łigaii 'ííł'íní, silversmith.

béésh łigaii sis, silver belt.

béésh łigaii sis ntseaigií, silver belt with large conchos.

béésh łigaii sis yázhí, silver belt with small conchos.

béésh łigaii yitsidí, silversmith.

béésh łitsoii, brass.

béésh ná'áłkadí, sewing-machine.

béésh naat'a'ii, airplane (also **chidí naat'a'í**).

béésh náhineests'ee'igií, coiled spring (in machinery).

béésh nit'i', railroad.

béésh nitł'izigií, steel.

béésh ńt'i'igií, that which is the railroad.

Béésh Sinil, Winslow, Arizona.

béésh tó bii' nilinigií, water pipe.

béésh tózháanii, mercury.

béeso, money. **T'áá béeso,** cash. **Jįįdą́ą́' naaki béeso yisétbá.** I earned two dollars today

béeso bá hooghan, bank.

béeso bik'é na'anishigií, wages.

béeso bizis, purse, wallet, pocketbook.

béesoigií, those that are dollars.

béeso yaa 'áhályáni, one who looks after money, treasurer.

be'estł'ǫ́, he is tied up, bound.

be'estł'ónéę, the one that was tied up.

bee tá'dígéshí, sheep shears, clippers.

bee wókeedigií, petition.

bé'ézhóó', hairbrush, comb, hair broom.

begochidi, a being regarded as possessing superhuman or supernatural qualities or powers; a divinity.

béhé—béhé, call a pet lamb.

béii'—béii', hyah—hyah (to call a dog).

bélch'iit, it is flaking off; it is peeling off (as paint or skin).

bénáhoosdzin, it was identified.

bénáhoosdzin, ké, the shoes turned up (were found).

bénálkéé', he was found out, discovered, caught.

bénínáá'dootą́, invented, discovered, found, originated.

bénínáá'deetánigií, that which was invented or discovered (like medicines, etc).

bénínáánáásnii', I recalled it to mind again.

be'ólta'igíí, that which is their school; his school. **Wááshindoon be'ólta'igíí.** The federal school.

bésdáago, he, she, is sitting looking after it, or caring for it.

bi, he, she, it, they, theirs. **daabí,** theirs. **T'áá bi,** he himself; just he.

bi'áłtsé, he, she first. **Bi'áłtse 'íiyą́ą́'.** He ate first. (He was the first one).

biba', for him (waiting). **Biba' sédá,** I am sitting waiting for him. **Shiba' na'ezką́ą́ lágo nánísdzá.** Supper was waiting for me when I came home.

bibąąhdi, at its edge; beside it.

bibąąhgóó, along its edge.

bibe', her milk; its milk; their milk; her teats.

bibee'eldǫǫh, his gun. **Shí shibee'eldǫǫh 'ádin.** I have no gun.

bibee'eldǫǫh bik'a', his bullets.

bibéegashii, his, her, their (two) cattle.

bibeehaz'áanii, his, its law.

bibéeso, his money. **Díí t'áá 'altso shi-béeso.** This is all my money.

bibéeso yigíí, that which is his money.

bibééxh, his knife.

bibid, his stomach.

bibijiyiit'aah, he teaches them, makes them learn it.

bí bikéyah, it is his land.

bich'ą́ą́h, in his way; in front of it, him; obstructing.

bich'ą́ą́h dahólǫǫgo, existing to prevent it; obstructing; hindering.

bich'ą́ą́hgi, in front of it.

bich'ą́ą́hji', in place of it. **Bich'ą́ą́hjí' haz-líí',** It replaced it.

bich'ą́ą́h naashá, I protect him.

bich'ą́ą́h nizhdookah, they will protect it.

bichaan, its feces; fecal matter; excrement.

bich'ah, his hat.

bicháhwíídéeni', to desire greatly; to have an extreme desire for; an earnest wishing for; needed badly; etc.

bichaii, his, her grandfather (maternal).

bich'é'é, her daughter.

bich'į', toward it, him, her. **bich'į'go,** being toward them. **bich'ijigo,** in the direction of it; on the side toward it.

bich'į' 'anídahazt'i'ii, those that are needy.

bich'į' aznízini, appetizer.

bich'į' dah diilyeed, sic 'em; jump on him.

bichidí, his, her car, automobile.

bichidí naat'a'í, his, her, their airplane.

bichidí naat'a'í bá haz'anígíí, ⁺heir airfield; their airport.

bich'į' dishwosh, I am yelling at him.

bich'į'gi, at a place before it; this side of it.

bich'į'go, toward it.

bich'į' hadeeshghaazh, I yelled to them.

bich'i' hasti', respectable.

bich'į' ho'distį, he is assigned to it; detailed to ——.

bichįįh, his nose. **bichįįh yee 'adilohii,** the one that lassoes with his nose (elephant). **bichįįh yee 'adilohii dit'oígíí,** hairy elephant, mastodon, mammoth. **bichįįh yee 'adilohii,** elephant. (also **chįįh yee 'adilohii**)

bich'iji, on the side toward it; on his side.

bich'ijigo, on the side toward it.

bich'į' kódaalyaa, they were given to them, delivered to them, distributed among them, etc.

bich'į' nahwii'ná, he is having trouble.

bich'į' nikiniit'áázh, we (two of us) started to walk toward it.

bich'iyą', his, her, food. **Nihich'iyą' k'adę́ę ádįįh.** Our food supply is getting low.

bich'iyą', its food; its feed. **Naa'ahóóhai bich'iyą'.** Chicken feed.

bicho', his genitals, testes.

bicho' hadahaas'niligíí, those that were castrated.

bicho' hadaha'niit, they are being castrated.

bich'ooní, his pal, helper, mate, partner.

bidéa'gi, on its rim, brink.

bidááh, in front of him, them, (so as to meet them) encountering them.

Bidáá' Ha' Azt'i', Grand Canyon, Arizona.

bidáahgi, in front of it (a moving thing).

bidááhjigo, on the front side of ——.

bidá'ák'eh, his field; his farm. **Bidá'ák'e-bę́ę,** his aforementioned field.

bidá'ák'ehgi, on his farm; at his field.

bida'alyaago, facsimiles of them; copies of them.

bidáá' ní'deeshchid, thick-lipped (pan, bucket, etc.).

bidaa' ní'deeshchid, thick-lipped (a person).

bidáashniyá, he met her.

bida'astł'ǫ, they were tied up, bound.

bida'astł'ǫ, they have tags on them (as for identification, or price tags).

bida'astł'ónę́ę, those that had been tied up.

bida'astł'ǫǫgo, since they were, or are tied up.

bida'atł'o'go, they were, or are, tied.

bidáda'ak'eh, their cornfields.

bida'deeshłoh, I will deceive them; I will trick them; I will fool them.

bidadéét'i', they have jurisdiction over it. **Shí doo shidéét'i' da.** I have nothing to do with it.

bidadéét'i'go, since they have jurisdiction or authority over it.

bida'deezhnish, they started to work on it.

bida'deezhnishgo, since they have started to work on it.

bida'diił'áago, since they are concerned about.

bidádi'níbaalgo, a container covering of cloth or paper.

bida'doonish, work will start on it.

bidah, downward.

bidah 'adaha'niiłgo, dropping them down one after another.

bidahasáahgo, they missed him, her, it (to feel the loss or absence of).

bidah ch'éélwod, he or it ran off of something and went down, crashed down.

bidah 'ee'nil, they were tossed down, (as bombs from an airplane).

bidah 'i'iiniiłii, bombardier.

bidahojiił'áá', they learned it. **bídahojiił-'á'igíí,** what they learned. **bíhooł'áá',** I learned it.

bídahojiił'aah, they are learning it; they are learning all about it.

bidahojiił'á'igíí, what they learned.

bidahojisáahgo, since they miss it (feel the loss or absence of —).

bidahónéedzáago, having possibilities.

bidahónéedzáá góne', into practical use.

bidahoo'aah, is, or are taught.

bidahoo'aahgo, the subject being taught.

bidahoo'aahii, subjects that are being learned or taught.

bídahoo'aahji, where it is taught.

bídahooł'aah, you (pl) learn, are learning, it. **bíhoosh'aah,** I'm learning it.

bidahosiilza', we missed them (in sense of not finding them present).

bídahwiil'áá', we learned it.

bidá'i, his, or her, uncle.

bida'néél'qqd, they were measured; measurements were made of it.

bidánidítįhí, its gate.

bidaniidlį, we are interested in it; we are enthusiastic about it.

bida'niilk'aii, they are getting fat.

ni'niilk'aii, you are getting fat.

bida'oodzá, descent.

bidaóółtq'go, including them; counting them.

bidazhdiilkaal, to stay with, keep after, keep at it, etc.

bidazh'neeł'qqhgo, since he has to measure it; or is taking measurements of

bide'édahoot'éhigíí, those that are needy; those who need aid.

bidee', his horn; his antlers. **Díí deenásts'aa' bidee' dįį'.** This ram has four horns.

bi'deelniih, to touch.

bidééłni, will have effect on. **Díí 'azee' dikos bidééłni.** This medicine is good for colds.

bidééłnii, doo — da, able to remain unaffected or undamaged by—etc.; to resist, withstand, repel. **Díí 'éé' bee'eldǫǫh bik'a' doo bidééłnii da.** This jacket is bullet-proof.

bideená, for it (in exchange for).

bidéét'i', he has the right to it; he is entitled to it.

bideiidę́ę'go, from above, or from the upper side of it.

bideiijigo, above it; upper (distant) side of it.

bidibé, his sheep.

bidibéhę́ę, what were his sheep.

bidideeshchił, I will release it; I will let go of it; I will touch it.

bidideeshniił, I will say to him; I will tell him.

bidi'doo'niit, he will be told (as to give a command to, etc.).

bi'diiltsood, he was taken into custody.

bi'diit'áágóó, doo, not worrying about it.

bídiiłjéé', I welded it to it.

bidíiniid, I said it to him.

bi'diisyį́, he was killed.

bi'diisyį́igo, since he was killed by someone.

bidiitsih, I pointed it at him, aimed at him (as gun).

bídin, to crave it. **Bidin dasiidlį́į́',** We needed it, craved it, could not get along without it. **Bidin nishłį́,** I need it, I crave it.

bídin, doo — hóyée' da, it is not scarce.

bidine'é, its, his, their people.

bídínéestah, I will try it.

bidine'é ya ndaakaii, those who represent their people, delegates, representatives.

bídin hóyéé', scarcity.

bidiní, you tell him (them).

bidi'nidzin, it is needed, in demand, etc.

bi'di'niigo, since he was told to.

bidininá, in their place; in return for them.

bidinínáágóó, in opposite direction from it; contrary to it.

bídin, t'áá, without.

bidishní, I told him.

bidiyin dine'é, their holy beings; their holy men, priests, etc.

bidi'yoolyééł, he will be killed.

bi'dizhchį, he was born.

bi'dizhchį́į́ dóó bik'iįj', after he was born.

bi'dizhchínę́ę, the one that was born.

bi'dizhchínígíí, bikáá', that upon which he was born.

bi'dizhchínígíí, nídizíid bini, the month of his birth.

bídó', he too; she too.

bidoh, his muscle.

bidookįįłii, provisions.

bi'dool'aadgo, since he was told to do something, given a command, etc.

bidoolch'ił, to peel or flake off of it.

bi'doolnih, bee, he will be told of it; the word of it will be passed on to him.

bidoolts'idígíí, the part that fell off, was lost, was wasted.

bidoołkaalgo, if you (two) will stick with it

bidoołkįįłii, that on which you (two) will subsist (your food supplies, etc.).

bi'doo'niid, he was told.

bi'doosdląądgo, he having been believed.

bi'doot'eezh, biih, they were led inside of it; they were conducted into it.

bidzaanééz, his mule.

bidziil, he is strong; his strength; it (problem, etc.) is difficult; it (problem, etc.) is hard.

bidziil, doo — da, he, or it, is not strong; weak. **Díí na'nizhoozh doo bidziil da.** This bridge is not strong.

bidziilgo, if, or since, it is strong.

bidziilii, that which is strong, tough, hard. **Naanish bidziilii.** Hard work.

bi'éé', his shirt, clothing.

bi'éé' danineezígíí, those of long gowns (Catholics).

bigaan, his arm; its limb.

bighá, through it. **Tséso' bighá di'nídíín.** The light is shining through the window.

bighaa', his wool.

bighąądídóó, part of it; a portion.

bighą́ą́'dóó 'adéest'į'í, watchtower. (also **bighą́ą́'dóó ha'alzídí**).

bighą́ą́h, in front of it; hitched, or joined to it.

bighą́ąhjį', afterward.

bighą́ą́h náádoodzoh, it will be added to it, increased (as written figures).

bighaa'ígíí, their particular wool, fur.

bighadayiis'nil, they took them away from them.

bighá hoodzą́, there is a hole through it.

bighajii'niiłgo, when one takes them away from him (them).

bighan, his home, dwelling, abode.

bighanáádeist'ą́, they again took it away from them, took another away from them.

bighanát'ą, they repossessed it from him.

bighandéé', from his, her house (home).

bighandi, at his home.

bighangóó, to his, her home.

bighanígi, at his home.

bighánlį, it flows through it.

bigi 'át'é, he is like him.

bigod, his knee.

bigodita', knee region, (also **bigodta'**).

bihétł'óól (or **bikétł'óól**), its, their roots.

bihidéénáá', to come into contact with, hit or strike lightly.

bihididoodzoh, it will be taken off, decreased (as in written figures).

bihidi'níiłgo, they are being taken away, culled, one after the other.

bihodiikaalgo, to keep after, or keep at it constantly; to persist.

bihodiilá, complication.

bihodi'nilchéehgo, since he was forced, or compelled, to do it, or ordered to do so.

bihojiił'ąą', he learned it.

bihojiił'ą'ąą, that of which he learned, or studied.

bihólniih, he is in charge of it.

bihólniihgi, the right to act officially, the right to command and to enforce obedience.

bihólniihgo, since he, she, it, has the authority, the right to act officially, etc.

bihólniihgóó, t'áá, just anywhere; somewhere.

bihoneedlį, exciting, with eagerness, with interest.

bihoneedlį, 'ayóo, it is very interesting; it has great interest.

bihónéedzą́, possible.

bihónéedzą́ą, doo — da, it is impossible; it is out of the question.

bihónéedzą́ągo, since it is possible; since it is agreeable to the eye, or to good taste; being of pleasing aspect.

bihónéedzáanii, that which is agreeable to the eye, or to good taste, etc.

bihónéésdlįįd, it became interesting, lively, etc.

bihoo'aah, is studied.

bihoo'aahgo, since it is studied.

bihoo'aahígíí, that which is studied.

bihoo'ąą'ii, knowledge.

bihoodzo, their boundary line.

bihóoghah, bii', there is enough room in it for him or it.

bihoohya'go, since it was missed, (failed to find).

bihooł'ą́ą', I learned it.

bihoosh'aah, I am learning it; I am studying it.

bihosésa', I missed it (failed to find).

bihwiideesh'ą́ą́ł, I shall learn it; I shall study it.

bihwiidíił'ą́ą́ł, you will learn it; you will study it.

bihwiidoo'áłígíí, lesson.

bihwiidoo'áłígíí binahat'a', curriculum.

bii', theirs, his.

bii', in, within, or inside of it (same as **biyi'**).

bii'adéest'į́į', mirror.

bii' 'áłah ńda'adleehé, chapter houses.

bii' 'áłah ńda'adleehígíí, that in which meetings are held.

bii' dah ndziiztą́, people are sitting up in it.

bii' da'neezk'azí, refrigerator, ice box.

bii' da'ólta'ágíí, kin, school houses.

bii'dees'eez, stirrup.

bí'i'eeł, k'adę́ę hot, he (they) are just about to catch up with him (in a boat); he (they) are about to overtake him.

biighą́ą'ask'idii, camel (the one with the mounded or humped back).

biighą́ągi, on its, their back(s).

biigháán, his back.

biighah, commensurate with it; proportionate to it.

biighahgi, beside it; alongside.

biighahgo, proportionate to it; up to it; equal to it; etc.

biighahgóó, along beside it; parallel to it.

bįįh, deer.

biih, within, or into it; into its interior. **Shighan biih díínáál.** You can move into my house.

bii' halts'aa', hollow.

bii' hazlįį'go, since it collected, or accumulated in it.

bįįh bidee', deer antlers.

biih daazgo', they flow into it; it leaks in several places.

bii' héél 'ádeeshłiił, I will pack them into it.

bįįhkǫ', buck (deer).

biih nááidziid, it was refilled (with fluid, or liquid).

biih náwo'i, pocket knife.

bii' hoodzá, tubular; hollow (as a log, or pipe).

bii' hoolts'aa', it is hollow (as a dish).

bįįhtsa'ii, doe.

bįįh yáázh, fawn.

bįįh yiljaa'í, bitterball (plant).

bii' 'iigisí, washtub.

bi'iil, its branches, brush; its needles; its bristles; its bough.

bi'iilzáąggi, the feeding of (it).

bi'iina', his, their living; his, her, their livelihood.

biil, Pueblo squaw dress.

bi'ilnii', they were advised, informed.

biiłkaahgo, while he was staying all night, camping.

biiłtsá, he (she) saw him (her).

biiłtsood, he grabbed him, took him into custody.

Biina, Ignacio, Colorado.

biínáál, he (she) saw what took place, he witnessed it, observed it.

bii' naaz'á, they are (lying) in them. **Díí chidí t'áá 'ałtso niłch'i bee hane'é bii' naaz'á.** All these cars have radios in them.

biínishghah, I measure up to it; it is within my ability.

biínishghah da, doo, I cannot do it; I am unable to do it.

bii' noot'įį', infection.

bii'oh, what is left, or remains.

bii'ooch'iizhgo, since it is grooved.

bii' shihóóghah, there is room enough in it for me.

biiskání, on the next day.

biisxį, it killed him. **Tó biisxį.** He drowned; he was drowned.

bii' tá'ádígisí, wash basin.

bii' yileeh, it becomes his, hers.

bííyis, handsome, good looking, pretty.

bííyisgo, because he was handsome.

bíízhdóókił, he will ask him for it.

biizhii, western nighthawk.

bíízhníiłdon, he shot at it.

bijááad, his leg; its wheels.

bijáágiizh, the space between his legs; his crotch.

bijaat'ah, the side of his head around the ear.

bijáátah dinishtáál, I tripped him.

bijeeh, its pitch, resin, wax, gum.

bijééhkał, his deafness; he is deaf.

bijéí, his pleura; his heart.

bijéí bąąh, on his heart; on his lungs.

bijéí bąąh dah nahaz'ánígíí, one who has tuberculosis.

bijéí yiłzólii, his, her lungs.

bijį, day for it. **Ts'ídá náháah bijį géne',** right on New Year's day.

bijiishjéé'go, since he kept (a herd of) them

bijik'ehgo, in accord with his own customs in, or after, his own way.

bijini, he said to him.

bíjí, t'áá, his own; after his own manner.

bijoosye', he was named after him.

bíká, for, after it, him.

bik'a', its arrow; his arrow; its bullets.

bikáá', on it; on its surface.

bikáá' 'ádahoot'éhígíí, the condition of it. **Naabeehó bikéyah bikáá' 'ádahoot'éhígíí** —, The condition of the Navajo reservation —.

bikáá'adání, table. (also **bik'i'adání**).

bikáá' dah 'anitéhí, bed. (also **tsásk'eh** and **bik'i dah 'anitéhé**).

bikáá' dah 'anitéhí 'áłts'óózígíí, cot, narrow bed.

bikáá' dah 'asdáhí, chair; seat; bench; (also bik'i dah 'asdáhi).

bikáá'dę́ę́', from above it; from upon it.

bikáa'gi, on it; upon it; at a place on its surface; or at a place above it.

biká'ágíí, what is on it (what is on that sheet of paper you have).

bikáá'góó, along its surface.

bik'ą́ą́h, against it (motion against it).

bikáa'jį', up to its surface; as far as its surface.

bikáá'jígo, the upper side of it.

biká 'aná'á!wo'gi, the status of his (her) help, aid, support, assistance, or relief.

bikáá' niijaa', they were placed on record; they are written up. Haadzíí' yę́ę́ naaltsoos bikáá' niijaa'. His talk was recorded on paper.

biká dideeshchił, I will reach for it.

biká 'é'é!'į, it could be ordered; it could be sent for.

biká 'e'elyeedigíí, one who is to receive assistance.

biká 'eeshwod, I helped him.

bikágí, its hide; its skin; its pelt.

bik'ahígíí, its fat; its oil; its suet.

bik'ah, łóó', cod liver oil.

biká 'i'doolwoł, he will receive aid.

biká 'i'oolwodgo, when he received aid.

bikázhdóya' 'át'éógóó, doo, since conditions are such that one cannot go after it.

bik'é, in exchange for it; for it, in payment; compensation for it.

bik'é 'aníídee', provided for the cost of.

bik'é 'azléago, since there is a charge for it.

bik'é 'azléago t'óó 'átsééd 'a'it'aah, for rent, lease.

bik'eda'eshchį, they are marked; they have writing on them; designs are stamped on it (as jewelry).

bikédaayah, their lands.

bik'edahół'įį, doo — de, they do not obey him, them.

bikéé', his, its tracks; his trail (single line); behind him; after them; in their tracks.

bikéé'góó, after, behind, them; in their wake.

bikee', his foot (feet); his footwear; his shoes; its tires.

bik'ee, on account of it; due to it.

bik'ee dadeeznih, they became angry with him; they turned against him.

bikéédę́ę́', from behind it; behind it, them, or him; after him. Chidí bikéédę́ę́' dah daalchí'ígíí. Red reflectors behind automobiles.

bikéédę́'ígíí, the one which is behind him.

bikée'di, sometime after it.

bikéé'góó, behind them.

bikéé'jígo, behind it; the rear end of it.

bikéé' nizhdiilwod, he started to chase him; he ran after it.

bik'e'eshchį, it is marked; it has writing on it; it is stamped.

bik'e'eshchįgo, since it is marked, etc.

bik'ee ti'dahojooznii', they suffered from it. Hak'az dóó dichin bik'ee ti'dahojoozníį'. They suffered from cold and hunger.

bik'e'éyéé', it is menacing, threatening, dangerous, risky.

bik'éézdiiłi', it glitters; it shines.

bik'éézdiiłi', bináá', his eyes shone.

bik'eh, according to it, him; in accord with it, him.

bik'eh 'adiłt'ohi, gun sight.

bik'eh deesdlį́į' lá, he overpowered him; he defeated him.

bik'ehdigóó, doo, concerning no one except me.

bik'ehgo, according to it, him; by his orders.

bik'ehgo na'abąqsi, driver's license; operator's permit.

bik'ehgo náhidizidí, calendar.

bik'ehgóó, in accordance with; in conformity with.

bik'eh na'nilkaadí, grazing permit; grazing regulations.

bik'ehodeesdlį́'ę́ęį́', to the time they were defeated.

bik'éí, his relatives.

bik'é 'íhwiidoo'áalii, tuition.

bikék'eh, their footprints.

bikék'ehjį', in their places. (also **bitsásk'eh-jį').**

bik'énda'jiiléego, they pay for them.

bik'e'neezgai, it hurts on account of it; it causes it to hurt. **Díí 'azee' doo bik'e'-neezgai da.** This medicine will not hurt you (will not cause burning, etc.).

bik'é ni'iilyé, payments are being made for it.

bik'ésdááz, it splashed on him. **'Ak'ah sido-go shila' bik'ésdááz.** Hot grease splashed on my hands.

bikétł'óól, its roots; his, her shoestrings.

bikétsíín, his, her, ankles.

bikéyah, his land; his country.

bikéyahą́ą, what was his land or country.

bikéyahą́ądi, in his former country.

bikéyahdi, in their country.

bik'i, on it; upon it. **Bik'i naaznil,** They lie about (here and there) on it.

bik'i 'at'eesí, gridiron.

bik'i 'atsidí, anvil.

bik'idaadzaaz, it snowed on them. (also **bik'ideichííl).**

bik'idadi'diitjįł, we will understand it.

bik'ida'di'doohtjįł, you (pl) will understand it.

bik'idadiilkǫ́, it (water or soil) covered them.

bik'idadziskáá', they tracked him down.

bik'i dah 'asdáhi, chair, seat (also **bikáá' dah 'asdáhi).**

bik'i dah 'asdáhi nineezígíí, sofa; daven-port; bench.

bik'i dah naazhjaa'go, with (separable) objects lying on top of them.

bik'idazh'diitá, they understood it; they realized it.

bik'i'deediz, we (two) wound it (as string); we bandaged it.

bik'í'deeshch'it, groping for it among things with one's hands.

bik'idideeshchił, I will put my thumb print on it.

bik'idi'deeshtįįł, I shall understand it.

bik'i diilkǫ́, it (water, soil) covered it.

bik'i hodidoonih, he will be pointed out, selected, or chosen.

bik'ihodiit'áahgo, when he was blamed.

bik'ihwiidoochįįł, it will be covered with silt (as after a flood).

bik'i 'iigisí, washboard.

bik'iijéé', they attacked him.

bik'iji', afterward.

bik'iji', 'áádóó, thereafter, after that.

bik'ijígháah, he is in the act of finding it; he is about to come upon it.

bik'ijigo, toward it.

bik'ijigóó, t'óó, aimlessly. **T'óó bik'ijigóó 'ádazhdííniid.** They said it just to be saying it (with no intention of doing what they said).

bik'ijiijéé', they attacked them; they at-tacked him.

bik'ijiiziid, he raked it over them.

bikin, his, their, house.

bik'ináájiisne', he chopped some more off of it.

bik'ináánéijahgo, when attacking them again.

bik'ináánísdzá, I came across it again; I found some more of it.

bik'inizdidlaad, shiny, lustrous.

bik'iniyá, I came across it; I found it.

bik'iósha', that I might come across it.

bik'is, his friend; his brother; her sister.

bik'izh'diitą́, he learned about it, came to understand it.

bik'izh'diitįįhgo, when one understands it.

bik'izh'nich'id, he came across it (while rummaging).

bikǫ', its fire; his fire.

bikǫ', bee'eldǫǫh, gunpowder.

bikǫ'ii, ch'osh, firefly, glowworm.

bikooh, arroyo, gorge, wash.

bikooh hatsoh, big arroyo, big wash.

biláąh, beyond it.

biláah 'át'éego, since it was superior to it.

biláahdi, at a point beyond it, farther than, later than that.

biláahgo, because there was an excess of.

biláahgóó, over beyond it.

biláahjj', to a point beyond it.

bilą́ąji', ahead of it (him): in front of him; before him.

bilą́ąji'ígíí, the one, or the ones, ahead of it.

Bilagáana, (fr. Span. Americano, American), white man; American.

bilagáana bizaad, English language.

bilagáanak'ehgo, after the fashion of the white man; white man's way.

Bilagáanak'ehji, in English.

biláhádi, t'ah — 'át'éego, more than.

bílák'ee, in his, their hands.

bílák'ediilnii', we (two) shook hands with him, her.

bílák'edoot'ą, it was turned over to him; they were authorized to take over.

bilasáana, apple.

bilasáana diwozhí, pineapple.

bíla' táa'ii, fork (three tined).

bilátah, its tip, end, peak, extremity.

bilátah da'iitsoii, they are in bloom; they have blossomed.

bilátahdi, at its tip; on its peak. (also **bí-látahgi**).

bilát'ahgóó, toward the tip; toward the top.

bilátahi, its tips; its blossoms; its flowers.

bilátahjj', up to its peak, end, tip.

bilééchąą'í, his dog.

bilį́'ę́ę, what was his stock.

bilį́į́', his pet, stock, horse.

bilį́į́' 'ádayiilaa, they made them their pets, domesticated them.

bił, drowsiness, sleepiness; with him; in his company.

bił 'ada'askaal, they are nailed down.

bił 'ada'jiłkaał, he is nailing them down.

bił 'adeesdǫǫh, he was shot with a gun.

bił 'ałk'iniikai, we met them; we ran across them.

bił bi'niiłhį, he is sleepy; he is drowsy.

bił dah náá'dii'éél, he set off in a boat again.

bił dah náá'diilyiz, people rushed off with it again.

bił dah nahaz'ą́ą́góó, in their areas; in their districts.

bił dahózhǫǫgo, since they were happy, glad.

bił dahweeshni', I told them about it.

biłeejin, their coal.

biłeejin haagééd, their coalmine.

bił 'é'él'íní, baking powder.

bił haz'ą́ǫgi, in their community.

bił hidideełgi, the art of catching them.

bił hodiilnih, we (two) will tell him (of it).

bił honeezgaigo, because he was suffering from pain.

bił hóóni'go, when he was notified (of it).

bił hóóyéé', he became afraid, frightened, scared, alarmed, terrified.

bił hózhǫ́ǫ da, doo, he is unhappy.

bił hózhǫ́, yaa, she, he, is happy about it; he is delighted with it.

bił hweeshni', I told him (of it); I notified him (of it).

bił 'ilį, he appreciates it.

bił kééhojit'iinii, neighborhood.

bił łeeh hoołdịáád, it was plowed under the ground.

bił łikan, he likes the tuste of it; he likes it.

bił nááhóóni', he was told (of it) again; he was notified (of it) again.

bił naaki danilį́igo, because they were confused.

bił nabéédahwiizįįh, they learned of it; they acquired knowledge of; they mastered it.

bił na'chinéshtą́ą́', I wrestled with him.

bił na'ahéónáád, to do or use improperly; strained.

bił na'ahisis'nił, I wrestled with him.

bił ndadzizne', they had a game with them; they played them

bił nída'alkadí, bias tape.

bił ni'diiłch'ah, yawn.

bił nigóó, t'áá, drowsily.

bił 'ó!ta'go, counting him; including him.

bił yik'ee nídiich'ah, he yawns.

bił yit'ą, it flew with him; arrived by it (flying).

bimá, his, her mother.

bimá sání, his, her grandmother (maternal).

bináá', his, her, their eyes.

bináá', its śeeds. **Tł'ohwaa'i bináá',** alfalfa seeds.

binaa, around it.

bináá 'ádaałts'ózi dine'é, slender eyes, Orientals (Chinese, Japanese).

bináá', chéch'il, acorns

binaadą́ą́', his corn; their corn.

bínáádahojiił'aah, they are learning (it) again; they again are studying (it).

binaadéę́, from around it.

binaadéę́' daniłíinii, outsiders.

bináá' digiz, cross-eyed.

binaagi, around it; near it; in the neighborhood of. (also **binaagóó).**

binaago, around it (go).

binaagóó, around it (him).

binááhai, his, her age. **Dikwíi ninááhai?** What's your age?

bínááhaigo, when he reached a certain age.

bínááhólníih, he again has the authority.

binaai, his elder brother.

bina'aldloosh, their livestock (quadruped).

binaaltsoosée, those that were their books.

binaalte', his slave.

binaaltsoos, his, their books; his, their papers.

binaalye'é, its, his property.

bináał, in their presence, before their eyes.

bínáánéidzogo, adding to it (as in figuring).

bina'anish, the work pertaining to it.

binaanish, their, his, job, work, profession.

binaashii, opposite side.

biná'ástłéé', jǫhonaa'éí, halo (of the sun).

biná'ástłéé', 'ooljéé', halo (of the moon).

binaat'áanii, their boss, chief; their leader.

bináá', tł'ohwaa'i, alfalfa seeds.

biná'ázt'i', it is surrounded by a wall or fence; it is fenced or walled around.

bináhááh, his (present passing) year.

binahagha', their profession, religion.

binahagha'ígíí, that which is their religion.

binahagha'jí, in their religion.

bináhásdzooígíí, their marked off, circumscribed area, reservation.

binahat'a', his plan.

binahat'a'ąą, what his form or system of government was; what his plan was.

bináhii'niiłgo, bá, because they are adding them one after another for them.

binahji', against it, the basis of understanding.

bínanihídídóokił, you will be asked about it.

bina'idikid, it is customarily asked.

bináká, through it.

binák'edaazgo', it (liquid) fell in their eyes; it (liquid) dropped in their eyes.

bináli, his, her grandfather (paternal), also used for grandmother (paternal).

binanihídídóokił, you will be asked about it.

bináníiji', to its slope; to its side (hill).

bina'niltin, it is being taught.

bina'niltingo, since it is being taught.

bina'nisktin, I am teaching it.

bina'nitin, his teachings.

binant'a'i, their leader; their chief; their supervisor.

binásdzid, I fear it; I am afraid of it.

bináz'á, it encircles it.

bináz'áhígíí, that which encircles it; its rims or tire.

binazh'niłtin, he teaches it.

binda'adlo', their tricks, grafts.

binda'adlo'go, since they were crooked, dishonest, tricky.

bindaanish, their jobs, professions.

binda'anishgo, since they are working on it.

binda'anishgóó, places where work is being done on it.

binda'anishii, that on which work is being done.

binda'azhnish, work was done on it.

bindabidi'niltin, what they are taught; subject taught.

binda'ididiilkił, we shall ask about it.

binda'idółkid, you (many) ask about it.

binda'idółkidgo, you (many) are asking about it.

bindajishnishigíí, that on which they have worked.

binidajókeed, they are asking him to return it.

bindazhdoolnish, they will do some work on it.

bine', behind it.

bine'déé', from behind it.

bine'di, behind it.

bineel'áágóó, doo, if it does not measure up to them.

binééł'qqd, I compared it with it; I measured it against it.

bineesá, she raised him, reared him.

bineeshdlí, I am interested in it, enthusiastic about it.

bineeshdlíjgo, I am interested in it; I am enthusiastic about it.

bine'jí, to, at, a point behind it.

bine'jigo, (toward) behind it.

bine' na'adá, fetish, protector (from the supernatural standpoint).

bine'na'ał'aash, the thirteenth (lunar) month of the Navajo year.

bini, in it; during it. **Ats'á Biyáázh bini shi'dizhchį.** I was born in February.

bíni', his mind; his desire.

Bini 'Ant'ą́ą́tsoh, September (the ninth month of the Gregorian year, having 30 days).

Bini 'Ant'ą́ą́ts'ózí, August (the eighth month of the Gregorian year, containing 31 days).

binichǫ'í, his goods, his property, his belongings.

binidabidi'niltin, they are being trained for it; they are learning it through instructors.

binidashishnish, bił, I worked on it with them.

binideeshchił, to embrace him; to put the arms around him.

bini'deesh'oł, I will sail around it; I will circumnavigate it.

bini'di, let him. **bini'di 'ánéidlééh.** Let him fix it.

binii', his, her waist; its middle; into it; inlay.

bi'niidlóohgo, when he gets cold.

bi'niighą́ą́', it has started to kill them.

bi'niighą́ą́', dichin, they are starving; they are very hungry.

biniijį́', in his face

binii'jigo, toward its center or middle.

bi'niiłhį, dichin, he is hungry.

bi'niiłhį, it has started to kill him; he got sick from it.

biniinaa, on account of it; because of it; for the reason that; since.

biniinaanígóó, t'áadoo, for no reason at all.

biniit'aa, alongside it. **Dził biniit'aa gódeg 'atiin.** The road goes up along the mountain.

biniiyé, for its purpose; in order to; for (the purpose of) it.

biniiyégo, for a purpose.

bini'jíst'í, he surrounded it with a wall or fence; he fenced it around.

biniiyéhégóó, t'áadoo, for no purpose, for nothing; aimlessly.

bini'jiyii'niił, he adds them to them usually.

bini' naaghá, let him go; leave him alone.

binishiit'éázh, we (two) went or walked around it, circled it.

bini' yá'át'ééh, sane; mentally sound; sober

biniyoldéé'go, on the windy side.

binjilnishgo, while he was working on it; while he was putting forth efforts on it.

bintsékees, his mind; his thoughts; his plans; his desire.

bintsékeesígíí, his thoughts.

bi'oh, less than it.

bi'oh neel'á, insufficient for them; too little for it.

bi'oonish, work is being done on it.

bis, adobe.

Bis Dah Łitso, Two Gray Hills (short distance east of Toadlena, New Mexico).

Bis Deez'áhí, Nava, also Newcomb, New Mexico (on U. S. 666).

bis dootł'izh, clay.

bisiláoo, their soldiers; their armed forces.

bisodizin, his prayer; prayer of ___.

bisóodi, pig; hog; bacon. (fr. Span. pitzote, fr. Nahuatl pitzotl).

bisóodi bitsį', pork; bacon.

bisóodi yázhí, shoat.

bist'e', his lunch, subsistence, etc.

bistłee', his stocking; his socks; his leggings.

bita', between them.

bit'a', its sails; its wing(s).

bit'ąą', its leaf, leaves.

bitaa, amongst.

bitaa 'a'niih, things are being distributed among them.

bitaa'as'nii', things were distributed among them.

bitaa daałniihgo, epidemic of; infestation of ___.

bitaadadoo'nihigíí, those which will be distributed among them.

bit'áahgi, near it; close to it; in the vicinity of it.

bit'áahji', to a point near it.

bitaa jigháago, going around among them.

bitaaná'niihgóó, how they are usually distributed among them.

bitaa ńdaa'nih, things are customarily distributed among them.

bitoańdaji'nih, they distribute them among them.

bitaas'nii'. they were distributed among them.

bita'gi, at a place between them; between them.

bitah, among them; included among.

bitahgi, at a place among them.

bitahgóó, among them; through their midst.

bitah hoditłid, he is trembling; he is shaking (as with fear, etc.).

bitahji', to a point among them.

bitah nááníłnii'go, they are again having an epidemic of it.

bitanáhádlah, they are usually picked out from among them.

bitáshjah, its handle, eye (of button with protrusion for eye).

bitát'ah, its ledge; its slope.

bitéél, his front.

bitééldéé', across their fronts, bellies.

bitiin, their trails; their tracks.

bitis, high over it. (also **bááṫis.**)

Bitł'ááh Bito', Beclabito, New Mexico (west of Shiprock).

bito', its water; his water.

bit'oh, its nest. **tsídii bit'oh,** bird nest.

bitoo', its juice.

bitoogi, at its water; at its spring.

bits'a', its pod; its shell.

bits'ąą', away from him, it.

bits'ąądéé', from it; derived from it.

bitsą́ą́di, in his belly; inside of it (in the body).

bits'ą́ą́di, at a place away from it; at a place apart from it.

bits'ą́ą́dóó, from it; out or it; deriving from it: stemming from it.

bits'ą́ą́hjį' (**bich'ą́ą́hjį'**), in place of it.

bits'ą́ąji', away from him.

bits'áda'deezdiin, gleaming; throwing off light; shining.

bits'áda'deezdiingo, they are sparkling, shining, glittering.

bits'ádi'nidiin, to shine (in sense of producing light).

bits'ádi'níliid, glittering; bright; shiny (i.e. glittering with reflected light).

bits'á'doo'oł, nihił, we will sail away from it.

bits'áhinidééh, they fall away from him.

bits'áho'dee'nígíí, those (people) that were selected, chosen, picked.

bits'áhoníyéé', tsin bee, a stick with which to frighten things away from him.

bits'áltáál, it popped away from it.

bits'á'ni'éél, shił, I sailed away from it; I left it by boat.

bits'ániikai, we went away from it; we departed from it; we left it; we abandoned it; we separated ourselves from it.

bits'ánilḍoi, it gives off heat.

bits'áshíni', I want to leave; I have a desire to get away from it.

bits'ázhníyá, he departed from it; he left it.

bitsé, before him (beforehand).

bitsee', his, their, its tail.

bitsee'é, frying pan.

bitséedi, previous to; before; before them; prior to it.

bitséedi, t'ah, even before it; before; before him; prior to it.

bitsee' hólóni, pear.

bitsee' yee 'adiłhałii, crocodile; alligator.

bitsį', his flesh; its flesh; its meat.

bitsį'ę́ę, that which was its flesh.

bitsi', his daughter; his niece (brother's daughter).

bitsii', his hair; his head.

bitsįjdi, at the base of it.

bitsiigháąą', his brain.

bitsiiji', up to his head.

bits'iil, its shell (also **bits'a'**).

bitsiin, its handle; its stem.

bits'íís, his body.

bitsiit'áád, pate, on top of the head.

bitsiit'áá tó 'áyiilaa, he baptized him.

bitsiits'iin, his head.

bitsiits'in, his skull; his cranuem.

bitsiji' níyá, t'áá, I arrived before him.

bitsiji', in front of, before, ahead of him.

bits'in, his (their) bone(s).

bitsoo', his (their) tongue(s).

bitsóóké, his, her grandchildren.

bits'os, its down (of a bird); its feather.

biwoo', his tooth (teeth).

biwoo' 'ádinii, one who is toothless.

biyaa, under it, him; beneath it.

biyaadi, at a place under it; beneath it; at its base; at the foot of.

biyaadóó, from under it. (also **biyaadę́ę́'**).

biyaagóó, along its base.

biyaajigo, toward its base; toward under it.

shádi'ááh biyaajigo, toward the south.

biyaajígo, below it.

biyáázh, her son; her nephew.

biyah, under it (supporting it).

biyaiijigo, below it; lower side of it; beneath it.

biyázhí, its (his) offspring; its young.

biye', his son; his nephew (brother's son).

biyéél, his pack; his burden.

biyęczhii, its eggs; its testes.

biyi', inside it; within it.

biyid, his chest.

biyi'di, at the interior.

biyi'di, in it; inside of it.

biyi'dę́ę́' (also **biyi'dóó**) from inside it.

biyi'dóó, from within it. (also **biyi'dę́ę́'**).

biyi'go, being in it.

biyi'góó, toward the interior of it.

biyi' 'iilnaahi, incubator.

biyi'jí, inside of it.

biyi'jigo, on the inside of it.

biyo', her necklace; its bell.

biyooch'ídi, liar.

biyooch'iid, he is a liar, his lie.

biyó, t'áá, a little bit; mildly; slightly; kind of. **T'áá biyó deesk'aaz díííj.** It's a little cold today.

bizaad, his language; his words.

bizaadjí, in his language; according to his language.

bizaad k'ehgo, at his word, his command, his orders.

biza'azis, his pocket.

bizadiikah, we will be devoured by him; we will fall into their clutches.

bizánághah, around the corner from it; around the bend.

bizánághahdóó, from around the corner.

bizázi, his ancestors.

bizdílid, shiny; glossy; lustrous.

bizéé', his mouth.

bizéé' hazlíį', deceased.

bizhání, t'áá, themselves; only; singly; nothing else; nothing but. **Díí tó t'éiyá t'áá bizhání 'át'é.** This is nothing but water.

bizhdiiĺkeal, he persists; he puts his shoulder to it; applies himself (to a task).

bizhdíiniid, he told them so.

bizhéé', his saliva; his spittle; its foam; his, or its froth.

bizhé'é, his father.

bizhéé' hólóní, beer.

bizhi', his name. **nízhi'**, your name.

bízhneel'ą́ągóó, doo, since it is too much for him; since it is beyond his ability.

bizid, his liver, (part of his body).

biziiz, his belt.

bizool, his windpipe.

bóhólnihigíí, one who is in charge; one who has the authority.

bóhólnihigíí, t'áá, anyone; anything.

bóholniíh, he is the boss; he is in charge; he is in authority.

bóhólniihgi, t'áá, anytime; anyday; anyplace.

bóhólniihgo, since he is boss; since he is in charge of it.

bóhólniihgóó, t'áá, to anyplace. (see **t'óó dzólniigóó**).

bohónéedzą́, possible; feasible; practicable.

bóhoneestą́ą', it was tried out; a test of it was made.

bóhoo'aahgo, learning it.

bóhoohya', it was missed; it was lost (failed to find it).

boo'ịį, doo — da, he doesn't see him.

bóóltą', (it) included.

bóóltą'go, counting, including them.

booshk'iizhdéé', from along its side.

booshk'iizhgi, (at) in his side.

- C -

choo', beaver.

chąą', fecal matter; excrement; feces.

chąą' báhooghan, toilet.

chąą' bee yildéhí, toilet paper.

ch'aa deeshááł, I will go on a tour.

chąą 'éé'ni', constipation.

ch'aa naagháhí, tourist.

chąąneiłhizii, scarcbee (also tsé yoo'áłí or tsénei'áhí).

ch'aa niséyá, I went on a tour.

chąąsht'ezhiitsoh, carrot.

chąąt'inii, canaigre (sorrel).

chách'osh, chancre, syphilis.

ch'agii, blackbird.

ch'ah hat; headwear; headgear., helmet; cap.

chahałheeł, darkness.

chahałheeł góne' bee 'anil'íní, fluoroscope.

chaha'oh, shadow; shade; ramada; brush shelter. (also chahash'oh).

chahash'oh, shadow.

ch'ah binázt'i'í, hat band.

ch'ah bítáa'ji' da'deez'áhígíí, cap.

chahóółhéél, darkness fell; it got dark.

chalééko, vest. (also dah ni'dishdǫ'ii).

ch'ał, frog.

ch'ał nineezi, large frog; bullfrog.

ch'ałtsoh, toad.

chánah niliinii, diné, a healthy person.

chá'oł, pinon tree.

chóshk'eh, an arroyo; a wash.

chashk'eh hats'ózí, gully, gullies. (also bikooh hats'ózí).

chátł'ish, phlegm.

chéch'il (tséch'il), oak, oaktree.

chéch'il bináá', acorn.

Chéch'il Łání, Cheechilgeetho, (south of Gallup, New Mexico).

chéch'il niłt'izí, scrub oak.

chéch'il niłt'izí yiłt'ąą'í, Oregon grape.

ch'é'édáá'. dooryard.

ch'éédabineeskaad, they drove them back out.

ch'éédildlohgo, when he starts laughing; when he giggles; when he smiles.

ch'ééh, in vain; futile; unsuccessful; failure.

ch'ééh 'áda'ahool'įįd, neither side won (as in a contest).

ch'ééh 'ádáát'įįd, they were unsuccessful.

ch'ééh 'adeesdzá, fatigue.

ch'ééh déyá, I am tired; I am exhausted.

ch'ééh didziih, gasping (for breath).

ch'ééh digháhii, turtle (also tsisteeł).

ch'éékai, they (three or more) survived.

ch'éénidzííd, you wake up.

ch'ééniłdoi, it (the weather) started to warm up again.

ch'éénisdzid, I awakened; I woke up.

ch'éénisííd, you wake him up.

ch'é'étiin, doorway.

ch'é'étiindóó, from the doorway.

ch'ééyá, he outlived; he survived; he lived through.

ch'éhékáahgo, while they come out one by one.

ch'éjeehgo, when they were about to come out.

ch'élwod, he ran out.

ch'ét'ééh, it will begin.

ch'íbi'dit'ááh, he was mentioned; he was in the news.

ch'idaaz'á, they are sticking out, protruding.

ch'ídadiit'ááł, we will carry it out (carry it along).

ch'ídahajeeh, they are running out one after another.

ch'ídahat'éésh, they are led out one after another.

ch'ídahidit'aah, something (as money) appropriated; to set apart for a particular use.

ch'ída'iiłdįįh, they usually survive.
ch'ída'iisdįįd, they survived.
ch'ída'iisdįįdígíí, survivors.
ch'ídajiiłkaad, they are bailing it (water) out; they are throwing them out.
ch'ídeesháął, I will go out; I will come out; I will survive.
ch'ídeeldlo', he laughed; he smiled.
ch'ídeesbąs, to drive it out (as a car from a garage).
ch'idí, buffalo robe.
chidí, automobile.
chidí 'ánál'įįgi, auto shop.
chidí 'ánéil'íni, automobile mechanic.
chidí bąąh dah naaztánígíí, license plates.
chidí bee dah ńdiit'áhí, jack (for raising an automobile).
chidí bitoo', gasoline.
chidí bitsiits'íin, engine (of a car).
chidí diné bee naagéhí, bus.
chidí naa'na'í, tractor.
chidí naat'a'í, airplane. (also béésh naat'a'íí).
chidí naat'a'í bikáá'déé' bee'eldǫǫh bikę' bidah 'adah...'niił, bombardment.
chidí naat'a'í ndonidaahágóó, airports.
chidí ndaełbąąsii, you drivers (you who drive cars).
ch'ídínéeshchééł, I will chase it out.
chidí 'ółta'í bee naagéhé, school bus.
chidítsoh, truck.
chidí yázhí, toy cars.
ch'ídi'yoolkił, a movie will be shown.
ch'í'dooldah, bik'ehgo, they will live according to, under, his authority.
ch'íhidínóodah, bá, it will be available for him.
ch'íhinidééhęę, bá, that which was available for him.
ch'íhodoolzhish, time will begin.
ch'íhonít'i', there is an exit; there is an outlet; there is a way out.
ch'įįdii, evil spirit; ghost; spirit of the dead; devil.
ch'įįdiitah, hell.

ch'įįdiitahgóó, damn——, to hell.
chįįh yee 'adilohii, elephant. (also bichįįh yee 'adilohii).
chííl, snowstorm.
chííl bił hááyoł, blizzard.
ch'iiyáán, food, groceries.
ch'íjíkai, they went out.
ch'íjóghá', that one might go out.
ch'íjóghá' 'ánáhoot'įįh, doo —— da, it (the weather) becomes such that one cannot go out.
ch'ikęęh, maiden.
ch'ikéí, maidens, young women.
ch'il, plant, weed.
ch'il 'abe'é, milkweed.
ch'il 'agháni, loco weed (poison weed).
ch'ílátyi', smokehole, chimney.
ch'il bee yildéhí, mattock.
ch'il bilástsii' dahólónigíí, cereals (bearded plants).
ch'il daadánigíí, vegetables.
ch'il deeninii, Russian thistle, tumbleweeds.
ch'ildiilyésii, snakeweed.
ch'il gohwéhí, Navajo tea (thelesperma gracile), wild tea.
ch'ilígíí, the (particular) plant.
ch'il łichxi'í, tomato, beet, carrots.
ch'il łigaaí, cabbage; cauliflower; lettuce.
ch'il łitsooí, orange. (also ch'il łitsxooí).
ch'il łitsooí dik'ǫzhígíí, lemon.
ch'il na'atł'o'ii, grapes; vines.
ch'il na'atł'o'ii bitoo', wine.
ch'il na'atł'o'iitsoh, prune.
ch'iłtaat'agii, marsh hawk.
ch'ilzhóó', sand sage.
chin, grime, filth.
ch'ínáádiníldlóóh, (you) smile again, laugh again.
chin 'ąąh 'ádin, cleanliness.
ch'ínááhoot'ánigíí, the word (news) we just now heard mentioned.
ch'ínáánát'aah, restatement.
ch'ínáhá'ááh, he tells the news (a story).
ch'ínádzid, he awakened; he woke up.

ch'inálwo', he runs out.

ch'inátdoh, it usually gets warm. (weather)

chin bąąh 'ádin, it is clean, free of grime or filth.

chin bąąh t'óó 'ahayói, it is grimy.

ch'i'ni'ą́, the sun is shining.

ch'i'ni'ééł, bił, he (they) sailed out.

ch'iníídee', left (after removal or destruction); remained. (see yidziih) Shibeeso naadiin ch'iníídee'. I have $20 left.

ch'iniijéé', we all ran out.

ch'iniikai, we walked out; we went out.

ch'iniítna'ígíí, surplus; left-over; excess.

Ch'ínílį, Chinle, Arizona.

ch'inílyeed, you run out; get out.

ch'i'nítdįįd, I, he, survived.

ch'i'nítdįįdígíí, survivor.

ch'inítdoi, it (the weather) started to get warm.

ch'íníyá, I went out; he went out; I walked out.

Chíshi, Chiricahua Apache.

ch'íshiibeezhii, chickadee.

ch'íshiisháshii, crested titmouse.

ch'iyáán, food; groceries; provisions (supply of food).

ch'iyáán 'ádaal'įįgi, art of cooking.

ch'iyáán 'ál'į, culinary arts.

ch'iyáán 'ats'íís bá yá'át'ééhii, diet.

ch'iyáán bił 'aa'i'íít'i', use of food tube.

ch'iyáán doo bidi'nidzinígíí, garbage, cast off food.

ch'iyáán 'íít'íni, cook, chef.

ch'iyáán t'áá bihólníihgóó ńdahadleehígíí, wild foods.

ch'iyáán ye'eniihii, dietitian.

ch'iyiijááh, he is carrying them out one after another.

chizh, wood; firewood; kindling.

chizhts'ósí, kindling; sticks (for firewood).

ch'ó, spruce,

chodaboos'įįd, they made use of him.

chodahoo'į, nihił, we have hope.

chodahoo'inígíí, doo biká, those that are nonproductive; those one cannot depend on.

chodajooł'į, they are making use of it.

chodajoos'įįd, they made use of them.

chodao'įįgo, since they are useful.

chodao'ínę́ę, those that were useful.

chodao'inígíí, the useful ones; those things that are useful.

chodaooz'įįd, they were put to use.

chodayooł'į, they make use of it.

chodeidooł'įįłígíí, the things which they will use.

chodeidoo'įįłígíí, those things which will be used; provisions.

ch'óhojilyę́ę́h, jimson weed.

chohoo'íní, kéyah doo bikáá', useless land, worthless land.

choideesh'įįł, I shall use it.

chǫǫh, wild rose.

choo'į, it is useful.

choo'įį da, doo, it is useless, not useful.

choo'iinii. the thing that is useful; the useful things.

chooł'į, it is being used.

chooł'įįgi, how to make use of it.

ch'óóshdą́ą́dą́ą́', originally; formerly; in the beginning; at first.

chooyin, menstrual discharge.

chooyiní, hunchback.

chooz'įįd, it proved useful; it was put to use; it became useful.

ch'osh, bug; worm; insect; maggot.

ch'osh 'ałchozhii, clothes moth.

ch'osh bikǫ'ii, glow worm; fireflies.

ch'osh ditł'ooí, caterpillar.

ch'osh doo yit'íinii, microbe; bacteria; germs.

ch'osh doo yit'íinii bee naatseedí, antiseptic; disinfectant.

ch'osh doo yit'íinii bee níl'íni, microscope.

Christ dayoodláanii, Christians.

Christ dayoodlánígíí, those who believe in Christ.

chxǫ́ǫ'i, to be ugly, filthy, worn, used. 'éé' chxǫ́'i, used clothing.

– D –

da', is it (question).

da, including; as well as; and.

daa —, what, how (also, haa —), daawolyé, what is it called?

dáábalii, shawl.

daabéezhgo, while they are boiling.

daabí, theirs.

daabíhéę, what was formerly theirs.

daacha, they are crying.

dá'áchaan, smut (on corn).

dąądą́ą́', last spring, (season).

dáádadeezbaal, hang loosely (a covering for an opening).

da'adánígíí, meals.

daada yidzaago, if something should happen to it.

dáádílkał, door.

da'adiz, they spin (yarn).

daadlánígíí, beverage.

dá'ághálii, rattle pod.

dąągo, in spring.

da'ahideeshchinéędą́ą́', when in the past they started to give birth; at the beginning of their existence.

da'ahidiits'a', they hear, understand one another.

da'ahigą́ągo, when they were, or are killing one another, or fighting one another.

da'ahigą́ęji', to the fighting area; to the war zone.

da'ahijigą́, they kill one another, fight.

da'ahijigą́ądę́ę́', from the fighting area; from the war zone.

da'ahijigą́ądi, at the battle front; at the fighting area.

da'ahijigą́ągo, when there was fighting.

da'ahijigánígíí, bee, those things with which people kill one another; weapons.

da'ahijoodlá, they hate one another, dislike one another, despise one another.

da'ahijoogą́ą́', there was war; when they

da'ahijoogą́'ąądą́ą́', during the war.

da'ahijoogą́ą́', bił, they fought them; they had war with them.

da'ahilghał, they (animals) are eating one another.

da'ahizhdoogą́ą́ł, there will be fighting; there will be a battle.

da'ahoogą́ą́', they fought one another.

da'ahoogą́ą́', yił, they fought them.

daahoot'éé lá, what is it (an area) like?

daahsą́, you (plural) are eating it.

dąąjį', as far as spring (season).

dá'áka', playing cards.

daak'ę́ęgo, having been ground.

dá'ákaz, corn stalk.

dá'ákaz bitoo', syrup.

dá'ákaz bitoo' łizhinígíí, molasses; sorghum.

dá'ák'eh, cornfield; garden; cornpatch; cultivated field.

Dá'ák'ehaláni, Many Farms, Arizona.

dá'ák'ehgo, since it was a cornfield.

da'ák'ehgóyaa, down toward the cornfields.

daakin, houses. Tsé bee daakingo, being houses of stone.

daalbáago, since they were gray.

daalchíí', they are red.

daaleeh, they become.

daalgaaígíí, those that are white.

daalgai, they are white.

daalgaii, the white ones.

daalgan, they are dried in the sun.

daalkango, since they are sweet, tasty, good.

daaltso, they are yellow.

daalzhin, they are black.

daalzhólí, they are soft, fluffy.

da'ałchin, they have the ability to detect scent.

da'ałchozhígíí, those that graze, eat leafy plants.

da'ałt'o', they suck.

daan, springtime (it is spring).

daane'é, amusements; playing; toys; playthings.

daani, they say.

daaniigo, because they are saying.........

daanínígíí, what they say.

da'asdzoh, they are marked off.........

daashǫ' yit'éego, how, in what manner.

daashch'il, they are curly.

daashjį nízáadjí', at an indefinite or unestimated distance; quite a ways.

daashłłizh, they are brown.

daaskai, they came; they arrived.

daaskaidą́ą́', if they came; if they should come; in case they come.

da'oslįį', yee lą́, they have accepted it; they have agreed to it.

doosti'go, since they were hesitant, uncertain about it.

da'ast'jid, yee, they got rich off them.

daasts'in, rigor mortis.

dá'át'ąą', cornhusk; cigaret paper; corn leaves.

daat'ees, they are roasting; they are broiling.

da'at'jigo, since they are rich.

dááłł'is, they hardened.

da'ałł'ó, they are weaving.

da'ałł'óogi, how to weave.

daatsaah, he is sick; he is ill.

da'atsaah, sickness; illness; infirmity.

daatsaahgo, because he is sick.

daats'í, may; possibly; maybe; perhaps; about.

da'atsid, they are silversmiths.

dá'átsiin, corncob.

daayit'eego, how, in what manner.

daa yit'éé shįį, a certain kind.

daazgan, they are dry, desicated.

daazlį́'ę́ę, those that became.........

daazlįį', they became; they came into existence.

daazlį'ígíí, those that have become.

daazlįį'ii, nááś, the older ones, more advanced ones.

daazt'é, they are done (cooking); they are roasted.

daaztsą́, he died; he is dead.

daaztsą́ągo, when he is dead.

dabi'ádígíí, the females.

dabididii'niił, we will tell him; we will say to him.

dabidii'ní, we call it.

dabidii'nínígíí, those that we call.

dabidi'nidzingo, since it is in demand.

dabidi'nínígíí, that which is said to them.

dabi'disnánę́ę, those that were captured.

dabidizhdooniił, they will tell them.

dabidoołkįįłii, that upon which you (pl.) will live; your subsistence.

dabidziil, they are strong; powerful.

dabidziilgo, since they are strong.

dabidziiligíí, doo, those that are not strong; the weak.

dabighan, their homes; their dwellings; they dwell.

dabighandóó, from their homes.

dabighanę́ę, what were their dwellings.

dabighanę́ęgi, where they formerly dwelt.

dabiisxí, they killed him.

dabiiyisii, the handsome ones.

dabijoołáá ńt'ę́ę', they used to hate him; they used to dislike him.

dabikáá', they are on it (written down on it).

dabiká'ígíí, what is on them (written).

dabik'is, their friend; their brother.

dabildeeł, they eat them.

dabilįį', their pets; horses.

dabiłniigo, they were saying to them.

dabiná'ę́ę, their eyes.

dabináłę́ę, those that were spectators, audience, bystanders, onlookers.

dabisnáago, when they captured him.

dabits'iini, they are skinny; they are poor.

dabiyooch'íid, they told lies; they tell lies.

dabizaadigíí, their language.

dabizáanii, their elders (women folks).

dabótą', they are holding him; he is in their custody.

dáda'ak'ehgo, there are fields all around.

da'deeldǫǫh, we fired; we opened fire.

dá'deeltł'inígíí, the dam that is being built.

dadeení, they are sharp.

da'deesdǫǫh, they fired their guns; they opened fire.

dadeeshnish, they began working.

dadeeskaidą́ą́', if they should start coming.

dadeeskai, náás, they started to go forward, advance, progress.

da'déest'íí'ígíí, tózis bee, telescope.

dá'deestł'in, dam, reservoir.

dá'deestsxah, lockjaw, tetanus.

dadeezbaa', they are going off to war.

dadeezdéél, shił, they have caught me; they have captured me.

dadeezhaazh, they are worn.

dadeezhaazhígíí, those that are worn.

dadeezlį, they flow out.

dadeezná, they were about to start moving.

dadéiit'íį', we looked; we are watching.

dadich'íízh, they are rough, scaly.

da'dideeshdǫǫł, bił, I will shoot them.

dádi'dooltł'íį́ł, a dam will be built.

dadighaał, they are opening their eyes.

da'diidííł, we will eat.

Jadiigisígíí, t'óó, those that are crazy mentally unsound. **T'óó dinigis,** You are crazy.

dadiilghał, we will eat it; we will chew it (meat) up.

dadiilid, they were burned up; they were burnt.

da'diil'oł, we will navigate; we will row a boat; we will sail.

da'diilzhish, we will dance; let us dance.

dadiiłhį'ę́ę, those that were melted; those that thawed out.

dadiiłhįį'go, because they are melted, thawed out, molten.

dadii'ni, we all say.

dadiiniid, they said.

dadii'niigo, we were saying, calling.

dadiit'a', dah, they flew off; they took wing.

da'diit'įįł, we will get rich.

da'diizts'ą́ą́', they all heard (something).

dadildon, they are popping (as firecrackers).

dadilkǫǫh, they are smooth.

da'diłdongo, they (people) are shooting.

dadiłdzid, they become rotten; they decay.

da'diłhałígíí, those that strike a blow, bat.

dadiłhįįhgo, since they are molten.

da'diłt'oh, they shoot an arrow.

dadinéest'áné̜e̜dą́ą́', 'ał'qq, when they increased.

dadíniidzįįł, we will start thinking.

dadíníil'įįł, we will look at him; let us take a look at him.

daditą́, they are thick, deep.

daditł'ooígíí, the hairy ones.

dadit'ódí, they are tender; they are soft.

dadiyinígíí, those that are holy; supernatural beings; the holy ones; the sacred ones.

dadoohts'įįh, k'adę́ę, you (pl.) are about to hear it; you wish to hear about it.

dadootł'izh, they are green; they are blue.

da'dooyįįł, they will eat; they will have a meal.

da'dzisiih, they missed, made a mistake.

dadzitsaahgo, when one dies.

dághá, mustache, whiskers, beard.

dághá bee yilzhéhí, razor.

dah, up; off; set out; at an elevation. **Dah yoo'ááł,** He or it is holding it up. **Dah diilwood,** He started off at a run. **Yił dah dii'áázh,** He started off with him.

dahaastł'ó, he or it is tied up (to something).

dahaastł'óógo, because he was tied up (to something).

dahaazlįį', they became, came to be.

dah 'adiidloh, pound (weight).

dah 'adiisool, puffed; inflated. **Bigąąziz dah na'asol.** She has puffed sleeves.

dah 'adiyéch'ą́ą́ł, suspension.

dahadlo', it is twitching.

daha'éé', their clothes.

dahajoobá'í, baa, they are poor, pitiful, miserable.

dahalni'go, when they tell.

dahalni', they tell, narrate, converse.

dahalni', yił 'ahił, they talk with one another about it.

dah 'alzhin, dot, speck.

dahani', the stories; the news.

daha'niigo, it is said.

dahasłįį', they caused it to come into existence. **Yaa saad dahasłįį',** They complained about it.

dahasłįį'go, yaa saad, since they complained about it.

dahats'íidgóó, doo nihił, since we were lonesome; since we felt badly; since we were homesick.

dah 'ats'os, conical.

dahazází, their ancestors.

dah 'azká, mesa.

dahazlįį, they became, came to be, came into existence.

dah dahidédlo', their weights (in pounds, etc.).

dah deii'éésh, they have.

dah dideesbąs, to start off driving it (car).

dah didoojah, they will stampede.

dah diighááh, he is about to start off.

dah diijaa', I took them with me (separable objects).

dah diijéé', they ran off, started off running.

dah diildloozh, he started off trotting (as a horse, on all fours).

dah diildoh, to waft.

dah diiná, he started to move (belongings).

dah dii'na', he started off crawling, he started off creeping.

dah diit'áázh, we (two) started off (walking).

dah díniilghaazh, fried bread.

dah ditsxiz, he is shivering, shaking.

dahéedeeł, 'ałch'į', it draws tighter, contracts.

dahéelghaał, they are crawling along.

dahidideełgo, they are breaking off (time after time), snapping.

dah hidideeshch'ął, I will suspend it (as by a cord).

dah hodidínéeshchał, to spade; to loosen it (soil).

dahidédlo', it weighs; pound. **Hastą́diindi dahidédlo',** (it weighs) sixty pounds.

dahideest'ą́, baa, they were allowed to have it (them).

dahideest'ánigi 'át'éego, baa, just like they were allotted one after the other to them.

dahidéjée'go, while they were suspended (by rope or cord, animate objects).

dahidénil, bąąh, they dangle from it; they are strung from it.

dahidiiná, dah, they started off moving, migrating, one after another.

dahidínóodahgo, baa, they will fall to them one after the other.

dahiina', they lived, survived.

dah 'iistł'ǫ́, loom (rug).

dah 'iistł'ǫ́ bá 'íi'áhí, upright pole (of the loom).

dahiná, they live; they are alive; they are living.

dahiná, yee, they live on; they live by means of it; it is their livelihood.

dahinii'ná, we live; we are alive.

dahinii'náanii, bee, those things upon which we live.

dahininéhígíí, those that usually die.

dahizhdookáahjigo da, t'áadoo dah, there is no place for them (several groups) to go.

dah náá'diildee', they (people) started off again.

dah nááneesdáhigíí, one who took office again.

dah naashch'ął, to hang suspended.

dah na'ayizii, leather pouch (worn suspended over one shoulder).

dah naazhjaa', they sit grouped.

dah nahéaztą́ągo, they are sitting up (at an elevation).

dah ńdinibįįh, they customarily sit up (at an elevation), they customarily take their seats.

dah ni'dishdo'ii, vest (a garment).

dah nteel, it has a wide end (as a blade of a putty-knife.

dahó'aahii, those who make plans; law makers.

dahodideezlįį', they started ·to become, came into existence.

dahodiik'ąąd, bił, they became lonesome, homesick.

dahodiilnih, bee 'ahił, we will tell one another about it.

dahodiína', bee, they have spent (enough) time.

dahodii'níigo, we are telling them, saying thus to them.

daho'dii'níił, biih, they are usually placed in it.

dahodilts'iid, yee, they support themselves by means of it.

dahodiłnih, yiih, they usually made him reach into it, put his hand into it.

dahodisingo, since they are religious.

daho'dókeedígíí, those that were called, summoned, or ordered to come.

dahojíyá, they are wise, smart, sensible, intelligent.

dahojoobá'ágo, baa, since they are poor.

dahólni', bił, you tell them.

dahóló, there are; they exist. **Bee dahóló.** They have it; they possess it.

dahólónéę, those that existed; what was in existence.

dahólónígíí, those that exist.

daholóogo, since they exist.

dahólóógóó, toward where they exist; toward where there are some.

dahóló ńt'éé', they used to exist.

dahółdon, they shoot at them.

dahołni', bee bił, you (pl.) tell him about it; you (pl.) tell them of it.

dahoneesná, they have won (in a contest).

dahoneesnáanii, the winners.

dahoneezdo, the places are warm.

dahoneezdogóó, in warm places; to warm places.

dahoniłnéegi, in their winnings.

dahoo'a', bąąh, he got sick; he became ill.

dahooghan, residence.

dahoo'įįgo, bá, they guide them.

dahoolni', yił, they told him; he told them; he passed the word around to them.

dahooltse', sightseeing.

dahoolyéego, the places are called thus.

dahóótááł, they sang songs.

dahootso, meadows, green pastures.

dahóóáyéé', bił, they got scared; they were frightened.

dahóóáyée'ii', t'óó bił, they had become terror stricken.

dahosiidlįį', we came into being.

dahótsaago, since they are big places.

dahóyáanii, those that are smart, wise, sensible, intelligent.

dahóyánígíí, the smart ones, sensible ones, intelligent ones.

dahóyéé', bił, they are lazy.

dahóyé'é, t'áadoo nihił, you (pl.) do not be lazy.

dahóyé'é, t'áadoo t'óó nihił, you (pl.) do not be afraid.

dahozhdootał, they will sing songs.

dahózhí, they call, name it (a place).

dahózhóní, they (areas) are nice, good, pretty, beautiful.

dahózhóogo, bił, since they are happy.

dahsání, porcupine.

dah sidá, he sits up (at an elevation).

dah sidáá ńt'éé', used to sit up (at an elevation).

dah sikéhigíí, the two that are sitting up (at an elevation).

dah sitą, it (a stiff, slender object) lies (at an elevation).

dahtoo', dew, dewdrop.

dahts'aa', mistletoe.

dahwee'aahii, governing body; government.

dahwiilni', we told; we related.

dahwiilni'go, when we told.

dahwiilni'igii, bee 'ahil, the things about which we have told one another.

dahwiinidzin, opinion of the people.

dahwiiniiłdon, they shot at them.

dahwiinist'jid, baa, they were tried (by the court); it was discussed; action has taken place (on it).

dahwiinit'jigo, baa, while being discussed; while they were being tried (in court).

dahwiinit'iinii, baa, subjects; defendants.

dahwiint'inigi, baa, where they discuss it.

dahwiint'inigii, baa, those actions that were taking place concerning it.

dahwiisxi, they killed him.

dah yidii'eezh, he lead them off.

dah yidiitą, he started to carry it off (stiff, slender object).

dah yidiyiinil, he hung them up, suspended them.

dah yidoochih, to flash (with a reddish light, as lightning, flashlight, etc.).

dah yiitą, crescent moon.

dah yiite', he dashed off.

dah yiitjhí, humming bird.

dah yiitjhidą́ą́', Indian paint brush.

dah yikahii, the organization, party.

dah.yisk'id, a mound.

dah yists'id, it suddenly appeared (at an elevation).

da'iidoodlaał, they will believe, be believers.

da'iidóołtah, they will study, go to school; they will read; they will count.

da'iigis bá hooghan, laundry.

da'iilzhiizh, we (many) danced.

da'iíłta', they have been to school; they are educated.

da'iíłta'igíí, the ones that are educated.

da'iinánigíí, life.

da'iíniil'eełęę, our sailing; our navigation; our going by boat.

da'iiníiłta', we are going to school; we are reading; we are counting.

da'iiníilta'igi 'át'éego, it is as we count.

da'iinółta'ii, you school children; you pupils; you students.

da'iitsoii, bílátah, blooms, flowers.

da'iiyą́ą́', they ate.

da'ilí, they are valuable; they are expensive.

da'iliinii, valuable ones, expensive ones.

daiłbał, they waved it (a flag).

da'iniísh, there is work being done.

dajichį', baa, they cherish it, protect it.

da'jiiłta', they have gone to school, received an education.

dajiiłtsą, they saw it, him.

dajiináago, while they are alive.

dajiináonii, bee, that by which they live, their livelihood.

dajiisxí, they killed him.

dajiisxínigii, the one which they killed.

da'jiiyą́ą́', they had a meal; they ate; they had a feast.

dajilghał, they eat it (meat).

dajiłjigo, since they are.

dajilínigii, whatever they are, those that are.........

dajiłbééxh, they boil it.

dajiłch'ilgo, they are (as usual) scorching it.

dajiniigo, when they are saying.

da'jist'jidgo, when they became rich.

da'jit'jigo, since they are rich.

da'jiłł S, they weave, are weaving.

da'jitł'óo dago, doo, since they do not weave; since they are not weavers.

dajitsaah, he is sick; he is ill.

dajiyą, they eat it; it is edible.

da'jiyáni góne', in a place where people eat, in the dining room, in the cafe, in the restaurant.

dajiyooznah, baa, they forgot about them.

dajixlį́į', they became, have come into being. **K'éé'didléhé dajixlį́į'.** They became farmers.

dajixtsą, he died; he is dead.

dajółta', they are counting them; they are reading it.

dajooba', they are kind.

dajooba', **doo — da**, they are unmerciful, mean.

dajooba', **doo yaa — da**, they are not nice to them; they are mistreating them.

da'joodlánigíí, those that believe it.

dajood!ánigíí, their belief.

dajood!ohgo, while they are laughing.

dajoo!yé, they are called.

da'joolzhiizh, there was a dance, people danced.

dajoozba', **yaa**, they treated them well.

Damįįgo, Sunday (Span. domingo).

Damįįgo Biiskání, Monday.

damiigo ná'ádleeh, Sundays come and go; weeks pass.

dandaazii, things that are heavy.

dánditįhi, gate (a movable barrier).

da'neest'ą́, things got ripe; they are ripened.

daanéet'įłęę, things that were growing.

danceyą́, they are matured, fully developed.

daneezná, they (three or more) died; they are dead.

daneeznánigíí, those that died; the dead ones; those that are dead.

dani'áhígíí, those that extend horizontally. **iził dani'áhígíí**, mountain ranges.

danichxǫ́ǫ́'ígíí, those that are ugly, undesirable.

danidiyooíhéél, they will kill you.

danidlį, they (three or more) are. **Ałk'éí danidlį**. They are all related to one another.

danihi'di'niigo, you (pl.) were told time after time.

danihighanigíí, your (pl.) homes.

danihijoolá, they do not like us; they hate us; they detest us.

danihiłni, they say to us, you (pl.).

danihini'go, if you (pl.) want to go; if you (pl.) wish to go.

danihinół'į, you (pl.) are looking at us.

danihizázi yę́ę, our or your ancestors.

danihizhdoolghałígíí, things that will eat us up.

daniid.į, we (three or more) are. **Naakaii łizhinii daniidlį**. We are Negroes.

daniidlínígíí, those of us who are.

daniidzįį', we thought; we wanted.

da'ni'įįh, yee, they usually rob them, steal from them.

da'niil'éél, we sailed, rowed, went by boat.

daniil'įįgo, as we look at it.

daniizįį'go, they having thought, wanted.

da'nijah, a place where people sleep; hotel; motel; dormitory.

da'nijahigíí, the hotel.

daniiį́, they are.

dani'į, they flow along horizontally.

donii'į, they are shown, exhibited.

daniłįįgo, since they are

daniłíinii, those that are.

dani'įį nt'éé', they used to be. **'Atah danilįį nt'éé'**. They used to be members.

danilínę́ędą́ą́', when they were.

danilinigíí, those which are.

danil'inígíí, exhibition; the exhibits.

da'niłch'ishídę́ę́', from all sides, converging (opposed to diverge).

daniłdáasgo, **'ahee**, they were of equal weight.

daniłtóligo, since they are crystal clear.

da'nilts'ą́ą́'góó, diverging, toward all directions.

danineez, they are long; they are tall.

danineezgo, since they are long; since they are tall.

danineezigíí, those that are long; those that are tall.

daniteeligíí, those that are wide, broad. (see **niteel**).

da'nítiinigíí, the roads.

danitsaa, they are big.

danitsaago, since they are large.

danitsxaaz, they are big and fat. **Dibé yázhí k'ad danitsxaaz**. The lambs are big now.

daniyééh, they grow up, mature, usually.

daniyol, winds blow.

daniyo!go, when winds are blowing.

danizaadgóó, to far away places; to distant places; to remote places.

danizaadi, at distant places; at remote places.

danizhóní, they are beautiful, pretty, attractive, charming, picturesque.

danizhónigo, since they are pretty, nice.

danízin, they think, want.

da'njahigíí, bee, bedding.

danlínęę, those that are (were).

danlinigíí, those that are.

danohsingo, you (pl.) think, want.

danohsinigíí, t'áá, whatever you (pl.) want; whatever you (pl.) wish; whatever you (pl.) think.

danół'į, you (pl.) look at it.

danół'įįgo, when you (pl.) look at them.

danoolch'iił, close your (pl.) eyes.

dantł'izigíí, those that are hard (opposed to soft).

da'ólta'ęę, what used to be schools.

da'ólta'ági, at the schools.

daolyé, they are called, their names are.

daolyéego, since they are called.

daolyéhęę, those that were called.

da'ólta', they study, read, count.

da'ólta'ęę, those that used to go to school.

da'ólta'édóó, from where they go to school.

da'ólta'í, pupils, students.

da'oodlá, they believe, are believers.

da'oo'į, they can see; they are witnesses.

da'oo'inęę, those that were able to see; those that were witnesses.

da'oosdląąd, they believed, became believers.

daosye', they were called, named.

das, weight.

desétsą, I am dead.

desétsęęgo, when I die.

dashdiikai, bił, they started off with him; they set out with him.

dashdiiyá, we started off; he set out.

dashidiizts'ą́ą́', they heard me.

dashidiyeołhééł, they will kill me.

dashidoolghał, they will eat me up.

dashidoołbish, they will cook me; they will boil me.

dashiłitsą, they saw me.

dashiłitséhí, t'áadoo, without their seeing me; before they saw me.

dashiisxį, they killed me. **Dashiisxįį dooleeł ńt'éé',** they would have killed me.

dashinół'į, you (pl.) look at me.

desidoots'ą́ą́', you (pl.) have heard, have heard of it.

da'sílizlih, bił, we (pl.) made a mistake with it.

da' t'áá 'aaníí, no kidding—is that a fact. (incredulity).

dawójfígo, when they are called (by name).

dayichxǫ', they were ruined, wrecked, spoiled.

dayidíínííd, they said to him.

dayidínéeshdǫǫ́ł, I will shoot at them; I will fire on them.

dayiłchįįh, they know how.

dayiłchįįhii, those that know how.

dayíłtaad, they made great number of them, made them many.

dayíłtchozh, they chewed them up; they eat them.

dayíłtchxǫ', they spoiled, ruined it.

dayíłtsą́, they saw it.

dayíłtsánęę, what they saw.

dayiinii', they heard of them; they were notified.

dayíiniłłden, they shot at him.

dayiiniił, yaa, they give them to them.

dayiists'ą́ą́', they are listening to it (as a radio).

dayiisxį, they killed him.

dayíiyą́ą́', they ate it.

dayiizh'eezh, yaa, they led them to them.

dayi'niiyą́ą́', they have started to eat them; they are going to eat them.

dayókeed, they ask for it.

dayókeedgo, when they ask for it.

dayółta', they count them; they read them.

dayółta'go, when they count it, read it.

dayoodlá, they believe in it.

dayoo'į, they see him (them).

dayooldééł, they ate them.

dazhdeesdęęh, they exploded them; they shot them off.

dazhdeez'á, baa, they turned it over to them; they relinquished it to them.

dazhdíílid, they got burned.

dazhdíítid, they burned them.

dazhdiítkǫǫh, they are smoothing them out.

dazhnił'į, they are looking at.

dazhnitá, bíka, they search for it; they are searching for it.

de (dei), up; upward. De'áyiilaa, He raised it up.

de'ádaadzaa, they raised their heads; they looked up.

de'ádajiilaa, they raised it up; they lifted it up.

de'áyiila, he raised it up, lifted it.

dééh, tea.

dééh bee yibézhí, teapot.

déé'įį', I looked; he looked.

deenásts'aa', ram, buck.

deeni, it is sharp, keen edged.

deesdoi, it (weather) is hot, warm.

deesdǫǫh, it blew up; it exploded.

deesdǫǫhgo, when it exploded.

deesháát, I will go.

deesh'ał, I will chew it (hard object).

deeshbish, to braid it (hair, rope, etc.).

deeshbish, I will boil it; I will cook it by boiling.

łeeshcha, I will cry; I will weep.

deeshchííł, to give birth to it, bear it.

deeshchįįł, I will smell it.

deeshch'it, to scratch it (as an insect bite).

deeshch'ish, I will file, rasp, saw, grate, brush, or sandpaper it. Shiwoo' deeshch'ish. I will brush my teeth.

deeshchosh, I will eat it (herbage).

deeshchxǫǫł, I will spoil, ruin, wreck, mar, ruffle, or disfigure it.

deeshdił, I will eat them (plural obj.).

łeeshghał, I will eat it (meat).

deeshgizh, gapped.

deeshįįł, I will eat it; I will make a meal on it.

deeshłeeł, I will or shall become, be.

deeshwoł, I will run; I will go running.

deeshzhaháą, dah, the foliage or protruding branches along the tree.

deesk'aaz, it (weather) is cold.

deesk'aazgo, when it (weather) was cold.

deeskai, they went, started on their way.

deeskai, yił, they have set out with him; they are accompanying him.

deesk'id, hill, ridge.

deestsiin, pinon.

deet'á, baa, it was given to them; it was relinquished to him or them.

deeteel, moose (wide horns).

deeyol, the wind began to blow.

deez'á, bluff (rock formation).

deez'ééł, it started to float along.

deezgo', he stumbled to the ground; he fell.

deezná, they, he, started to move, migrate.

deezt'i', it started to extend, (as a wire); it began (as a story).

deezt'i'éé, it started off, it had its beginning.

dégo', I tripped.

dei, up; upward.

dei'áshłaa, I raised it up.

deideesdǫǫh, they fired it off.

deidíítid, they burned it.

deidiits'a', they understand it fully (as a language); they have heard of it.

deidiłhįįhgo, when they melt it.

deidínóoł'įįł, they will see it; they will look at it.

deidiyiilo', dah, they hung him; he weighed them.

deidlą́ą́', we drank it.

deidoo'ał, they will eat them; they will chew it.

deidooyįįł, they will eat it.

deighánidi, doo, far, far away.

deigo, upward.

deigo dah diildoh, ascension, ascent.

deiildzis, ravines.

deiilníísh, they are working.

deiiłkaah, they are tracking it along, following its trail.

deiiłtsánéę, those that I saw.

łeijááh, dah, they are holding them up.

łeiji', upper part.

deiji'éé', shirt.

deiji' 'éé yaago deezt'i'igii, shirt tail.

deijoolá, they hate them.

deijooláago, because they disliked, or hated them.

deikódaadzaa, they came up thus.

deikónééh, they increase in quantity, weight, size.

deil'áhąą, those that used to extend, stand (as timber).

deildeel, they eat them.

deilée, dah — dooleel, they will have it in their possession.

deiléhęęgi, dah — 'át'éego, like that which they had in their possession.

deilghal, they eat it (meat).

deiltse'góó, t'áá, whenever they are seen.

deilchozhigii, those that eat it (leafy plants)

deilni, they say to them, call them.

deinéehgo, while they are moving, migrating along.

deinééł'įį', they looked at it; they examined it.

deinééł'įį', ya, they looked up; they looked skyward; they examined it for him.

deinéełkaadgo, while they were driving them along (as a herd of sheep).

deineez'įį', they stole them.

deini'įįhgo, yee, they usually steal them from them.

deiniiji, we called, named, or mentioned, it.

deiniikeedéę, what we had asked for.

deiniiłkaad, yaa, they drove them to them.

deinił'į, they are looking at it; they are examining it.

deinił'įįgo, when they look at it.

deinízin, they want it.

deinó'ááh, they deceive them.

deinohdlą, you (pl.) believe it. (believe ye it.)

deinóolta', you (pl.) study, or read it.

deist'įįd, they got rich in it.

deistį, yaa, they brought him to him.

deit'íinii, these who are rich in them.

deitł'óogo, because they weave it.

deits'ǫǫs, they suck (not in the sense of the young being fed from a nipple).

deiyą, they eat, or are eating it.

deiyánígíí, those that they eat.

deizháashgo, as they are wearing.

deizhniíłdon, they shot at him.

deizlóóz, he (they) came leading him; they came with him in tow.

déłí, sandhill crane.

Denihootso, Denehotso, Arizona.

deniníyá, ké, the shoe turned up (curled up).

désh'įį', I am looking, observing.

désyiz, I got frightened; I dodged.

désyiz, bik'ee, I was startled by it.

déyá, I am on my way; I am going; I am going to go.

—di, at. (also —gi)

dį'ąjį, the fourth day; for four days.

dibáá', thirst.

dibé, sheep.

dibé bighan, sheep corral.

dibé binaʼłtsoos, sheep permit; stock permit.

dibé bitsį', mutton.

dibé bitsį' 'ásaanaasdziidgo, fried mutton.

dibé bitsį' shibézhigií, mutton stew.

dibé bitsį' sit'éhigií, roasted mutton.

dibé biya', sheep tick.

dibé biya' dootł'izhí, sheep lice.

dibé cho'ádinii, wether (sheep).

dibéhéę, what were sheep; aforementioned sheep.

dibé nii'į, say phoebe (name of bird).

dibé tsa'ii, ewe.

dibé yázhí, lamb.

dích'íí', hot (as pepper), bitter.

dich'íízh, it is rough, coarse, chapped, asperate.

dichin, hunger.

dichin 'ooghééł, starvation.

dichxosh, stubby; bushy; shaggy.

dideesbąs, to start rolling it along.

dideesh'ááł, I will start carrying it.

dideeshbał, to hang it up (as curtain).

dideeshbah, to start on a raid.

dideeshch'ah, to open one's mouth.

dideeshchii', inflammation, inflamed.

dideeshdǫǫł, I will explode it; fire it; blow it up; detonate it.

didéesh'įįł, I will (take a) look.

dideeshtłił, I will set it afire.

dideests'įįł, I will hear it; I will hear about it.

didííłjéé', I built a fire.

didiit'įįł, we will look; we will take a look.

didooch'ih, a breeze of air will come up.

didoochííł, it will start to snow.

didooch'ish, it will become rough; it will get chapped.

didoodlóós, dah, he will be led off.

didookah, náás, they will start forward, start to progress.

didooljéé', a fire was built.

didoołdzil, it will decay.

didoołhjh, it will melt.

didooniił, he will say.

didooyįįł, to be holy, supernatural; to bring about.

didzé, berry, berries.

didzé dík'ǫzhii, chokeberry.

didzé dit'ódii, service berry.

didzétsoh, peaches.

didzétsoh dik'ǫzhígíí, plum.

didzétsoh yázhí, apricot.

díghaał, open your eyes.

digháhii, ch'ééh, turtle, tortoise. (see tsisteeł).

digiz, it is crooked (not in the right position).

eigohgo, when it starts to flow.

díí, this; these.

dįį', four.

dii'áázh, yił dah, he started off with him; he set off with him.

diichiłi, abalone shell.

di'jdi, brittle; fragile.

diidí, this one; these.

dįįdi, four times.

diidiígíí, particularly this one.

diidííłjéé', he (they) built a fire.

dįįdi mííl, four thousand.

dįįdi neeznádiin, four hundred.

díigi 'át'éego, in this way, like this, in this fashion.

diigis, insane.

diigis báhooghan, insane asylum.

dįį'go, four of them.

diijéé', dah, they started off at a run.

diijeeh, dah, they are just about to start off running.

díí jį, today; this day.

Dį'įjį Ndaʼanish, Thursday.

diikai, dah, they started off.

diik'ǫsh, it is rotten, it is spoiled; yeast.

dí'il, it is hairy (as angora goat). (also dits'oz).

—díil, to be large (man, animal, mountain, etc.).

diildǫǫh, it is about to burst.

diilid, it burned; it is burnt.

diilidígíí, what has been burnt.

diilkǫ', it became smooth.

diiltła, it started to burn; it caught fire.

diilwod, dah, he started off running; he started to run.

diilyésii, ch'il, rabbit brush.

diiłdzid, it decayed; it is rotten; spoiled.

diił'éél, dah, I sailed it off.

diiłhįį', it is molten, melted.

diiłkǫ', I made it smooth.

diináół, you will go, you will come.

diiná, dah, he, they started moving, migrating.

dííniid, I said it; he said it.

dííniidii', he said it and....; I said it and.....

diish, this? this one?

diish jįįdóó, from today (on).

diishkǫǫh, I am making it smooth.

diishtįįh, ch'ééh dah, I cannot pick it up; I am unable to lift it. (a stiff slender object).

diitaa', they, it, fell apart, went to pieces, shattered.

diit'ash, we two will go, come, arrive; let us go.

díí'ts'áadah, fourteen.

díjyáál, half a dollar, four bits, fifty cents.

diiyá, dah, he (or i) started off, set out.

díízéíí, it broke to pieces, shattered.

díízhíní, this summer.

dijah, expectoration.

dijool, spherical (ball like).

dikah, náás, they start forward, progress, usually.

dik'ǫ́ǫ́zh, sour, alkaline, salty.

dikos, cough.

dikos 'azee', cough syrup, cough medicine.

dikostsoh 'ání'iishiłígíí, whooping cough.

díkwíí, how many? how much?

díkwíídi, how many times?

díkwíígo, how many of them?

díkwíígóó, to how many places?

díkwíí shą', how many are there?

díkwíí shįį, there are several.

díkwíí shą' bą́ą́h 'ílį, how much is it worth?

dilch'il, crackling; popping; static (on radio).

dilchxosh, effervescent (as pop).

dildǫ', tinkling (as the sound of a thin sheet of tin).

dili', it usually burns.

dilk'is, juniper, cedar.

dilkǫǫh, it is smooth; smoothed surface.

dilkǫǫhgo, smoothly.

diltłi', it is burning; it is afire.

dilt'óshii, gray titmouse (bird), or sparrow.

dilwosh, he is shouting; he is hollering.

dilyéhé, Pleiades—Seven Sisters.

dilyíhí, lead (metal).

dił, blood.

dił 'adeidááchil, congestion of blood.

dił 'aheełt'éii bééhoozįįh, blood typing.

dił 'álnééh ndoolkah 'biniiyé, Wasserman (test).

dił 'ats'iistah naazlįįgi, circulation (of the blood).

dił bii' noot'įį', septicemia.

dił bitoo', blood serum.

dił biyi' naa'eełí, corpuscle.

dilch'il, dense (as hair, wool).

diłdánii, quail.

dił dilyilii, blood clot.

dił dineestał, hemorrhage.

dił dootł'izhi, venous blood.

dildxid, it will spoil; it will rot.

diłhįįh, it is melting.

diłhił, dark, jet-black.

dił 'iih nádzííd, blood transfusion.

dił 'iih yiłt'ood, blood transfusion.

dił na'ałkidigii, blood pressure.

dił nilk'įh, the clotting of the blood.

dił t'éiyá, bloody.

dił wólta', blood count.

dił yíchxǫ', septicemia.

dina', it lasts; ability to endure; to hold out.

dina' da, doo, it does not hold out, or last.

diné, a being; person; man; Navajo; the people.

diné biya', human louse.

diné dadiyinii, the holy people; holy men.

diné da'iigisí, laundry man.

diné daninéhigii, the corpse (of a human being).

diné daninéhigii hasht'edeile'é, undertaker, mortician.

dine'é, tribe; people; nation; race (of men).

dinééh, young man, youth.

dínéeshch'il, to close one's eyes, to blink one's eyes.

díinéesh'įįł, I shall look at it.

dínéest'ą́, it started to grow.

dinéhęę, the man who; the man; the men that were.

dinéhigíí, particular man.

dinéji, with respect to man, concerning man.

dinénáhódlóonii, here used as a convenient term to denote the Northern Athabascan people. Literally it means "the other Navajos in existence" and refers to the people in the north related to the Navajo, and according to others to the Canoncito Navajos.

dinétah, the old Navajo country. (v. Van Vaulkenburg's **Diné Bikéyah**)

dini', wild game.

dini, you say.

diniibįįh, dah, we sit.

diniih, pain, ache.

díní'įį', keep your eyes open; stay awake, look.

díníil'įį, we will look at it.

dinilbá, light gray.

dinilchíí', pink.

dinilgai, cream colored.

dinishch'ah, to hold the mouth open.

dínísh'įį', I am looking; I am awake.

dinishwo', I can run fast; I am a runner.

díníyá, you have set out; you are on your way; you are going to go.

dinóochał, it will swell up.

dinooltł'izh, greenish.

dínóot'įį, they will grow, mature, get ripe.

dínóozįįł, he will think, want.

dísáás, you are in the act of starting to dribble it along (as sand).

diséts'ą́ą́, I have heard; I have heard of.

diséts'ą́'í, t'áadoo — da, I heard nothing; I heard not a sound.

disháhí, t'áadoo háájída, I did not start off anywhere; I went nowhere.

dishch'id, eczema.

dishníigo, I said thus.........

dishch'id, kee' bąąh, athlete's foot.

disho, hairy (as fine hair on one's arm).

dissǫǫs, reed whistle.

disxǫs, glittering.

ditą, it is thick, deep (as water).

dit'in, dense, close together (as leaves on a tree).

ditłéé', wet, damp, humid.

ditłid, tremulous (as jello); shaky (as a palsied limb).

ditł'o, it is hairy (as a dog, sheep); hirsute.

ditł'ooí, the hairy one; shaggy one.

dit'ódi, soft; tender; fragile; pliable; perishable (as fruit).

dits'id, tough, sinewy.

dits'oz, hairy.

dits'oz, hairy (as angora).

ditsxiz, jerky, shaky, trembling, shaking (with fear, etc.), quivering.

diwol, it is rough, uneven.

diwozh, thorny.

Díwózhii Bii' Tó, Greasewood, Arizona.

díwózhiiłbáíí, chamizo, chamiso.

díwózhiishzhiin, greasewood.

diyeeshhééł, I will kill it (him).

diyin, the holy being, supernatural being; it is sacred; he is holy.

Diyin 'Ayóó 'Át'éii, Almighty Holy Being.

diyinígíí, that which is holy; the one who is holy.

diyinii, the holy one

diyogi, Navajo blanket, Navajo rug.

diyoolyéłę́ę, bee, that with which it will be killed; weapon.

diyoolyéłígíí, the one who will be killed, the intended victim.

diyóół, wind (to come up)

diyóósh, bullsnake.

diz, a pile of trash or driftwood caught in a stream by the whirling waters.

dizdiin, forty.

dígdiindi, forty times.

dízdiindi 'adées'eez, forty paces, forty feet.

dizéí, crumbly.

dláád, mold, lichen.

łeesh, clay (white).

dłǫ'átah né'éshjaa', burrowing owl.

Dłǫ́'áyázhí, Thoreau, New Mexico.

dloh, laughter.

dłǫ́ii, weasel.

dłǫ́ǫ', prairie dog.

dlozishzhiin, black pine squirrel.

dloziłgaii, pine squirrel.

dó', too, also. shi dó', I also, me, too.

dólii, mountain bluebird.

dóliiłchíí', chestnut breasted bluebird.

dóó, and.

—dóó, from (a definite point).

doo, not. (Precedes a negation, and is usually followed by da, which comes after the negative word or phrase. As: Doo yá'át'ééh .da, It is not good).

doo (abbreviated form of **dooleeł**), it will be.

doo 'áhályáni, blockhead, a stupid person.

doo 'ak'éhól'įį da, disobedience.

doo 'ákó 'iishłaa da, I did it wrong.

doo 'ákót'ée da, it is wrong, incorrect.

doo'ash, they (two) will go, come.

doo baa 'ákohwiinidzin da, to be unaware.

doo bą́ą́h 'ílíní da, valueless (as imitation necklace); worthless.

doo ba'jóolíí' 'át'ée da, he is unreliable.

doo be'ádadíláah da, they behave well; they are not troublesome; they are not full of mischief.

doo beehaz'ą́ą́ da, it is forbidden.

doo bídin dahóyée' da, they are plentiful.

doo bik'i'diishtįįh da, I do not understand it (comprehend).

dóó bik'iji', after, thereafter.

doo bił hats'íid da, he is lonesome, homesick.

doo hózhǫ́, not quite.

doo hoot'įį da, obscure.

doo bił ntsíhákeesígi 'áhoodzaa, accident.

doobish, it will boil.

doo bitah dahats'íidii bá haz'ą́ą́ góne', infirmary.

doo bízhneedlįį da, he is not interested.

doo bohónéedzą́ą́ da, it is impossible, or impracticable.

dooch'ih, to blow, or arrive (as a breeze).

doochííł, to snow (i.e. the arrival of a snowstorm).

doochxǫǫł, it will be ruined, wrecked, disarranged, spoiled.

dooda, no (in refusal), not.

Doodaatsaahii, Jesus Christ.

doodaii', or; or else; if not; otherwise.

doo da'íljį da, they are valueless, worthless.

dooda shą'shin, I do not think so.

doo deidiits'a' da, they do not understand It (as a language); they cannot hear it; they have not heard of it.

doo deighánígóó, far off; long way. (also **nízaadgóó**)

doodįłígíí, that which will be eaten.

doo ditą́a da, it is shallow, thin.

doo diyíiłhéeł da ńt'ę́ę́', you should not have killed him.

doodlįįłii, that which will be drunk.

doo doogáał da, he will not come, he will **doohęs,** it will itch.

doo hináágóó, being lifeless.

doo hah, slowly. (also **tąądee**). not be here.

doo hááji da, nowhere.

doo 'idéét'i' da, unconcern.

doo 'ih'onéedzą́ą́ da, impossibility.

dóó'įį', that you might look.

dooildinę́ę́ (doo **yildinę́ę́**), the aforementioned despised one.

doo 'ił 'ééhózin da, unconsciousness.

doo 'iłhats'íi da, lonesomeness.

doo 'iłna'adáá góne', isolation ward.

dook'ą́ą́ł, it is burning (also **diłtłi'**).

dook'áłigíí, naadą́ą́' bee, that with which corn will be ground; something with which to grind corn.

Dook'o'osłíid, San Francisco Peaks (near Flagstaff, Arizona).

doo lá dó' — da, boy oh boy, what a......... **Doo lá dó' nighan hózhóni da,** Boy oh boy, what a nice home you have!

doolchį́į́ł, to scent along, follow his nose (as a dog).

dooleeł, it will be, it will become. Used with verbs in present tense to futurize them, with verbs in past tense to form future perfect, etc. **naashá,** I am walking about. **naasháa dooleeł,** I shall be walking about. (It is often abbreviated to **doo**).

dooleełę́ę́, I wish that it would be.

dooleełgo, so it will be.

dooleełígíí, that which will be.

doolk'ool, to be (or it is) undulating, wavy (as wool, terrain, etc.), corrugated, wrinkled (as rambouillet sheep).

doolnihéégóó, dah, toward where he was pointing (with his finger).

dool'oł, it will be floated; it will be sailed (rowed, paddled, etc.).

dooltsos, baa (haa), it (flat, flexible object) will be given to him.

doo naagháhi da, there is no one around, no one home; it is deserted, uninhabited.

doo naaki nilíígóó, without doubt.

doo náldzidii, one who is brave.

doo ndayiilée da, they are not paying it.

doo ndi, not even.

doo ndiists'a' da, I do not understand you; I cannot hear you.

dóone'é, clan.

doo nii'eeł da, he does not perspire, he does not sweat.

doonííł haada, it will act in some way; it will do something; it will injure.

doonííł, ła', it will be successful; it will be completed, finished.

doo ninit'i'i, endless.

doo nisin da, I do not care for it, I do not want it.

doo shaa náhát'íí da, I am not supposed to be bothered.

dootííł, it will freeze, (an object); it will get cold (freezing).

dootł'izh, green, blue.

dootł'izhii, turquoise.

doo ts'ídá baa yinít'íí da lá, it does not affect them (as disease, etc.).

doo yá'ádaashóonii, the evil ones, the bad ones.

doo yá'áshǫǫ da, a bad person; not good; dangerous; wicked; worthless.

doo yá'át'éeh da, a bad omen; evil; not good.

doo yee 'oo'íí dago, since he cannot see with it.

doo yiits'iłii, unbreakable.

doo yił da'ahidiits'a'góó, since they cannot understand each other's language.

doo yinízin dago, he does not care for it; he does not want it.

doo yit'íí da, obscure.

doozhǫǫhii, unbroken horse, wild horse, bronco.

dósh'eeł, let me be on my way floating.

dzǫǫdi, over here.

dzaanééz, mule.

dzaanééz yázhí, young mule.

dzédzi', in the fire.

dzééh, elk.

dzidiłháshii, scorpion.

dzidiyoołhééł, he will kill him.

dzidza yíinil, he put them into the fire.

dzigai, flat; plain; prairie.

dziil, strength, to be strong.

dziiłhaal, it rushed on (away). **Tó nihik'i dziiłhaal,** the water rushed over us; the waves dashed over us.

dziiłtsą́ągo, when he saw it.

dzi'izi, bicycle.

dzi'izh bijááł tá'igíí, tricycle.

dzi'izitsoh, motorcycle.

dzilí, hawk (Cooper's).

dził, mountain.

Dziłghą́'á (also **Dziłghą́'i**), Arizona Apaches (general name given to White Mountain and San Carlos Apaches).

dziłgóó ndaakaaigíí, those that live in the mountains; bears; wild beasts.

Dziłibái, Gray Mountain.

Dziłijiin, Black Mountain.

Dził Ná'oodiłii, Huerfano Mountain.

dziłtsíjigi, at the base of the mountain, or at the foot of the mountain.

Dziłyi', in the mountains; Intermountain.

dzizį, one (person) is standing.

dzizti, one (person) is lying down.

dzólníígóó, t'óó, aimlessly.

- E -

'eda'astł'ónígíí, naaltsoos bee, paper twine.

'éé', clothing; garments; shirt.

'a'e'aah, west.

'a'e'aah bich'ijigo, westward.

'a'e'aah biyaadi, in the west.

'a'e'aah biyaajigo, westward, in the far west.

'a'e'aahdéé'go, from the west.

'e'e'áahgo, when the sun goes down, when the sun sets.

'a'e'aahjí, on the west side.

'a'e'aahjigo, westward.

'e'e'aah, k'adéé, the sun is setting; the sun is about to set.

'éé' biih ná'nilí, clothes cabinet.

'éédahodoosįįł, they will recognize the place.

'éédahoozin, bił, they found out, came to know, things.

'éédahózingo, bił, because they know things.

'éédoohah, to spend the year.

'e'e'eeł, shił yóó, I am sailing away.

'ééhéestł'inígíí, parts.

'éého'dílzin, fame.

'ééhodoozįįł, there will be knowledge.

'ééhodoozįįłigíí, bee, that with which there will be knowledge.

'ééhodoozįįł, shił, I shall know things.

'eehólónígíí, possession.

'ééhoozįįh, inspection; examination; test.

'ééhoozin, bee, with it there came to be knowledge.

'ééhózingi, t'áadoo bił, at a place unfamiliar to him.

'ééhózinii, bee, compass; sextant.

'ééhózini, t'áadoo, unbeknown to anyone; without anyone's knowing.

'éé'ilnii', released.

'é'él'į, the custom of making, or doing something.

'e'el'įįgi, photography.

'e'elneeh, swallow.

'eelwod, he ran; he made a run.

'e'elyaa, photograph.

'éé' naats'oodii, sweater, knitted garment.

'éénééz, topcoat, overcoat.

'éé' neishoodii, clergyman.

'éé' neishodii bi'éé' 'ádaołts'íísigíí, Protestant minister.

'éé' neishoodii bi'éé' danineezigíí, Catholic priest.

'éé' neishoodii binahagha', white man's religion.

'eesh'oł, I am sailing, rowing, along.

'eet'a', it flew away. (also dah diit'a').

'éétsoh, coat, or overcoat.

'éétsoh 'áłts'íísiigíí, jacket.

'éí, that; that one ('éí generally refers to something remote from the speaker.)

'éí beego, on account of that, for that reason.

'eidí, that one (near you). (also 'eii).

'éidiigíí, that very one.

'éigi 'át'éego, in that fashion, in that way, like that.

'eii, that, that one, that one there. ('eii generally refers to something close at hand.)

'éiida, jó, instead of it, him, them.

'éik'ehgo, according to that, after that fashion, in that way, in that manner.

'éí lá t'áá 'éí ni, very well; fine; swell. (in the sense of being grateful).

'éiyá, only (a restrictive element); exclusively; specifically.

'énáhoosdzin, there was a return of knowledge; (we) got our bearings again; (we) re-oriented ourselves.

'éłłohí 'ak'ah sisi'igíí, camphorated oil.

– G –

ga', expletive; this (not that—used emphatically).

gáagii, crow.

Gáamalii, Mormon.

gad, juniper.

Gad Deelzha, Mesa Verde, Colorado.

gad ni'eełí, red juniper, cedar.

gah, rabbit.

gahtsoh, jackrabbit.

gałbáhi, cottontail rabbit.

ge', silence, hush, hark, listen, attention.

géeso, cheese.

ghą́ą́'ask'idii, camel. (also bííghą́ą́ 'ask'idii)

ghaai, t'áá 'ákwíí, every winter; every year.

Ghąąjį', October.

gha'diit'aahii, a lawyer, attorney.

—gi, at. (also —di)

—gi 'at'éego, like.

gidi—gidi, kitty—kitty.

giinisi, fifteen cents.

giníłbáhi, western goshawk.

ginítsoh, desert sparrow hawk.

gish, digging stick, walking cane.

—go da 'át'é, it is possible that.........

góde, upward.

gódei, up.

gódeig, upward.

gohwééh, coffee.

gohwééh hashtł'ishí, cocoa.

golchóón, comforter, quilt.

gólízhii, skunk.

góne', inside.

gónaa, across; around here; hereabouts; in this vicinity.

góne'é, inside (an enclosure); in the interior; indoors. (also wóne'é)

—góó, to; along the extension of; toward.

Góóhníinii, Hualpai, Havasupai.

góóldi, court (a place of justice).

góyaa, down into, down along.

- H -

há, for him, her, it, one, them (i.e. for sake of).

haa, about, to, him, her, them.

ha'qq, over the hill.

háá'á, it sticks up out.

ha'a'aah, east.

ha'a'aahdi, in the east.

ha'a'aah bich'ijigo, eastward.

ha'a'aah biyaadéé' naaghái, easterner.

ha'a'aah biyaajigo, toward the east.

ha'a'aahdéé', from the east.

ha'a'aahdi nahat'á yiniiyé dah ńdinibjjhii, Congress.

ha'a'aahjigo, eastward.

haa 'ádahayą, they are being cared for, they are under supervision.

háá'ált'e', exhumation.

háá'áyjjh, to rest.

hááchaii', he cried out and (then); he let out a cry and.........

haada, somehow; in some wise; some way; in some manner or another.

háádaadzih, they speak out (one after another).

ηáádaalyjhi, t'áadoo, without resting.

háádabii'niilgo, while they dig them up.

háádadidoo'niil, they will put their clothes back on, they will dress up again.

ηáádahaashchii'go, since they are sharp pointed

ηaá daha'niil, they are taken out again, exhumed.

háádahiniséégóó, where they (plants) come up one after the other.

háádahinisééh, they (plants) grow back up.

haadahoot'jjhgo, when something happens.

haa dahwiilzhiishgo, when their turn comes.

háádajiishée'go, he whetted them to a point.

háádajiizhk'aazh, he ground them to a point.

haadashą' yit'éego, how in the world?

háádéé', where from?

háádéé'goshjj, from some direction.

háádeeshyjh, I will rest; I will take a vacation.

haadeinééh, something is about to happen to it.

haadei'nééh, what shall we do?

háadi, where; where?

háadida, somewhere; wherever.

háadida t'áá hoolzhishgi, sometime in the future.

háadi, where, where?

háadida, somewhere, wherever.

háádóó da, from some point; from somewhere; from some place.

haadzihgo, when he speaks.

haadzii', he spoke out; he exclaimed; he made a speech. **T'áadoo haadzii' da.** He said nothing. **Yee yich'j' haadzii'.** He mentioned it to him.

haadzii'go, when he made a speech; when he spoke out.

haagedígi, where it is dug out, where it is mined.

ha'agééd, mine.

haagééd, it is mined.

háághal, he turned his eyes.

háágiz, tó, turned on the water faucet.

haagizgo, while it was turned on (as water from the faucet).

háágóó shjj, toward some place or another; to some destination or other.

hqqh, upon him; alongside him.

haah, here (as in asking one to hand something here).

hááhaashchii', it is sharp pointed.

hááhágo, soon, without delay, in a speedy manner.

hááhék'aashí, bee, that with which to grind it; a grindstone.

hááhályjjhgo, while it rests usually

hááhgishjj, sometime (future).

hááhgóóshjj, strongly; hard; energetically; with force; diligently.

haa'í yee', let us see; show me.

háájída, in some direction; toward wherever.

háájigo, which way; in what direction.

háájil, it came out (protruding).

háájílyjh, one rests.

háájíshǫ', which way? where to? where did it go?

hááji shjj, in some direction, somewhere.

hááji' shjj, to a point (as far as somewhere).

háájit'ash, they (two) go up out; they (two) ascend.

Haak'oh, Acoma, New Mexico.

háálá, because, for, the fact is.

haalá 'áhánééh, well—well—well (mild and pleasant surprise, as in meeting an old friend).

haalá 'áhoodzaa, wake up (as when one is not paying attention).

haalá 'ánínééh, what is the matter with you? (as one would say to a child who spilled its milk).

haalá yit'é? what seems to be the matter?

háálj, it flows up out.

ha'altsédii, walnut.

haalzíid, it is being watched.

ha'alzíid, reconnaissance.

ha'áłchíni, his, their, children, family.

haa néelt'e', how many, how much (in number). (also **díkwíí**).

háánídááh, you come back up out.

hááhideeneez, tapering to a point.

hááhinoot'jjł, they (plants) come up one after another.

hááhwiildóóh, bii', he is regaining consciousness; he is coming to, relaxing.

haa'í? where?

haa'ída, wheresoever; whenever; sometime; somewhere.

háá'iidziih, exhalation.

haait'éegosha', how.

haa ninádahajeehígíí, something which one gets by mail.

haa ninádahajeehígíí, naaltsoos, mail.

hááni yee', someone.

háánoot'á, it grew back; they (ants, etc.) propagated.

haa ntsáhákees, consideration of him.

ha'asdzá, ascension; ascent.

haasdzíí', I spoke out; I spoke up; I made a speech.

haashǫ? how? **Haashǫ' yit'éego?** Just how? In just what manner?

haash? how?

haa sha yit'éego? how?

haashjj, indeterminate, indefinite.

haashjj néeláá', a great many; numberless.

haashjj yit'éego, how; how? In what probable manner; by some device.

hááshóhłeeh, pull me back up (as one says when he is at the end of a rope).

haasht'eezh, they were led up out; they were conducted up out.

ha'asidí, watchman; inspector; guard; sentry; sentinel.

ha'asiid, I am watching; to be constantly on the alert; to give earnest heed; to be observant.

haaskai, they went up out, ascended.

haas'na', he crawled up (out); he crept up. **Tsin yąqh haas'na',** He climbed the tree.

haas'na', yąqh, he climbed it.

haastihgo, when he became old; since he was old.

haat'ánęę, that which was brought up out (an object).

ha'át'éegi, where (specific location).

ha'át'éegi da, wheresoever; somewhere (also **haa'ída**)

há'át'éegishą, where?

ha'át'éego, how? why?

ha'át'éegoshą, why? how?

ha'át'iida, something, anything.

ha'át'iish, what, what is it?

ha'át'iishǫ, what is it?

ha'át'iishǫ biniiyé, why? what for?

ha'át'iishįį, something.

háát'i' silį'ígíí, origin.

haayá, he went up out, ascended.

haayáhą́ągi, where he had come up out; where he had ascended.

hááyiis'nil, she took them back out; she redeemed them.

haayit'éego, how?

haaz'éél, it floated up out.

ha'az'éél, nihit, we sailed out.

haaz'éí, ladder.

haazhjé'ę́ę, those that ran up out.

haazhjéé', tsin yąąh, they ran up the tree; they took to the tree.

habee'eldǫǫh, one's gun.

habe' gónaa, across one's bust region, or breast region.

habídazh'dooɫjish, they will cause them to move out, crush them out, force them out.

habi'doo'nil, they were eliminated; they were taken out.

hach'ah, his hat.

hach'é'édą́ą'góó, in his dooryard, along his dooryard.

hach'į', to him, toward him.

hachidí, his automobile.

hach'į' yaa danichį', they would not let him have it, they barred him from it.

hach'ooní, his partner, his comrade.

hádą́ą́', when (in the past).

hadaagééd, they are mined.

hadááhjigo, toward his way, toward his front.

hadaaits'idgo, when it fell down (an object).

hadaalzheeh, they are hunting it (game).

hadaalzheehígíí, what they hunt.

hadaalzheehgo, because they hunted for it.

hadaalt'é, it is in a proper state, normal, as it should be.

hadaas'áágóó, to where there are a great many of them.

hadaasdzíí', they spoke out.

hadaasdzíí', t'áadoo — da, they did not speak out; they did not utter a word.

hadaasgaigi, where they (areas) are white.

hádą́ą' shą', how long ago? when?

hádą́ą́' shį́į, at some time in the past.

hadaastłhígíí, those that are old, worn out.

hada'astsood, they fed him; they gave him some (food).

hadaaz'á, they protrude up out.

hada'ázheehígíí, those things that are hunted, game.

hadaazlį, tó, the waters flow up out, many springs spurt, flow up.

hadabi'diit'éeshgo, when they are led up.

hadadéébjid, they filled, became full.

hadadeeskǫ' deposit (coal, rock, etc.).

hadadeezbiingo, since they are full (like boxes full of apples, etc.).

hadadiidzaa, they are all dressed up.

hadadiilghaazh, we shouted; we let out a yell.

hadadiniilkał, we will drive them up out.

hádadit'é, they dress.

hádadóh'įį', look for it (you many).

hadah, down, downward.

hadaha'niił, they are taken out, extracted.

hadah ch'éégo, he fell down (like off the roof, etc.)

hadah góyaa, down an incline.

hadahiidleehgo, when we pulled them out one after another; when we catch them (fish).

hadahiilį, waterfall.

hadáhodiník'ą́ą́', he was trapped in the fire.

hadahoneeshchaad, yit, they make trouble for them, stir up trouble among them.

hadahoneeyánígíí, mirage.

hadahoniye', banded calcareous aragonite.

hadahwiisdzooígíí, the designated areas, the marked off areas.

hada'iil'eeł, we are going after something in a boat.

hada'íínóɫni, (you pl.) be patient.

hadajilzheeh, people hunt them (game).

hada'jisíid, bíká, they were on the lookout for him.

hadanáádzá, he again went down; he again descended.

hadanáálwod, he ran down again.

hadaneesá, they came up, sprouted.

hada'nithosh, they spurt out, spew, emit, gush (intransitive).

hadashidees'íí', they discovered me; they found me out; they caught me in the act.

hadazdees'íí', they discovered it.

hadazhdínóotaal, they will hunt (or look) for it; they will search for it.

hadazhneeztą́ą́', they looked for it, searched for it.

hadazhntáhą́ądą́ą́', when people used to search for it.

hade'ádahoodzaa, things overwhelmed them, got out of control for them; they were in trouble.

hadéébįįd, it got full; it filled up.

hadeesbąs, to drive it (car, wagon) up out (as from a hole, uphill, etc.).

hadeeshch'il, to scratch it up out (as in scratching or digging with the hands for water).

hadeeshghaazh, I let out a yell, I screamed.

hadeeshwol, I will run up.

hádeeshzhee', he has started to hunt it; he is hunting it; he is going to hunt it.

ha'deet'ą, he was given permission, allowed to.

hadeezbin, it is full.

hádeidéez'íí', they are looking for him (them).

hadeidiilaago, when they drafted it.

hadeigédigii, what they are digging out; whatever they mined.

hadeiikai, we went down; we got down.

hadeiznil, they took them out.

hadideeshbįįl, to fill it with it.

hadidlą, abdomen.

hadidooniil, it will be dressed, equipped.

ha'diijááh, take your clothes off, undress.

ha'diilk'ąą', t'áadoo kó' bee bii' —— da, I did not hollow it out by burning it.

hadiilwol, you will run up out.

hadiilyaa, it was drafted (as a constitution, paper, etc.).

ha'diishjaa', I undressed.

ha'diishjaa' dóó néti, I undressed and lay down.

hadiishlaa, I drafted it; I prepared it

ha'ditch'ali, chatter-box.

hadine'é, his people.

hadinéeshchat, I will card it (wool)

hadi'ní'ą, he came to terms; he gave him his permission.

hadinisht'é, I am all dressed up.

hadinóo'wosh, to boil, bubble.

hadit'e, he is dressed; he is equipped.

hado, heat.

hadoodzih, bąąh 'ílįį góne' yee, he will speak its value, appraise it.

hadóólgháásh, do not yell.

h-doolghaazh, he let out a yell; he shouted; e screamed

hadoo'kééz, he coughed.

hadoot'áál, niwoo', your tooth will be extracted.

hadziil, his strength; he is strong.

hadziiyá, bump; swelling; hernia. **Shitáá' hadziiyá.** I have a bump on my forehead.

ha'éé', his shirt; his clothing.

haghan, his dwelling.

haghandi, at his home.

hágo, come here. **Hágo yidiiniid.** He summoned him..

hágoshįį, go ahead, ok, all right, very well.

hágoshįį, bééhodoozįįl, we'll see (disbelief or acceptance of a challenge).

hah, quickly, immediately, rapidly, fast, promptly.

hahaashch'iizhée, those that were sawed off.

hahaaskai, they came out one after another

hahadleehigii, the catching; the pulling out one after another.

hahajeeh, they usually run out one after the other.

hahakááh, they walk, come, out one after the other.

hahałkaadí, łeezh bee, shovel.

haha'niił, they are usually taken out one after another.

hahasááł, they flew out and floated (as sparks, feathers, etc.).

hahasáłigii, something that flies out and floats around in the air (as sparks, paper, a feather, etc.).

hahashkaah, I am scooping it out; I am shoveling it out.

hahgo, when.

hahgo da, sometime.

hahgodashį́į, sometime perhaps (in future)

hahgoshą́? when?

hahí, rapidly, quickly, immediately.

hahidisóóh, expectorate, spit out.

hahiikaad, it hangs out (as his tongue).

hahinidééh, they fall out one after another.

hahi, t'áá, pretty soon.

hahodiid'áád, there was a commotion, excitement.

hahodiil'á, it (area) extends out.

hahóó'á, noise, yelling.

hahoodzo, it (area) is marked out.

hahoodzooigii biyi', inside or within the marked off area.

hahóół'á, they make noise, they make a din.

háhóółchįįd, he was angered by him; he made him angry.

hahwiigééd, excavation.

hahwiishgédę́ę, the hole I was digging.

hahwiis'niligi, excavation.

hai, winter.

hái, who.

hái bi, whose.

ha'idínish'į́į', I am standing and looking for something; I am keeping watch.

háidi shą́? which? (Also **háidish**).

haidoo'ááł, biyaa, he will take it out from under him; he will get it before he does.

haigééd, he is digging it out; he is digging for it; he is mining it.

háiida, anyone; someone; somebody.

háiida, t'áá, anyone; whosoever.

háiishą' dó'? who else?

hainitáago, ch'ééh, since he is searching for it in vain.

háishą' who? (also **háish**).

háishą' 'ánit'į, who are you?

háishį́į, someone, somebody.

hajisííd, he is keeping an eye on it; he is observing it; he is watching it.

hajizh'áázh, they two went up out; they two ascended.

hajoobá'ágo, finally (after much struggle).

hajoobá'í, baa, he is poor.

háká, for him; after him.

háká 'análwo', he helps him.

haká 'eelwod, he helped him.

háká nikidadiibaa'go, since they set out to subdue them.

hak'az, coldness; chill; frigidity.

hak'az doo bínísdzil da, I cannot withstand the cold.

hakéé', behind him; along behind him; after him.

hakee'gi, at his feet.

hakéé' nálwod, it ran back following him; it followed him back.

hak'ehdadeesdlį́į', they overcame them; they defeated them.

hak'ehdeesdlį́į', he overcame him; he defeated him.

hak'eh náádeesdlį́į', he defeated him again.

hak'éí, his relatives; one's relatives.

hakéyah, his, one's land

hak'ihodoot'ah, he, or they, will be accused.

hak'iijéé', they attacked them.

hak'ináánádzá, he, it, came upon him again; he, it, came across (met) him again.

hak'ináánijéé', they ran upon them again; they came at them again.

hakinji', as far as his house.

hála', his, one's hand.

hálák'eet'ą, it was placed (a bulky, hard object) in his hands.

háláshgaan, his, one's fingernail.

halbá, gray (an area).

halbáago, because it (an area), was gray (with fog, etc.).

halchíí', red (an area).

Halchíítah, Painted Desert, Arizona.

halchin, there is the odor of; it smells.

haleeh, it (area) becomes.

haleehgo, since it (an area) becomes.

halgai, prairie, plain.

Halgai Hóteel, Great Plains.

halgai hóteelnii, people of the plains.

halíí', one's pet; one's stock; one's horse.

halni', he tells.

halni'go, when he tells (a story).

hálwod, she came running for or after it.

hályeed, yiníká, it runs through, penetrates. passes right through it (one after another).

halgizh, forked (as a tree), V-shaped.

halt'eeh, yiih, it usually puts him into it. **Té'é'įį yiih háált'eeh.** It usually puts him into poverty.

hamá, his mother, one's mother.

ha'naa, across (area).

hanáá' bee, with one's eyes.

hanáádahaas'ná, they again moved up out one after another (migrated).

hanáádahaas'ná, they again moved up out one after another (migrated).

hanáádaneesá, it again sprouted up.

Hanáádlí, Carson, New Mexico (30 miles southeast of Farmington).

hanáádoot'ih, it will be taken up again (as in discussion); it will be resumed.

hanááhodoogaał, it will start again (as a program, meeting, etc.).

hanááhojiizgeed, he dug another hole.

hanáá'íí'eezh, he led up out again.

hanáájiich'ish, one saws out again.

hanáák'is 'álnééh, to wink.

hanaalte', his slave.

hanaaltsoos, his books; his papers.

hanáát, in his, or their, presence.

hanáá'na', he crawled back up out.

hanáánéádzíí', he again spoke out; he again exclaimed.

hanáánáásdzíí', I again spoke out.

hanáánáát'i'igíí, resumption.

hanáánájeehi, t'áadoo 'ááji', before they could again run up to there; before they could run that far again.

ha'naa naní'á, it spans across.

hanáánáyoł, the wind blows again.

ha'naa nihonít'i', a way across (an area); a crossing.

ha'naa niniit'áázh, we (two) went across (an area).

hanaanishígíí, his duties; his work.

hanáánoot'ánígíí, those that again grew out, the next generation.

hanááshyįį', I rested; I took a vacation.

hanááyiiłkáągo, when day dawned again; at the beginning of the month.

hanááazhnítá, he is again looking for it; he is looking for another.

hanádáhígíí, yikáá', that with which he climbs up out.

hanályįįhgo, while he was resting.

hanáshdááh, I go up out; I ascend.

hanás'na', he has crawled back up out.

hanáz'éél, it floated back up.

handínéeshchééł, I will chase you up out.

hani', story; news; tale.

hanéilkááh, day starts dawning again and again.

hanéi'nił, he takes them out.

hanéisi', he examines, inspects it.

hanéiyol, I let my breath back out.

háni', his mind; his desire.

háni' 'ásdįįd, to become unconscious.

hanii, apparently; seemingly (a particle difficult of translation. **Doo hanii kót'éego 'áníléeh da.** Why don't you make it this way?)

haniibą́ą́z, full moon.

haniídee', they fell out (separable objects).

ha'níigo, it being said; it being told about.

ha'niihgo, baa, since he was praised.

ha'níił, baa, they are given to him one after another.

ha'nilchaad, carding.

ha'nithosh, it is gushing out; it is bubbling.

hanínáánályįįh, he is resting again.

ha'nínéé, what was told; what was said.

ha'nínígíí, what is called; what was mentioned as.........

ha'ntá, search.

haoh, yes. (see **'aoo').**

ha'oodzí'éé, what was said.

ha'oodzíí', enunciation.

ha'oodzíí', bee, what was announced; announcement of it was made (orally).

ha'ooldee', baa, undertaken.

hasbídí, mourning dove, turtledove, a pigeon.

hasé'éél, I floated up out; I came up out of the water.

haséyá, I went up out; I came up; I ascended.

hashk'aan, yucca fruit; fig; banana; date.

hashké, he is mean, fierce, angry; he scolds.

hashké daniidzįį'go, because they were angered.

hashkééjí naat'ááh, war chief.

hashni', nil, I am telling you; let me tell you something.

hasht'e', in order; settled.

hasht'e dahoolyaa, they were prepared.

hasht'e dahwiilyaa, we prepared it (an area).

hasht'e danile', you prepare them; you make them ready.

hashtedeiilyaa, we made it ready; we prepared it (them).

hasht'ediidzaa, 'altso, we (two) are, or he is, all ready.

hasht'ediisdzaa, I got ready.

hasht'edít'é, is is still, calm.

hasht'éé doo'nííl, it will be put back in order.

hasht'ééjídlééh, he is getting them back into order; making them ready.

hasht'eelyaa, it was prepared; it was made ready.

hasht'eeshłééh, I am getting it ready.

hasht'e halnééh, (a place) is being prepared, or being fixed.

hasht'ehodíít'e', it became calm, still.

hasht'ehodi'nééh, preparation.

hasht'e hólzin, to keep the place in order, tidy, neat.

hasht'ehoolaa, he prepared a place.

hasht'ehoolyaa, bá, a place was prepared for it (him).

hasht'ejiléhí, t'áado 'altso, before they could finish getting it ready.

hasht'e nááxhdiidzaa, he again got ready.

hasht'e' nihidi'nííl, put them away; store them away (for future use).

hasht'e' nininá, I, he, settled down, or established self to live.

hasht'eyiilaa, he prepared it.

hashtł'ish, mud; mire.

hashtł'ish łigaígíí 'ąąh niit'aah, plaster cast.

hashtł'ish tsé nádleehé, concrete; cement.

hastą́ą́, six.

hastą́'ácdah, sixteen.

hastą́'ádahdi, sixteen times.

hastą́ądi míil, six thousand.

hastą́ągóó, to six different places.

hastą́ąyáál, six bits, 75 cents.

hastą́diin, sixty.

hastą́diindi, sixty times.

hastą́diingóó, toward, or about, sixty.

hastą́:t'é, there are six of them (animate objects).

hast'e', his lunch.

hasti', baa, sensitive, delicate.

hastiin, man, Mr., elder. **bahastiin,** her husband.

hastiinéé, aforementioned man.

hastói, elders, menfolk.

hastói dahóyáanii, scientists, wise men, savants.

hastói náhást'éíí siniligíí, a committee of nine men, Advisory Committee of the Navajo Tribal Council.

haszéé', noiseless.

hatáál, ceremony.

hataałii, chanter, shaman, singer.

hataańdaa'nih, they are customarily distributed among them.

hatah góne', into their midst.

hatah yá'ádahoot'ééh, they are all in good health.

hátásiil, perspiration, sweat.

hatéél, front side of body.

hats'ą́ą́', away from them; from them (against one's wishes or desire).

hatsą́ądi, area inside of one's body.

hats'idigi, kwe'é doo, here in this lonely place; here in this awful place.

háts'ihyaa, sneeze, ker-choo.

hats'íídgóó, t'óó doo bił, he seemed to be lonely, unhappy.

hatsinaa'eełę́ę, what was their boat.

hats'ózí, a narrow area.

hayázhí, little areas.

haye', his son (See **biye'**).

hayid, one's chest.

hayííghaz, he scratched it.

hayiiłką́, twilight (faint light from darkness to sunrise only); day dawned out.

hayiiłką́ągo, at dawn.

hayiiłką́ągo ch'éédeesdził, I will wake up at dawn.

hayiiłts'ǫ́ǫ́d, he pulled it up out.

hayiiniiłgo, as he was pulling them up (like pulling up carrots from the ground).

hayisiid, he is watching him, watching it.

haz'ą́, there is space, room; it is possible; can do or be; being able; could; been able. **Doo ná haz'ą́ą da.** There's no room for you. **Doo bee ná haz'ą́ą da.** You have no right. **Doo bee shá haz'ą́ą da.** I have no right.

hazaadk'ehgo, in accord with his word; his command; in accord with his instructions.

haza'aleehtsoh, wild celery.

haz'áanii, bee, law; regulations; ordinance.

haz'ánígi, where the place is; where there is room.

házdéez'íj', one is looking for it; it is being sought: he is looking for it.

hazéists osii, chipmunk.

hazéítsoh, squirrel.

hazgan, dry (an area).

hazhdeel'íj', it came to his knowledge; he found out; he discovered that.

hazhdiich'ish, one saws along the side of it; one rips it with a saw.

hazhdiilaa, he dressed him up.

hazhé'é, his father.

hazhnitá, he is looking for it, searching for it.

hazhntáago, one searching for it.

hazhó'ó, carefully.

hazhó'ó, baa hani', explanation.

hazhó'ógo, carefully, slowly, cautiously.

hazhóó'ógo, softly; slowly.

hazkééh, t'óó shił, I am merely confused.

hazlį́'ę́ędą́ą́', t'óó, when it first came into existence.

hazlį́į', it became, came to be; it came into being, came to exist.

hazlį́'ígíí, that which came into being.

héél, pack, burden.

heeneez, tapered.

heeskai, yaa, they came to them one after another.

heesne', they were cut one after another; they were chopped down, or off.

heets'óóz, tapered; conical.

héí, hey (as in shouting to attract a person's attention).

hidees'náá', it quivered, trembled, shook, quaked, moved.

hidideeł, yił, he catches them (one after another.)

hidideeshchah, to start to hop along.

hidideeshłoh, dah, I will hang him or she (to execute on the gallows); I will weigh it.

hidiilo', dah, I hung him or her (executed on the gallows); I weighed it.

hidikááh, náás, they usually advance one after another.

higéeshgo, as he cut them off (with knife, etc.).

hiidoołch'ííł, to be mid-afternoon.

híiłch'į'go, in mid-afternoon.

hijiyeekai, baa, they went to challenge them, to oppose them.

hijiyoochah, to be hopping along.

hiłiijíí', twilight (from sunset to darkness only).

hiná, he is alive; he is living.

hináago, while he, it, was alive.

hináóh bijéí, cell.

hináóh bijéí bijéí, nucleus (of a cell).

hináóh bijéí łahnált'éego nida'iiłnáanii, tissue (body).

hináanii, the living things.

hináni, one that lives.

hineezdee', they came. **Béeso haa hineezdee'.** He realized some money; he came into possession of some money.

hinidéehgo, baa, since he acquired them.

hinishná, I live, or am alive.

hinishnáago, t'ahdii, while I am still alive.

hinishnáanii, bee, that by which I live; my livelihood.

his, pus.

hishne', I am cutting (with an ax); I am chopping them off.

hoda'doolniił, they will be photographed.

hódah, up.

hódahgo, upward, at a higher elevation.

hódahólníih, they are in authority.

hodeesdzo, it (area) was marked off, a line was drawn, a boundary line was made.

hodeeshnih, I will tell my story.

hodeeshnihígíí, baa, what I will tell about; what I will relate.

hodeeshxhiizh, time started to pass; a period of time was in course.

hodeeshxhiizhgo, as time goes by.

hodeeshxhiizhgóó, náás, as time goes on, in the future, in the course of time.

hodeet'ą, baa, it (area) was given to him, them; an area was turned over to them or him.

hódéét'i', he has a right to it.

hodéezyééł, noiseless.

hodichin, hunger-strickened area; starvation.

hodideezlįį', there started to be; it started to come into being.

hodi'dooltsołgo, because he will be arrested, or taken into custody.

hodiilnih, we (two) will tell our story.

ho'diiltsood, he was arrested, taken into custody.

hodiiłid, it burnt him; he burnt an area (as one burning weeds).

hodiina', time passed; a long time.

hodiina'go, after a while; soon; after a time.

hodiina'í, t'áadoo, before long; after a while; soon.

hodiiniid, he said to them; I said to him.

hodiinísin, I observe it, keep it; to comply with (religiously).

hodilkǫǫh, it (area, surface) is smooth.

hodilzhíísh, time usually moves on; a period of time usually passes.

hodiłch'il, dense (an area).

hodina'í, t'áadoo, soon (in future), as soon as possible; right away; before long.

hodine'é, his, their people.

hodiłłéé', the place is wet, damp.

hodiłtlid, shitah, my body trembles, I am shaking (as of fear or surprise).

hodiwol, it (area, as a road) is rough, bumpy, rutted.

hodiwosh, clamor; shout; to yell.

hodiyin, the place is holy, sacred.

hodiyoołhéełgo, since it will kill him.

ho'dizhchįįgi, birthplace.

hodoochįįł, to rebel; to revolt.

hodoołchį́į́ł, it will smell; it will have an odor.

hodooleeł, it will come into being; there will be.

hodoolk'ool, undulating (an area).

hodoolnih, yee yił, he will tell him about it.

hodoonih, bee bił, he will be told about it.

hodoo'niid, it was said.

hodoo'niidgo, since it was said.

hodooniił, haada, something will happen; something might happen.

hodootjjł, it will freeze (the ground).

hodootł'izh, it (area) is green, blue.

hódzá, to be wise.

hódzáągo, wisely, cautiously.

hóhí, t'áá, he himself.

hóhóoghah, bii', there is room in it for them; it is big enough for them; it is roomy enough for them.

hóhóólnííh, bee, he will have charge of it (area).

hojilni', baa, he tells about it.

hojiyąągo, mindful; thoughtful; heeding; considerate; sensible; readiness of comprehension.

hojólni', baa, that one might tell about it. **Doo hojólni' 'át'éégóó,** in a way impossible to tell about.

hojoobá'ágo, poorly; dire straits; with great difficulty; perplexed.

hojoo'í, he sees it (area); he is familiar (with the area).

hók'ąądóó, from a hilltop. (Also **wók'ąądóó** and **yók'ąądóó**).

hók'ąągi, on a hilltop. (Also **wók'ąągi** and **yók'ąągi**).

hók'ąąji', as far as a hilltop. (Also **wók ąąji'** and **yók'ąąji'**).

hóla, I don't know.

hóle', let it come into being; let there be.

hólni , you tell (a story).

hóló, there is, or are; it exists. **Tó hóló.** There is water. (see **ádin.** There is none).

hólónéé, what was in existence.

hólónéégóó, to where it used to exist.

hólónígíí, that which exists.

hólóogo, because there are.

hoł, with him, her, one. (accompaniment).

hoł 'ééhózin, he knows things; he is educated; he is conscious, aware.

hoł diiltłago, because it started to burn with him in it.

hoł doołtłáád, set it afire with him in it.

hoł hadíínóód, it burst into flame with him in it.

hoł 'ilí, he appreciates it.

hoł ndinínóód, he was overcome by sniffing (poison fume, vapor, gases, etc.).

honááhai, the years he passed; the years he has spent; his age.

honaanish, his work.

hónáásii', finally, at last. (Also **wónáansii'**).

honázt'i', they surrounded them; they have them encircled.

honeeni, fun; merriment; sport; frolic; amusement; entertainment.

hóneesdin, he is attached to him; he is used to him.

honeesná, he won; he gained victory.

honeesnánígíí, the winner.

honeezdo, it is warm (space or area).

honeezk'ází, it (an area) is cool.

honeezná, to prevail (in a contest); to win.

honeeznáa da, doo, a draw (an indecisive contest); a tie (in a game).

honeeztł'ah, delay; interferred with.

honibąąh, fireside.

hóni'dii, let him; let them.

honiidoii, bee, he got hot.

honiigahgo, when (an area) gets unbearably hot.

honiigaii, it (an area) got considerably warm.

honiik'aaz, the weather became cold.

honiildóóh, to warm up (a room or an area).

honiilziił, to warm up.

ho'niiłhįįgo, because he threatened to kill him; because he took ill from it.

honishgish, fire poker.

honishłó, I exist.

honooji, rugged (area); corrugated (area).

honoołchééł, he is chasing him.

honoołchééł nahalingo, ła' da, as though someone were chasing him; like one who is being chased.

hoo'a', space was made. **Doo bá hoo'a' da.** There came to be no room (space) for him.

hoo'a', bee, it (law, regulation) is agreed upon.

hoochah, he is hopping along.

hóóchį', there came to be trouble.

hóóchįįd, bá, he got angry.

hoodzaa, haa, what happened? (see **haa hóót'įįd**).

hoodzá, biih, there is a hole in it.

hoodzo, zone (marked off area); boundary line.

hoodzooígíí, the demarcation line which was drawn; the boundary line.

hooghan, dwelling; home; hogan.

hooghandi, at home.

hooghangóó, toward home, homeward.

hook'eeghan, haunted house; hogan in which death has occurred.

hool'á, so far; area extends on; time has passed.

hool'áágóó, forever, always.

hoolni'í, t'áadoo yił, without his having told them (or him).

hoolni, shił, she told me.

hoolts'aa', a hollow place.

hoolyé, it (an area) is called.

hoolyéedi, at a place called .... (Also —gi).

hoolyéédóó, from a place called ....

hoolyéégóó, to a place called ....

hoolzhiizh, time passed.

hoolzhiizhgo, baa, when it is time for it; when it was his turn.

hoolzhish, time is passing.

hoolzhishgi, at a period of time.

hoolzhishgo, as time goes on.

hool'aah, make room (as when one wants to enter a crowded car).

hool'aah, shá, make room for me.

hoołtsá, he saw the place; I saw him; he saw him.

hóółtsei, the place is dry.

hóóni'ę́ę, what was related; what was told.

hooshch'į', t'áá, immediately; on the spot; right then and there.

hooshdódii, whip-poor-will.

Hooshdódii To'í, Whip-poor-will Mesa.

hoos'įįd, it became daylight; it got light.

hoostse' laanaa, I wish I could see the place.

hoot'áałii, the plan; the policy; the government.

hootah níyá, he or I came for a visit, came to visit.

hoot'į, there is visibility; things are visible.

hoot'įį da, doo, there is no visibility, the ceiling is zero.

hoot'įįgóó, doo, since there is no visibility, since the visibility is poor.

hoot'įįji', to where there is visibility.

hootso, meadow.

hooyání, t'áadoo, suddenly; all of a sudden; without warning.

hóóyéé', it became dreadful.

hoozdo, warm (an area).

Hoozdo, Phoenix, Arizona.

hóózhǫǫd, baa shił, I became happy about it; I cheered up on account of it.

hóózhǫǫd, bił, he became happy; he cheered up.

hoozk'az, it (a place) is cold (as in ice box).

hosélįį', I came into existence, I was born.

hosh, thorn, cactus.

hosh bineest'ą', cactus fruit.

hosh niteelí, prickly pear.

hóteel, it (an area) is wide. **'Atiin hóteel.** The road is wide.

hóteeldi, halgai, on the Great Plains.

hóteelgo, over a wide area.

hótsaa, a big place.

hótsaaígíí, that place which is big.

hótsaago, over a wide area. (See **hóteelgo**).

hóyá, he is wise, intelligent, smart.

hóyéé', awful, dreadful.

Hóyéé', Steamboat, Canyon, Arizona.

hoyoo'nééh, forgetfulness.

hoyoo'néhégi, baa — 'ádzaa, it would be forgotten, would fall into oblivion.

hoyoos'nah, baa, it was forgotten.

hózhǫ́, very; extremely; well; very much. **Doo hózhǫ́ yáłti' da.** He does not talk much; he does not talk well.

hózhǫ́, bił, he is happy.

hózhóní, it (space or area) is beautiful, clean, nice.

hózhóóniish, hani' baa, is it good news?

hwááh, whew (as when one is hot or tired, or when one sets a burden down).

hwee, with (through the medium of).

hwee 'ádingo, since they have none.

hwéédááhai, they spent years.

hwéédoohah, he will spend years.

hwéé hodoozįįł, knowledge of him will be gotten or obtained; he will be tested.

hwééhoozingo, when everything is found out about him.

hwéé'ílnii', they were released, were turned loose, given freedom, freed.

Hwééldi, Fort Sumner, New Mexico. (Span. Fuerte, fort, pronounced juerte colloquially).

hwee náháah, for him the year is passing.

hwe'ena'í, their enemies.

hwe'esdzáán, one's wife; his wife.

hweeshni'ígíí, the story I told; my testimony.

hwiidéeltǫ', slippery (place).

hwiih, inside him; satisfaction. **Hwiih yiłk'aaz lá.** He caught cold. **Hwiih siłį́į́'.** He became satisfied; he had plenty; he got full, had enough.

hwiiná, it (a place) is alive, or full of animation and spirits; it is cheerful (an area).

hwiináa, doo shitah — da, I am weak; I am feeble.

hwiinidzin, is is though; it is believed opinionated.

hwiinidzinę́ę, what was thought; what was believed.

hwiinidzingo, the opinion.

hwiiniiłt'óóh, k'aa' yee, he is about to shoot at him with an arrow.

hwiiniiłt'įįd, baa, an action on it; discussion of it has taken place.

hwiinist'įįdę́ę́', baa, at the time of the discussion (of it).

hwiinit'į́, baa, it is being discussed; action (on it) is in progress.

hwiinit'į́įgóó, doo baa, since no one is doing anything (about it or for it).

hwiinit'íinii, baa, the subject (of the discussion).

hwii' siziinii, soul.

hwiisxį, it killed him; he killed him.

– I –

'ichxǫ́ǫ́'i, to be ugly.

'idahojiit'aah, they are learning; they are getting an education; they are being trained.

'idahoo'aahigíí, the training.

'idahool'ą́ą́', they learned things; they took training.

'idahwiidoot'áłígíí, those that will be trained; those that are going to be taught.

'i'deesdlo', fraud.

'i'didlech, t'áadoo le'é bee, larceny.

'idiiljeehí, plaster.

'i'diit'á, t'áadoo le'é, to worry.

'i'diishyaa, I made myself (into........).

'i'dílzool, whistling.

'idi'níyįįd, reaction.

'i'dit'ood, to wean.

'idlįįgi, being .....

'i'doo'ol, shił yóó, I will sail away.

'ihiniidééh, extras; in addition to what is already there.

'ihodéélni, susceptibility.

'ihodiilá, complication.

'ihónéedzą́, possibility.

'ihoo'aah, education; learning; training.

'ihoosh'aah, I am learning.

'ihwiideesh'ááł, I will learn.

'ihwiidool'áałgo, he will learn.

'ii', within, inside of.

'ii'á, it sticks up; it juts up; it stands (a tree. pole, etc.).

'ii'áázh, yił yeh, he went in with him; he entered with him.

'ii'adziid, injection.

'ii'alt'ood, injection.

'iich'ąh, epileptic fit.

'iich'ąhii, gypsy moth, moth.

'iidą́ą́', then (in past) long ago, at that time, during that time.

'iidą́ą́'dą́ą́, if, if so. (See lá dą́ą́').

'iidánígo, t'áadoo bits'ą́ą́' — yá'át'ééh dooleeł, it will be best if we do not eat off him, best if we do not eat his food.

'iideeł, yił, he grabbed it; he went for it.

'iideeshbįįł, I will win (at gambling).

'iideeshhosh, I will sleep; I will go to sleep.

'iidéeshtah, I will go to school, I will read, I will count.

'iidéetą́ą́', its thickness, depth.

'iidéetą́'igíí, the thickness of it.

'iidláád, it ripped.

'iidookáłígíí, yah, what he will bring in (in a vessel); what he will serve.

'iidoolííł, he will make it.

'iidoołdįįł, he will destroy them; he will cause it to become extinct.

'iidzo, was added (to it).

'ii'eeł, it is floating away.

'ii'ééł, yóó, it floated away.

'iigqah, semen.

'iigeh, wedding.

'iigháah, going in (into enclosure or behind something).

'iigháahgo, when it goes down, when it goes in.

'iigháah, yah, he is about to go in.

'iigháán, backbone, vertebra. (See 'iishgháán).

'iigháán bi'deeskǫ́ǫ́', lumbago.

'iighą́ą́tsiighąą', or 'iigháán tsiighąą', spinal cord.

'iighą́ą́tsiighąą' dideeshchii', spinal meningitis.

'iigis, to wash.

'ii'ha'al'eeł, irrigate (medical term).

'iih yiłk'aazgo dikos 'idoolna', a cold.

'iih yisháah, I am about to enter (into a car or train, etc.).

'i'íí'ą, the sun set.

'i'íí'ąągo, when the sun set.

'i'iidziih, inhalation.

'i'iijool, it moved in (fog, smoke, gases, fumes, etc.).

'i'iilgháásh, anesthesia.

'i'iilkeedí góne', in the theatre (where movies are shown).

'iijahgo, yah, when they all go in.

'iijéé', they ran into.

'iijéé', yiká, they helped him.

'iijííłt'o, he took a shot with his arrow.

'iikááh, sand painting.

'iikai, we went away; we went in.

'iilééh, he is making them.

'iiléehgo, while he was making it.

'iiléehgo, 'áłah, while he was gathering or assembling them together, or calling them to assemble.

'iilghaazh, we (two) went to sleep, we (two) dozed off.

'iilts'ą', his ...., empyemia. (medical term).

'iilyé, assassination; murder.

'iilyeed, yiká, the help he was going to give him.

'iiłhaazh, he or I went to sleep; he slept.

'iiłhéehgo, when he kills.

'iił'jid, ch'ééh, I could do nothing with it, I acted in vain concerning it.

'iiłni, he says (said) to him.

'iiłnii', it became the middle; mid.
shį'iiłnii', mid-summer.

'iiłnii', it (as a disease, fad, etc.) passed away.

'iiłnii', tł'éé', the middle of the night came; it became midnight.

'iiłta'ii, one who has gone to school; the educated one; one who counted.

'iiłt'e', yah, I put him inside; I put him in jail.

'iiná, life.

'iiná, they moved away, migrated off.

'iinááji, ways of life.

'iináanii, bee, resources; livelihood.

'iiná·bá siláii, resources (from which a living can be made).

'iinánigíí, a particular life, way of living.

'ii'ni', thunder; lightning.

'iiníiłta'go, as he starts counting, reading; as he starts to go to school.

'ii'nííyąą', infection.

'iininízin, you have in mind; your thinking.

'iinishta', I am counting; I am reading; I am going to school.

'iinisin, I have in mind.

'iinisin, I keep it; I maintain it.

'iinisinęę, what I had in mind; my intentions.

'iiniyá, you went (in or out of sight).

'iishch'id, womb, uterus.

'iishch'id bii' ni'iłts'id, tumor of the uterus.

'iishch'id hasht'e' nináłtsóós, suspension of

'ii'shéłjaa'igi bee, t'áá, with all my might.

'iishgháán, backbone, vertebrae. (See 'iigháán).

'iishjání, t'áá, clearly; quite apparent; it stands to reason that.

'iishłaa, I made it.

'iishłaaígíí, what I made; the one that I made.

'iishnih, I am milking (a cow, etc.).

'ii'sinil, heald sticks (in Navajo loom).

'iisisdląąd, I believed it.

'iists'ąą', he listened.

'iisxíinii, killer; murderer; assassin; slayer.

'iisxíinii bíka'algizh, autopsy.

'iił'í', it extends; stretches; runs; goes (extends).

'iił'jid, I acted; I did.

'iił'jid, ch'ééh, I can do nothing with it.

'iiłs'a', it sounds; it makes a noise.

'iiłs'a'í, t'áadoo, noiselessly; without being heard.

'iiyá, it went away (out or sight). Ha'ąą 'iiyá. He went over the hill.

'iiyąą', I ate; he ate.

'iiyá, yah, he or I went in; he or I entered.

'iiyisíí, very; chiefly; mainly; greatly; particularly; extremely.

'iiyisii, t'áá, really; very.

'iiyol, it (wind) stopped blowing; the wind died down.

'ilį, thought exists, it is the thinking, it is costly; it is expensive; it is valuable; it brings a good price.

'ilįį, doo — da, it is cheap, or inexpensive; it is worthless, phoney, fake.

'ilįįgo, because it is valuable, or expensive.

'iliinii, genuine; precious; valuable; something that is held in esteem.

'iliinii, béésh, precious metals.

'ilíní, t'áadoo haada dooniił, without thinking what will happen; with no consideration of consequences.

'ił, conifer needle; evergreen branch.

'ił 'adaagizí, bolts; screws.

'ił 'adaalkaałí, nails; tacks.

'ił 'adaalkaałí 'áłts'íísíígíí, tack; brad.

'ił 'anaa' hazlį́į', declaration of war.

'ił ch'aa hazlį́į', stun

'ił ch'ihwii'aah, he informs.

'ił ch'ihwii'aahii, informant, informer.

'ił dah nát'áhí, padlock; button (for fastening garments).

'ił 'ééhózin, wisdom.

'ił ha'agéés, to unscrew.

'ił honeeni, enjoyment.

'ił hóóyéé', panic, terror.

'iłhosh, you are sleeping; you are asleep; sleep.

'iłhóyéé', laziness.

'ił hózhǫ́, happiness; joy; gladness; blessedness; good fortune; good luck; prosperity.

'ił 'iidis, to wrap.

'ił na'aash, cousin (son of one's paternal aunt, or of one's maternal uncle).

'ił náhodééyá, dizziness.

'ił náhodigháah, dizziness.

'ił nanitł'ah, difficulty.

'ił náshjingo hatáál, corral dance, or fire dance.

'ił názt'i', circular brush shelter.

'ił 'oo'oł, voyage.

'ina'adlo', trick; cheating; fraud; lure.

'inaanish, profession.

'iná'ázt'i', fence; fenced enclosure.

'iná'ázt'i'ígíí, that which is a fence; fenced enclosure. 'iná'ázt'i'go, it having been enclosed by a fence.

'inálkáá', conviction.

'ináółtǫ'í, interest fee.

'inchxǫ́'í, property; belongings.

'inda, then; and then; only then; at that time; and.

Indians Yinant'a'i, Commissioner of Indian Affairs.

'i'neel'ąąh, measurement.

'i'niiháhí, t'áádoo, before winter begins, pre-winter.

'i'niihai, to become winter.

'i'niilzhiizh, he started to dance.

'i'niiyą́ą́', pollution.

'i'niłdzil, resistance; endurance.

'ini' niliinii, determination.

'inót'ááh, deception.

– J –

jaa'abaní, bat (mammal).

jááá bąąh niná'nilí, leggings.

jááá łánii, centipede.

jaa'í, coffee pot. (Also bidaa'í).

jaatł'óół, earring.

jádí, antelope, pronghorn.

jádishdłǫ'ii, prairie wren.

jástis ts'in bił 'ahąąh ní'áhígíí, fibula.

jeeh, resin; pitch; chewing gum.

jeeh dígházii, rubber.

jeeh sáá', dried pitch, dried resin (rosin).

jeełid, soot.

jeeshóó', turkey buzzard.

jéí 'ádjih, tuberculosis (of the lung).

jéí 'ádjih báhooghan, tuberculosis sana-
torium.

-ji', as far as; up to.

-jí, on the side.

jí, day.

jidéé'jí', he looked; he took a look.

jideeskaiígíí, náás, the progress they made.

jideeyá, ch'ééh, he is tired.

jideezh'áázh, they two have started on their
way; they two are going to go.

jidéez'jí', he is looking.

jidigháahgo, when one goes; when one
starts off to.........

jidiiłkǫǫh, to make it smooth or even on
the surface.

jidiizts'ą́ą́', he heard it.

jidilkos, coughing.

jidiłid, to burn it.

jidizhah, to spit.

jighááhgo, if one goes.

-jigo, toward.

-jigo, in the direction; on the side of it.

jííbįį', bąąh, he picked them from it
(berries).

jíídą́ą́', today (the part already past).

jíídóó, díísh, from today on; beginning
today.

jíigo, during the day.

jííiéé', kįįh, they ran into town.

jíík'eh, t'áá, free, gratis.

jíiłąąd, they became numerous. Baa jíiłąąd.
They tackled it in numbers (i.e. they all
helped bail out the water).

jíiłąą, hasht'e', he prepared it; he put it
in order; made it ready.

jíiłįh, to taste it, to sample it (by tasting).

jíiłtsá, he saw him (it).

jíiłtsánéędą́ą́', when he had seen him.

jíiłtsánéęgóó, to where he had seen it.

jíiníba'góó, doo, if you are not kind, good,
nice; if you have no mercy.

jíinil, biih, he put them into it.

jíisxį, he killed him.

jíizhgizh, bá, he cut them off for him.

jíízhi', he named it; he called to him by
name.

jijoołá, to hate.

jíikai, they came, went, arrived.

jíleeh, one usually becomes; to become.

jílį, he, one is.

jíliinii, one who is, he who is.

jilt'é, there are .... of them.

jiłąąh, to increase.

jiłhazhí, hackberry.

jineesk'oł, he blinked (his eyes).

jiní, he says; it is said.

jinii'éél, to perspire; to sweat.

jiníigo, while he was saying.

jiniizjí', he thought, wanted.

jiniizjí'go, when he thought.

jiníyá, he came; he went; he arrived.

jinízin, he wants; he thinks.

jinízinéé, what he thought; what he wanted.

jí'ólta', day school.

jisgan, he dried them; he dessicated them.

jish, medicine pouch; medicineman's pouch.

jishbéézh, bił, he boiled it with it.

jishcháá', grave, graveyard.

jishcháádéé', from the grave.

jishgish, lightning flashed. (Also **łe'dool-ch'il).**

jishjįzh, he crushed it.

jit'áázh, bił 'ałdááh, they two met each other (moving toward the same point from a different direction).

jitseeł, he is chopping it; cutting it with an ax.

jiyooznah, baa, he forgot it; he forgot about it.

jizdá, he stays, sits.

jizghad, he shook it; he shook it out; he spilled it out (allowed them to fall out).

jizįigi, at the place where he is standing; where he stands.

jizké, they (two) are sitting; they (two) sit together.

jizlįį', he became; he came to be.

jiztį, he is lying; lying down.

jizyį, dah, he placed it (a bundle or a bag of separable objects) up.

jóhonaa'éí, sunbearer; sun; watch; clock.

jóhonaa'éí 'áłtsíísíígíí, pocket watch.

jóhonaa'éí biná'ástłéé', ring around the sun; halo (around the sun).

jóhonaa'éí bitł'óól, watch fob, watchchain.

jóhonaa'éí daaztsą́, eclipse (of the sun) (lit. the sun is dead).

jóhonaa'éí hálátsíín naaz'ánígíí, wristwatch.

jóhonaa'éí 'iíł'íní, watchmaker.

jóhonaa'éí ntsaaígíí, clock.

joodłą́ą́góó, doo, if one does not believe him, it; for not believing him, it.

joogáál, he is walking along.

joo-á-ł~o, náá;, when one keeps going; if one keeps going; as one goes along.

joogii, crested blue jay.

ʼooʼih, he is carrying them along.

joo'd'osh, he is creeping along (on all fours).

joo'óós, to lead (one animate object).

joolyé. he is called........; his name is ....

jooł, ball.

jooł bee nda'a'néegi, game of ball; ball playing.

joołmas, to roll (a spherical or animate object).

jóółta', doo — 'ánéełą́ą' da, so many one cannot count them.

jooshba', I am kind.

- K -

k'aa', arrow.

k'aabéésh, arrowhead, arrow point.

K'aabizhii, Cove, Arizona.

káá' digóní, small pox.

k'on'igíí, a particular arrow.

k'aalógii, butterfly.

K'aałání, China Springs, (near Gallup, New Mexico).

k'aasdá, poison; arrow poison; toxin.

k'aasdá beeyigá, anti-toxin.

k'aayééł, quiver (for arrows).

k'ad, now.

k'adéé, almost; nearly; about to.

k'adí, that is all, quit it, that is enough.

k'ad láą, there ....(as when one has finished a task).

k'adshą', what about now?

k'ad, t'áá, right now.

k'ad t'éiyá, t'áá, now is the only time; now is the only chance.

k'ai', willow.

K'ai' Bii' Tó, Kaibito, Arizona (water in the willows).

K'ai' Ńt'i'í, Two Wells, (South of Gallup, New Mexico).

kanaagháii, sickly person; an invalid.

k'asdą́ą́, almost; nearly.

kázh, grinding sound.

k'é, friendship; peace; relationship.

ké, foot; feet; shoe (bikee, his feet or shoes).

ké'achogii, galoshes; overshoes.

kébąqh ntł'izgo dah naazniligíí, corn (on foot); callous (on foot).

ké bee néilchíhí, shoe polish (red).

ké bee néílgáhí, white shoe polish.

ké bee néilzhjhí, black shoe polish.

ké bikétal danineezígíí, high heel boots; cowboy boots.

ké bił 'adaalkaałi, cobbler's nail.

k'édahidi'níí ńt'éę́', yił, they were friendly with them.

k'édanidzin, they are friendly, polite.

k'e'deesh'ał, I will loosen it (a knot); I will untie it.

ké deigo danineezí, boots (high-topped); engineer boots.

k'éédadidii'níił, we will get even; we will take vengeance.

k'ééda'didléeh, they cultivate; they farm; they till the soil.

k'ééda'didléehgo, since they farm.

k'ééda'didléhígíí, planters; farmers; agriculturalists: tillers of the soil.

k'éédadiidzaa, we got even.

k'éédadilyéehgi, where they are planted; where they are cultivated.

k'éédadilyéehii, what people planted; what people raised on their farms; farm produce.

kéédahat'į, they live; their homestead; they dwell.

kéédahat'jįgo, since they live.

kéédahat'jįgóó, to where they live.

kéédahat'inéę, those that lived.

kéédahat'inéę, what used to live.

kéédahat'inígíí, those who live; inhabitants.

kéédahoht'į, you (pl) live.

kéédahojit'į, they live; people live.

kéédahwiit'į, we live.

k'éédazhdidlééhęę, what they planted.

k'ee'deeshchxǫǫ́ł, I will erase it; I will rub it out.

k'éédeididléehgo, since they raise them.

k'éé'didléhé, farmer.

k'éé'dilyééh, planting; agriculture; cultivation.

k'éé'dishdlééh, I plant; I farm.

kééhasht'ínídi, where I live.

kééhat'íinii, resident.

kééhat'ínigi, where he lives.

kééhat'ínigíí, he that lives; those who live; inhabitant(s); resident(s).

k'ééhodi'nééh, to take vengeance on.

kééhót'į, you live.

kééhwiit'į, we live.

kééhwiit'ínigíí, bikáá', the land on which we live.

k'é'éltǫ', fractured (as a bone); it broke in two; it was broken in two.

k'eclyáı, seeds (for planting).

k'éé'oolchxǫ', erasure.

k'a'et'áád, to untie.

k'eet'áán, prayerstick. (in Navajo ceremonies).

k'eet'oh, bowguard.

k'éézh'dídlééh, he plants; he farms.

k'éézhdoodlá, he replanted it.

Kégiizhí, Papago.

k'éhdahidi'ní, they are friendly with one another.

k'ehgo, in accordance with; after the fashion of; in the way or manner of.

k'éhózdon, straight ahead.

k'éididlééh, he plants it.

kéjeehé, tennis shoes.

kék'eh, footprint.

kélą́ą́d, tips of the toes.

kélchi, moccasin.

kénááhat'í, they live again; others live.

k'éńdahasdlį́į́', they became friends again; they restored peace.

ké ndoots'osii bikétal nineezi, cowboy bootshoes.

kénidoots'osii, high topped shoes.

k'énidzin, friendly; polite.

k'énínáádahasdlį́į́', they came back to a state of friendship; they made up all over again; peace has been restored.

kénitsaaigii, high-topped moccasin (women's).

késhgolii, club-footed.

késhjéé', moccasin game.

Kéeshmish, Christmas (from English Christmas).

Késhmishgo, During Christmas.

Késhmish Yázhí, Thanksgiving.

Kétł'áhí, Pima.

kétł'óól, shoe lace, shoestring.

kétsíín, ankle.

kéts'iiní, oxford (shoes).

kétsíín niná'nilí, shackle for the ankle; fetter.

kéyah, land; country; terrain.

Kéyah Binant'á'í, Secretary of the Interior.

kéyahgi, on the land, on land.

kéyahgóó, toward land; toward homeland.

kéyahigíí, a specific land.

kéyahjigo, toward land, landward (as if one was out in the ocean).

kéyah yaa 'ádahalyáanii, soil conservationist.

k'ézdon, straight.

k'ézt'i', continuation.

k'ida'deehya', planting has been done.

k'idadeehya'ii, what has been planted; things that were planted.

k'idadiilyá, we planted it.

k'idahoneezláago, since the area is level.

kidahonii'ą́ą́góó, on the slopes.

kidahonii'ánigíí, the slopes; the grades. (See niinah).

k'idajizhgizh, they cut them in two; they severed them.

k'idazhdoonish, they will break it in two (by pulling); they will pull it apart.

k'ideeshch'ish, to saw or file it in two.

k'idinidéél, fracture (of a brittle bone or other object); snapped off; it broke off (with a snap).

k'idinidéél dóó binaa tidílyaa, compound fracture.

k'ihineestah, at full speed ahead.

k'ihoditééh, boredom.

k'ihoneezlá, an area is level; leveled place.

k'ii', sumac.

kįįh, into town. Kįįh yiyá, I went into town; I entered town.

kįįh dadoobah, to storm a city; to raid a city.

kįįh dahidoobah, to storm city after city.

Kįįh dayiijáahii, what they bring to the trading post; what they bring to market.

kįįh yíyá, I entered, or went, into town.

k'iiłtsoii, rabbit brush.

K'iiłtsoiitah, Cornfield, Arizona. (near Ganado)

k'iinigizh, he cut it in two; he cut it off; he severed it.

Kiis'áanii, Pueblos.

k'iishzhinii, ironwood.

kin, market; house; town; cabin.

k'ináázh'doodlá, he again planted; he again farmed.

kin bee daadleeshigii, house paint.

kin bii' da' nijahígíí, hotel, motel.

kin bii' nii'oh nida'aldahígíí, outside toilet; privy.

Kin Dah Łichi'í, Kinlichee, Arizona. (near Ganado).

kin dah naazhjaa'dóó, from towns.

kin dah naazhjaa'góó, towns.

kindi, at the house; in town.

Kin Dootł'izhí, Towaoc, Colorado.

k'íneedlíshii, stink beetle.

k'íneeshbízhii, dumpling.

k'inídláád, broken (as a string).

kinigíí, a specific house.

kéédahat'íinii, those that live; inhabitants.

kíniizhoozh, leaning side by side against something (slender objects as planks, logs, poles, etc.).

k'ínijił'ahí, currant.

k'inítne', I chopped it in two; I pounded it in two.

kin łání, town, city.

Kin Łání, Flagstaff, Arizona; Durango, Colorado.

Kinłichíí', San Juan Pueblo, New Mexico.

Kinłichíí'nii, San Juan (people of the Pueblo of San Juan).

Kin Łigaai, Baca, New Mexico; Moenave, (near Tuba City, Arizona).

kin nii'niłéégi, where houses were built.

kin shijaa', city or town.

kintahdi, in town, downtown, in the city.

kintahgóó, to town, to the city.

kintahji', in town (to a point).

Kinteel, Pueblo Pintada, New Mexico; Wide Ruins, (near Chambers, Arizona); Aztec Ruins (Aztec, New Mexico).

kin yąąh sizíní, prostitute, whore.

k'ish, alder.

k'íshishjíízh, poison ivy.

kits'iil (or 'ásaats'iil), potsherds.

k'izhdilééh, one plants it.

k'ízhdooch'ish, one saws it off; one files it off.

ko', fire.

ko' bee niltsési, fire extinguisher; fire hydrant.

kóbidishní, this is what I say to him; I speak thus to him.

kóbizhdíiniid, he said (thusly) to him.

kódaolyé, they are called thus; their names are.

kodéé', from here; through here.

kódeeshłííł, I shall make it thus; I shall do thus to it.

kódei, up this way.

kódeiidzaa, we did this way; we acted thus.

kódeiilyaa, we did thus to it.

kódeile', they do thus to it.

kodi, over here; right here; here.

kudi, kodi, help, help.

kódíji', t'áá, just this far; just to here and no farther.

kodóó, from here on; from here; thence; from now on.

kódooníił, he will do thus.

kódooníłígíí, the future happening; doing thus.

kódzaa, he did thus; it happened thus.

kohąo, this much; this big.

kóhoniłtso, it (area) is this big.

kóhoot'é, the place looks like this.

kéhoot'éedą́ą́', a year ago; last year.

kóhóót'įįdgo, because it happened thus.

ko'ígíí, the specific fire.

koji, this side; this way; in this direction.

koji', as far as here.

kojigo, this way; this direction.

kójiit'jih, one does this way.

kójiit'jihgo, one usually does thus.

kójíní, he said thus.

kójíít'į, he did thus: he is doing thus.

kǫ'k'eh, fireplace.

kól'jih, thus it is done.

kónaa, across here.

kónááhoot'éhé, next year by this time.

kǫ' na'atbąąsii, train.

kǫ' na'atbąąsii bitiin, railroad; railroad tracks.

kǫ' na'atbąąsii ninádaaltti'góó, at train stations; where the trains stop.

kónáánádzaa,. 'ąą, it swelled up some more; it expanded again; it opened again.

kónádzaa, náás, it increased again.

kóndoo'níít, yaa, it will decrease, get smaller in size, shorter in height.

kóne', here inside.

kóne'é, in here.

kóní, he says (thus); this is what he says.

kónighánigo, at short intervals.

kónigháníjį', for a little while; for a short time; at a short distance.

kónigháníjį', t'óó, for a little while.

kóníigo, while he was saying thus.

kónishéíí, that small.

kǫ́ǫ́, here; hither; this way; through here; hereabout.

kóoni, hereabout.

kó'óolyéenii, so and so, (a person).

k'ǫ́ǫ́zh, body odor.

k'os, cloud, clouds, cloudy.

k'osh, to sour; to spoil.

kót'é, it is this way; it is thus.

kót'éego, in this way; thus.

kót'é, t'áadoo — 'ilíní, without warning; all of a sudden; unexpectedly.

kót'jih, they do thus; it happens thus.

kóyaa, down here.

kǫ' yiniltsési, fire engine.

kwá'ásíní, friends.

kwe'é, here; right here. (See **kwii**).

kwii, here (less closely defined area than that denoted by **kwe'é**); hereabout.

- L -

lá, it is; it occurred to me (a particle, usually indicating recently discovered knowledge).

lą́, approval; agreement; correct; all right; yes; O.K.

—lą́ą, surely.

lą́'ąą', O.K.; yes; I see (understand); yeah; I agree; correct; all right; you are welcome (in answer to thank you).

laanaa, wish that it would.

ládą́ą́', if; in case; if so.

lą da'azlį́į́', it was agreed; agreement was made.

lą'í, much; numerous; many.

lą'í 'altah 'ádaat'éii, many kinds.

lą'ídi, many times.

lą'ígo, since there were many, or was much; lots of it.

láiish. glove; mitten.

lashdóón, ribbon.

látah 'adijoolí, flax.

látsíín, wrist.

látsíín názt'i'í, wrist-band; cuff (shirt).

látsíín niná'nili, handcuffs.

látsíní, bracelet.

látsíní bináá, set (in bracelet).

le'dólt'e' góne', average.

le'é, t'áadoo, things; something; anything.

léi', (a particle indicating lack of familiarity with); a certain; some.

lók'aa'. reed.

Lók'aah Niteel, Ganado, Arizona.

lók'aatsoh, cane reed.

Lók'a'deeshjin, Keams Canyon, Arizona.

Lók'ai'jígai, Lukachukai, Arizona; Sheep Breeding Laboratory near Fort Wingate, New Mexico.

ła', a; one; some; someone; the other one.

łą́, many; much.

ła'ą́ą, what was the other one.

łą́ą́góó, t'áá, many things; in many ways; a great deal; a lot.

łáá'íí, one (in counting). łáá'íi góne', in the first place; first.

ła'atł'éégo, overnight; in one night; just one night.

ła'binááhaaí, yearling.

ła'da, someone.

łah, once; once upon a time; sometimes; at one time.

łáháda, seldom; rarely; occasionally; at rare intervals; once in awhile.

łahda, sometimes.

łahdi, elsewhere.

łahgo, in another way; a different part; differently; otherwise; at another place.

łahgo 'áhoodzaa, there was a change; the weather underwent a change.

łahgo 'át'éego, in a different way; in a changed way.

łahgo 'é'énééh, metamorphosis.

łahgóó, elsewhere; in some places; in other places.

łahji', part of it; part of them.

łahjí, on the other side; the other way around.

łahjí' deinít'jjgo, they were busy at something else; they were occupied with something else.

łahjigo, in another direction.

ła'hoodzaa, accomplished; completed; finished; success.

ła'igíí, the other one; the other part.

łá'í'idlį́, bee, cooperation; unification.

łá'í ndi, not even one; none at all.

łá'í niidlį́, we are united.

łá'í siidlį́į', we united.

ła' nááná, another; some more; more.

ła'óójį, in one day.

ła'ts'áadah, eleven.

ła'ts'áadahdi, eleven times.

ła'ts'áadahí, t'áá, only eleven.

ła' yilyaaígíí, accomplishment.

łe'doolch'il, lightning flashed (Also jishgish); thunderbolt.

łééchąą'í, dog.

łééchąą'í bighan, kennel.

łééchąą'í biya', dog lice.

łééhchąąłgaii, greyhound; Greyhound bus.

łééchąą yázhí, puppy.

łeeh, into the ground, soil, earth, dirt, or ashes.

łeeh bi'dilteehgo, when he was being buried in the ground, or grave.

łeeh daho'dii'niiłgi, graveyard, cemetery.

łeeh dooł'eez, cancer root (plant).

łeeh ho'dooltį, his body was buried.

łeeh yiyíinil, he buried them; he placed them in the ground.

łeejin, coal.

łeejin haagééd, coal mine.

łeejin haigédi, coal miner.

łees'áán, bread (of the type baked in ashes, or in an outdoor oven).

łees'áán yiłzhódí, Milky Way. (See yikáísdáhi).

łeeshch'ih, ashes; cinders.

łee'shibéézh, barbecued corn; chicos.

łeets'aa', pottery; chinaware; earthenware

łé'étsoh, rat.

łeetsoii, yellow ochre; uranium.

łeeyáán, alkali.

łé'éyázhí, colt.

łeeyi', in the ground; underground; in the soil.

łeeyi'di dahólóonii, minerals (as ores, rocks etc.).

łeeyi'di, at a place in the ground; within the soil.

łeeyi'igeed, trench.

Łeeyi'tó, Klagetoh, Arizona.

łeezh, dirt; dust; soil.

łeezh bee hahalkaadí, shovel; spade.

łeezh bił háayol, sandstorm.

łeezh dah naaztą́ągo, dikes.

łeh, usually; customarily.

łe' hasin, jealousy (of spouse).

łe'oogeed, cellar; storage pit.

—łí, could it be that (question)? Lók'aah Nteelgóó dó' diníyáashłí? Could it be that you are going to Ganado?

łibá, gray.

łichíí', red.

łichíí' 'ałna'asdzoh, Red Cross.

Łichíí' Deez'áhí, Sanders, Arizona.

łichíí'go 'qqhadaajeehígíí, measles.

łid, smoke.

łid yiiłgááh, make a smoke signal.

łigai, it is white; white.

łį́į́', pet; livestock; horse.

łį́į́' bee, horseback.

łį́į́' bee yilzhóhí, curry comb.

łį́į́' bighan, horse corral; stable (for horses).

łį́į́' bihétł'óól, hobbles.

łį́į́' biką'ii, gelding.

łį́į́' bikee', horseshoe.

łį́į́' bita'góó ní'áhígíí, wagon tongue.

łį́į́' bitsis'ná, horsefly.

łį́į́' biyééł, saddle.

łį́į́' biyééł bidą́ą́hdę́ę́' háá'áhígíí, saddle tree, saddle horn.

łį́į́' biyééł bikéédę́ę́' háá'áhígíí, cantle (of the saddle).

łį́į́chogii, studhorse, stallion.

łį́į' da'ałchini, wild horses (lit. horses that can scent).

łį́į́' na'ałbąąsii, work horse; team of horses.

łį́į́' na'ayéhé, saddle horse.

łį́į́tsa'ii, mare.

łį́į́' yii'a'aałí, feed bag.

łik'aii, it is fat, corpulent, plump, obese. (See neesk'ah).

łikan, it is sweet, tasty, good, palatable.

łikizh, spotted.

łikon, inflammable.

łitso, it is yellow; nickel coin (five cent) of U.S.

łitsoii, bile; acidity of the stomach.

łizh, urine.

łizh 'eghánílí, polyuria.

łizh ' áshjjhłíkan t'éiyá, glycosuria.

łizh bee dah siyinigíí, bladder (urinary).

łizhin, it is black.

łizhinii, the black one.

łoh, noose.

łóó', fish.

łóó' bik'ah, codliver oil.

łóód, sore (inflamed skin).

łóód dineesdlíí' lesion.

łood doo nádziihii, cancer.

łóód na'agházhigíí, ulcer.

łóódtsoh, small pox.

łóó'tsoh, large fish; whale.

– M –

mǫgi, monkey.

mǫgitsoh, gorilla, ape.

mǫ'ii, coyote.

mǫ'iidą́ą́', ironwood; wild privet.
(Also k'iishzhinii)

Mǫ'ii Deeshgiizh, Jemez Pueblo, New
Mexico.

Mǫ'ii Deeshgiizhnii, Jemez Indians, people
of Jemez Pueblo.

mǫ'ii dootł'izhí, kit fox.

Mǫ'ii Tééh Yiłtizhí, Coyote Canyon, New
Mexico.

mǫ'iitsoń, wolf.

mǫ'iitsoh bee yigą́, strychnine.

mandagyiiya, butter; oleomargarine.

masdéél, pie.

Méhigo, Mexico.

Méhigo Biyéého, Old Mexico.

miil, a thousand (Span. mil). (Also míil).

miilgo, a thousand of them.

mósí, cat. (Also gídí).

mósígi 'ániłtso, as big as a cat; the size of
a cat.

mósíkǫ', tomcat.

- N -

na', here (in handing something to a person).

ná, for you.

naa —, to you; about you; around.

naa'aash, they (two) are living; are walking about.

naa'aashéé, yił, the one with whom he was going about; his companion.

naa'aash, shił, my cousin (male speaking); he goes about with me.

naa'ahineezkaad, they fell over (as timber, pole, house).

naa'ahóóhai, chicken.

naa'ahóóhai 'aleeh, rodeo. (Also **'ahóóhai**).

naa'ahóóhai bi'áadii, hen.

naa'ahóóhai bikǫ'ii, rooster.

naa'ahóóhai biya', chicken lice, or mites.

naa'ahóóhai biyázhí, chicks.

naa'ahóóhai haalteeh, chicken pull (sport event).

náá'áłdó, repeat, again. (Also **nááná**).

náá'áłníí'dóó, łahji', from the other half.

naa'anáágo', he fell over again; he toppled over again.

naa'aniídee', they fell over (from a standing position).

náá'ásdlíí', it was again thought; the opinion again was; it again occurred.

náá'ásdlíí'go, since it occurred again.

naabaahii, warrior.

Naabeehó, Navajo.

Naabeehó binant'a'í daniłíinii, Navajo leaders.

Naabeehó dine'é, Navajo people.

Naabeehóji, according to the Navajo; Navajo customs.

Naabeehók'ehji, in the Navajo way.

náá' bee yiłtłahi, eye ointment.

náábi'ni', he again desires; he again wants to.

náábiyi', in it again.

náábiyi', ła', there is some more of it in it.

na'acha', heat (sexual).

na'ach'ǫǫh, art; decoration.

na'ach'ǫǫhí, artist.

naach'id, handling; managing.

na'adá, to walk.

naadą́ą́', corn.

naadą́ą́' bit'ąą', corn leaves. (also **dá'át'aa'**)

naadą́ą́' bitsiigha', corn silk.

naadą́ą́' biwoo', corn kernels.

naadą́ą́' bizóól, corn tassel.

nááda'ahijoogą́ą́', there was war again.

nááda'asdlíí', they again became.

nááda'deeldǫǫh, we again fired.

nááda'deest'a', they again flew off; they again took wing.

nááda'diibaa', dah, they started to make war again.

nááda'dijnééh, dah, they started on the move; migrating again.

nááda'dinéesh'įįł, I will look at them again.

nááda'dinóoséél, they (shrubs, etc.) will again grow.

nááda'hazlíí', they again came into being.

nááda'hidinisééh, they usually come up, grow, or sprout again.

nááda'hodiilnih, we shall tell again.

nááda'ínóolta'go, when you all go to school again.

nááda'jidlíinii, those who again are.

naada'jooba', they are nice, or good to you; they treat you well.

nááda'niidzjj'go, they again thought, again wanted.

nááda'yííkeed, they again asked for it.

nááda'yííłbįįh, they again earn, win, gain.

náádazhdiijih, they gather, reap, or harvest them.

náádeesdǫǫh, it again went off; it again exploded.

náá'deesdǫǫh, yił, he again shot him, it.

náádeesdzá, hadah, he started on his way down again.

náádeesnii'go, it passed again (as a disease, fad, etc. **'iiłnii').**

náádeet'ą, baa, it was again given to them; another was given to them.

náádeeyol, the wind again started blowing; the wind came up again.

náádeidi'ááh, yaa, they usually turn it over to them.

náádeinidzingo, since they want another, or again want it.

náádeiniildon, we again shot at him.

náádeistséeh da, t'ah doo, I have not as yet seen them again.

naa dideesh'ááł, I will turn it over to you; I will relinquish it to you.

náádiidza', he recuperated, recovered, regained health.

naadiidzá, dah, he again started off; he again set out.

náa ḍii'eezh, dah, he again started off leading.

náádiilkǫ', shik'i, it (water, sand, etc.) covered me again; it again spread over me.

naadiin, twenty.

náádiiná, dah, they again started off migrating.

naadiin 'ashdla', twenty-five.

naadiindi, twenty times.

naadiin dįį', twenty four.

náádii'nił, 'iih, you will again put them in; you will again load them.

naadiiní, t'áá, only twenty.

naadiin naaki, twenty two.

naadiin náhást'éigóó, toward twenty nine different places.

náádiisdzáago, when I recuperated.

náádiisdzá, dah, I again started off; I again set out.

náádildziił, try hard again.

náádilt'éehgo, another is being run or stretched (as a wire, rail, etc.).

náádínéesh'įįł, I will again look at it.

naadiní'ą, I turned it over to you.

náádishnish, I again start to work.

ná'ádleeh, the recurrence.

ná'ádleehígíí, bą́ą́h, their usual value in trade; whatever they are usually worth.

naadlo'gi, with regard to steering it.

naadlo'í, bucket, pail. (Also **tó bee naakáhí).**

naadlo'í, bee, rudder; steering wheel.

na'adlo'ígíí, steering; trickery.

na'ádódlii, doo — da, he does not expect to live; he has no hope.

naadooboo'iinii, small ground squirrel.

náádoochǫǫł, it will again spoil; it will again be wrecked or ruined.

náádoo'niid, he said thus again.

náádoo'nił, haa, they will again be given to him.

náádzá, yiih, he again went into it.

naa'eeł, dah, it floats.

na'a'eełígíí, navigation.

na'a'eeł, nihił, we are sailing about.

naaghá, he goes about; he is living; he is walking around.

naagháádą́ą́', if he is around; if he is about; when he was alive.

naaghéa da, doo, he does not walk about; he cannot walk.

naagháagi, wherever he is.

naagháhą́ądą́ą́', t'ah, when he was still living.

naagháhą́ągóó, doo, to where he has never been.

náágo', it flowed downward; it fell down.

nááhai, a year completely passed; a year passed.

nááhaidą́ą́', łǫ'í, years ago; many years ago.

nááhá'néhí, t'áadoo haada, without another event.

naqh dah haz'ą́, haayit'éego, what are your symptoms?

nááhidees'náá', it (earth) again shook, trembled, quaked; it moved again.

na'ahínítaah, wrestling.

ná'ahinoolchéełgo, when they (two) were running back.

nááhodé'ą́, I originated new plans.

nááhodeeszhiizh, time again passed; another period of time passed.

nááhodeez'áanii, one who originates new plans.

na'áhodiidlá, he loiters about.

nááhodíínísin, I again observe it (as observe the Sabbath).

ná'áhodíłt'jjgóó, doo nihaa, when he was not paying any attention to us, or was disregarding us.

nááhodilzhish, another period of time usually starts to pass.

náádóhdlǫ́, it again exists; another exists; there is another.

nááhódlǫ́ǫgo, since there is another.

nááhodoolnih, yił, he will again tell him; he will relay the information to him.

nááhoneesnáá lá, he won again; he took first place again.

nááhoo'aahí, t'áadoo shąąh dah, before I get sick again; before I again have trouble (physically).

nááhoodzaoí, t'áadoo haada, without any

nááhoolzhish, time is again passing; another period of time is going by.

nááhóóyéé', shił, I became terrified again.

na'áhozhdilziidgo, because he was taking his time.

nááʼíídéeshtah, I shall go to school again.

ná'ájeeh, lubrication.

náájidzá, baa, he again went to it; he again visited them.

náájiské, they (two) are again sitting.

na'ajoołí, gas.

naajóshłí, I trust you; I have confidence in you.

naakaaígíí, yaa, what are they doing; with what are they busying themselves.

naak'a'at'áhí, cotton cloth; cloth; material.

naak'a'at'áhí dishooigíí, velvet (cloth).

naak'a'at'áhí disǫsígíí, silk (cloth).

naakai, they walk about; live.

na'akaigi, at a (ye'ii bichaii) dance.

Naakaii, Mexican, Spaniard.

Naakaii Bito', Mexican Springs, New Mexico

naakaiik'ehjí, in Spanish.

Naakaii Łizhinii, Negro; colored people.

na'akéé', there is someone's footprint.

na'akéé'ę́ę, the footprints (he saw around).

náákę́ęz, it fell (a slender, stiff object).

naaki, two.

naaki 'asdzo, two inches.

naakidi, twice; two times.

naakidi míil, two thousand.

naakidi neeznádiin, two hundred.

naaki dootł'izh, twenty cents.

naakigo, since there were two; two or them.

naaki góne', in the second place; secondly.

naakigóó, toward two; two ways.

naaki jį nda'anish, Tuesday.

naakishchíín, twins.

naakits'áadah, twelve.

naakits'áadahdi, twelve times.

naakits'áadahgo, dozen.

naakits'áadah yáál, twelve bits ($1.50).

naaki yáál, two bits (twenty-five cents).

ná'ákwi, nausea.

naal'a'gíí, bá, his servant, slave, errand boy, messenger, or helper.

naalchi'í, agent; ambassador.

naaldeeh, they live, exist.

na'aldeehééédą́ą́, baa, when these things were being done.

naaldloosh, it is trotting about.

naaldlooshii, quadrupeds; animals; beasts; livestock.

naaldoh, it floats about (as a gas or cloud).

na'al'eełę́ę, the voyage; the matter of sailing about.

na'al'eełgi, concerning navigation.

naal'eełí, duck; goose.

naaljį́íd, paraplegia.

naalkaah, inspection; examination.

na'alkaah, trial (at law); investigation; research; to trail.

naalkaahgo, tracking; studying.

ná'álkadgi, with regard to sewing.

ná'álkadgo hála' bąąh naaz'ánígíí, thimble.

na'alkid, temperature; time (by the clock).

na'alkidí, clock; watch.

naainish, he is working.

naalnoodi, fleet lizard.

naalté, slave.

ná'áltłah, lubrication.

ná'áltłeeh, to get wet.

naaltsoos, book; paper. ,

naaltsoos 'ohi'niił, voting (by paper ballots).

naaltsoos báhooghan, post office.

naaltsoos bee 'ach'iishí, sandpaper; carborundum paper; flint paper.

ncaitsoos bikáá' 'e'eiyaaígíí, picture: photograph.

naaltsoos bik'ehgo na'abąąsígíí, driver's license.

naaltsoos bik'i nda'a'nil, photography.

naaltsoos dadiłdonígíí, firecracker

naaltsoos 'íił'íní, clerk; stenographer; secretary.

naaltsoos 'íił'íinii, printer.

naaltsoos neiyéhé, mail carrier.

naaltsoos ntł'izígíí, cardboard.

naaltsoos tsits'aa', carton; paper box.

naaltsoos yik'i nda'anilí, photographer.

nááíwoł, he is running back.

naalyéhé, merchandise; goods; wealth; property.

naalyéhé há hooghan, trading post: store; warehouse.

naalyéhé ya naazhádi, store clerk; traders, storekeepers.

naalyéhé yá sidáhí, store keeper; trader; store clerk; merchant.

naalzheehgo, while he was hunting.

naał'aashii, tarantula.

ná'ał'ahí, butcher.

Naatáni, Comanche.

na'albąąsii, the driver (of a car, truck, etc.).

na'ałcha', to be in heat.

naałchid, he is motioning.

na'áłchíní, your children.

na'ałdoni, oil drum; can (large).

naałdzid, cancer.

na'ał'eełí, sailor; navigator (on water).

na'ałkǫ́ǫ́', he is swimming.

na'ałniih, epidemic.

naałniih yił naagháii, carrier (of disease).

nááłtą', to fall (referring to moisture from the sky).

na'ałt'a'í, aviator.

nááłtánígíí, it fell (referring to moisture from the sky).

nááná, again.

nááná, t'ááłáhádi, once more.

naanáájah, to run around.

naanááłwoł, he is running around.

naaná'ás'éél, he turned around (in a boat).

náánááshgį, 'iih, to put in again (referring to bundles or packages).

naaná'áskǫ́ǫ́', he turned around (while swimming).

naanáát'ahgo, while flying around.

naa nahiilniih, we will buy it from you.

náánákai, they came back.

náánákwii, try here; here again.

náánáła', another; another one; to give some more.

náánáłahdę́ę́', from another place.

náánáłahdi, at another place. (See **náánáłahgo).**

náánáłahgo, elsewhere; furthermore.

náánáłah góne'é, in another room.

náánáłahgóó, in other places.

náánáłahji, another topic; in another direction.

náánáłahji' 'aho'dool'a', transfer (of a person).

náánáłahjigo, in the opposite direction.

náánáłah kéyahgóó, to another land.

naanánoogoh, yiká, he is rushing around for it.

náánásdá, he is again sitting.

náánásd'įį', to again become; that which again became.

náánásdlį́į'go, since it again became.

náánásdlį'ígíí, that which again became.

náánásdzíinii, to again hold a position.

náánáshjaa'ígíí, a specific group.

nááná̌s'nil, group (a few inanimate objects lying close together).

nááná:'niłígíí, group (specific). (See náá-nás'nil).

nááná̌st'á, another (a similar hard object) lies.

nááná̌st'ánígíí, another (specific similar hard object) lies.

nááná̌stį, to see again (a similar animate object) lying down.

naané, he, she, or they (two) are playing.

nááneesdáhígíí, an occupant that again fills a position.

na'anéhígíí, migratory.

nááné̌igo, shik'i, flowed again and covered me.

nááné̌ilwod, ła' hak'i, attacked by another.

nááné̌iłtsá, I saw him again.

nááné̌iská, days passed.

nááné̌iská̖ą̖go, when night, or nights, have passed.

nááánídá̖, eat some more of it.

naanídeesbą̖s, turn it around (referring to a wheeled vehicle).

naaní'deesbą̖s, to turn around (referring to driving a wheeled vehicle).

nááʼnίʼééł, bił, to again arrive by boat.

naanii, sideways.

naaniidínéeʼá̖, it is leaning (as a house).

naanii dínéetį, leaning (without support).

náániidzį̄į̄', to reconsider (two); we again believed.

naaniigo, crosswise.

naaniigo k'é'éłtę', crosswise fracture.

na'a'niih, distribution.

naaniiłts'id, shikétsíín, I turned my ankle.

nááníił'į́į', ła' 'łih, I sneaked another one in.

nááníiłʼóazhgo, when we (two) return again.

náání'nííł, ła' baa, give them some more (hard separable objects).

naanísétbą̖ę̖z, chidí, I turned the car around.

naaní'séł'ééł, I turned around (in a boat).

na'anish, to work.

naanish, job; business; employment.

naanish bá 'adinii, unemployed people.

naanish binaałtsoos, Social Security card.

naanish daniłíinii, work one does.

na'anishí, bee, tools.

na'anishígíí, work one does.

naanishtsoh, a big job, a heavy responsibility.

naanísisdzá, I turned back (walking).

nááanítaahgo, yaa, to investigate repeatedly.

naa'ołí, beans.

naa'ołí nímazí, peas.

náá'ółta'ígíí, one who goes to school also.

nááas, forward; from now on

na'asbą̖ą̖s, I can drive.

na'asdee', round trip (by many people).

náasdi, at a later time; further on.

nááas dookahgo, to go (many) forward.

náasee, to go forward.

náasee, lengthwise; length

náasee ts'in 'ałk'iniizhoozh, lengthwise fractures.

naashdeeł, choo'į, I am looking for cil.

náasee ts'in 'ałtániizhoozh, longitudinal fractures.

nááasgóó, in the future.

naashá, I am alive; I am walking about.

nash'aash, nił, I go around with you.

naasháa dooleeł, I will be walking around.

naashá, baa I am working on something.

naashch'ąą', painting; drawing; design.

naashch'id, my ability to handle it.

ná'áshdį́įh, I eat.

Naashgali dine'é, Mescalero Apache.

naashjaah, I am carrying them around.

naashdeeł, I am throwing it about.

na'ashjé'ii, spider.

na'ashjé'ii bijáád danineezi, grandaddy long legs (spider).

na'ashjé'ii bitł'óól, spider, web; cobweb.

na'ashjé'ii diłhiłí, black widow spider.

na'ashjé'ii nahacha'ígíí, jumping spider.

na'ashjé'iitsoh, wolf spider.

naashkaah, I am tracking it; I am investigating it.

na'ashkǫǫ' I can swim.

naashło', to guide (wheeled vehicle or an animal).

naashné, I am playing.

naashnéhé, bił, my playmate.

naashnishígíí, bá, my employer.

na'ashǫ'ii, reptiles (lizard).

na'ashǫ'ii da'ałchozhígíí, herbivorous reptiles.

na'ashǫ'ii dich'izhii, hornèd toad.

na'ashǫ'ii dishch'izhii, horned toad.

na'ashǫ'ii doo da'ałchozhígíí, non-herbivorous reptiles.

na'ashǫ'ii dootł'izhí, green lizard.

na'ashǫ'iiłbáhí, gray lizard.

na'ashǫ'iiłtsoh, dinosaur; big reptile.

Naasht'ézhí, Zuni, New Mexico (both the pueblo and the people).

Naasht'ézhídi, at Zuni.

Naasht'ézhígóó, to the pueblos of Zuni.

naashzheeh, I am hunting.

náásidi, t'ah, at a place still farther on.

nááś jookah, they are progressing.

naaskáá', it has been investigated.

naaskai, to go and return (three or more).

naastsooz, lying around (flat flexible object).

nááś yit'ih, continuation.

naat'á, portable.

naat'ááh, orator.

naat'áanii, leader; governor; superintendent.

Naat'áanii Nééz, Shiprock, New Mexico.

naat'áanii t'áálá'í, general superintendent.

naat'a'í, something that flies.

na'at'a'í, dah, flag.

naat'a'ígíí, some specific thing that flies.

náát'i', it is hanging down (as rope, wire or piece of string).

na'atłeeh, impetigo.

na'atł'o', cat's cradle.

na'atł'o'ii, something that entwines.

na'atł'o'ii, ch'il, grapes.

ná'át'oh, smoking (a cigarette). **Doo ná'át'oh da,** no smoking.

naat'ood, flexible.

Naatooh Sik'ai'í, Grants, New Mexico.

Naatoohó, Isleta, New Mexico.

naatsédlózii, roadrunner.

na'atseed, killing.

na'atseedji, bee, for the purpose of killing.

nááts'íílid, rainbow.

Naatsis'áán, Navajo Mountain, Utah.

naats'ǫǫd, elastic; resilient.

nááts'ó'ooldisii, whirlwind.

na'ats'ǫǫsí, mouse.

Nááts'ózí, oriental people (especially Japanese or Chinese).

Naats'ózí dine'é, people of the orient.

naayá, round trip (taken by one person).

naayáago, after the round trip (made by one person).

naayáhǫǫ, the round trip (made by one person).

nááyidiizts'ą́ą́', heard again (he).

nááyiiłbįįh, to earn.

nááyiiłbįįhgo, earning (he is).

nááyiiłbįįhgo, yee, gaining from something.

nááyiiłbįįhígíí, what he earns.

nááyiiłbįįhíí, gain made from something specific.

nááyiiłbįįh, yee, gain made from something.

nááyiiłtsá, he saw it (or him) again.

nááyisgo, while he or it was turning.

naayízí, squash; pumpkin.

nááyoogį, yiih, to pack or load again.

nááyoołkáál, time passing (day or night).

naaz'á, they lie about (inanimate objects).

naaz'ánígíí, the ones that lie around.

naazbaa', he has been to war.

naazdá, to sit about (animate objects).

naazdáago, since they are sitting about.

naazdáágóó, places where they are sitting around.

naazdáhígíí, sit about; those that are sitting.

naazdahígíí, naalyéhé yá, those who operate a store.

na'az'éélgóó, place where a round trip by boat was made.

na'az'éál, hoł, a trip by boat (made by one person).

naazghal, he looked around.

naazh'áázh, round trip (made by two).

nááxh'dees'éligii, his starting on another voyage.

ná'áxhdiilyé, suicide.

nááxhdiiłtj, it was recovered (animate object).

na'azheeh, hunting.

naazhjaa' lying about (several bunches).

naazhjaa'go, since they were lying about (several bunches).

naazhjaa'góó, places where several bunches lie.

naazhjéé', lying in groups (animate objects).

naazhjéé'ii, those that are lying in groups.

naazhjé'igii, the ones that are lying in groups.

naazj, they are standing.

naazínéé, those that stood.

na'azísí, gopher.

naazkaad, they are standing about (trees, brushes, etc.); they are spread out (on the floor, rugs, etc.).

naaznilgo, since they are lying around.

naaznilgo bikáá', on top of those that are lying around.

naazniligii, lying around (specific things).

naazniligii, 'ahqqh, those that are lying side by side.

naazni'i-ii, t'áá bini', lying around empty or unused.

naaznilii, those that are lying around.

naaztá, lying around (one hard elongated object).

naaztą́ago, because each was lying around (hard elongated object).

naaztą́ą́góó, places where they are lying (hard elongated objects).

naaztániaii, those that are lying around (hard elongated objects).

ná'ázt'i', a fenced enclosure.

naaztseed, they were killed.

na'aztseed, massacre.

naazvíioo, since there are bodies of water.

nabé'é:dee', they were destroyed (animate objects).

nabéaili, wheelbarrow.

nabidaniitaahao. when we were testing it.

nabidanitaah, they are testing him.

nabidanohtaahao, when you (three or more) are trying it out.

nabideeshłaoł. I will destroy them.

nabidiiłaoł, you will destroy them.

nábi'dii'nil, they (people) were picked up.

nabidi'neestą́'áa, what he was taught.

nábidíníi'aa', he started to distract him by false pretense.

nábidíníitą́ą́', he began to teach him.

nabidi'ntingo, while he was being taught.

nabijískai, they destroyed them.

nabikéé', tracks (his) are around.

nabik'í, about (concerning).

nabik'íyájiłti'go, while he was discussing it.

nabineeztą́ą́', he was taught.

nabisésá, I destroyed them.

nabistseed, it killed them.

nabitiin, their tracks (about).

nabitiingo, since there are tracks about.

nabizhnigizh, cutting it with a knife (in no definite pattern).

nabóhonitaahigii, that which is being tried out.

nádááh, he will come back.

nada'didiit'áál, we will come to terms with you; we will permit you; we will give in to you.

ná dah hidideeshłoh, I will weigh it for you.

nádleeh, hermaphrodite.

nádleeh, it becomes.

nádleehigii, that which becomes.

nédzá, he returned.

nádzáago, when he returned.

nádzas, it snows.

nágeeh, they will be hauled back.

naghái, that one.

náhááh, the year is passing.

naha'áhą́ą, his aforementioned plans.

nahaashdeeł, choo'j, I am looking for aid.

nahaaznii', has been sold.

nahaaznii'ę́ę, bá, that which was bought for him.

naháaztą́, they are sitting about.

naháaztáanii, those which are sitting about.

naháaztánigíí, those who are sitting; the ones that are sitting.

nahacha', dah, he is jumping up and down.

nahachagii, grasshopper.

náhád!áʌhgo, when they were being chosen, or picked up.

náhádleeh, it (usually) becomes.

náhádzid, danger; fear.

náhádzidgi, wilderness.

nahaghá, performance; religious ceremony.

náháhí, t'áadoo, before the year passed.

náháhí, t'áadoo lę'í, before many years.

nahak'izii, cricket.

náhá᷄áá', I picked them out; I gathered them, or it.

nahalin, looks like, it seems.

nahalingo, resembles.

nahalni', yaa, he is going about telling about something.

nahalyé, to be paid.

nahalzhiishę́ę, bił, the time that used to be required; time formerly required.

nahaʼin, barking.

nahaltin, it is raining; rain.

nahaltingo, because it was raining.

naha'náágóó, doo, because it was motionless.

náháni'go, to await information.

nahaniihgo, from the sale of.

náhá'niligii, 'atah, to put back with a group.

nahasá, performed (referring to a religious ceremony).

nahasdzáán. the earth. (Also **nahosdzáán**).

nahasdzáánigíí, the one which is the earth.

náhásdzo, marked off; zone (an area).

náhásdzogo, since it is marked off (an area).

náhásdzo hayáxhi, an acre.

náhásdzooígíí that which is marked off (an area).

nahashcha', to hop around.

nahashch'id, badger.

Nahashch'idí, Naschiti, New Mexico.

nahashkáá', close to the ground; low.

nahasht'e'ii, kangaroo rat.

nahasht'e'ii 'áłts'íísígíí, kangaroo mouse.

náhasin, amusing.

náhasin, baa, to be amusing; to be interesting.

nahasni', he told his story.

nahasni'ę́ę, yaa, the things he told about.

náhást'éí, nine.

náhást'éí dah nídinibįįh, a committee of nine.

náhást'éidi, nine times.

náhást'éidiin, ninety.

náhást'éigo, nine of them.

náhást'éígóó, nine times (to go out).

náhást'éíts'áadah, nineteen.

náhást'éíts'áadahgóó, nineteen times (to go out).

náhást'įįd, baa, action concerning it took place; he was tried.

náhást'įįdgo, baa, when action concerning it took place; when he was tried.

náhástł'ah, corner.

nahat'á, plan, system, or form of government.

nahat'áhígíí, those plans.

nahateeł, slippery (area).

nahat'i', to joke or jest.

nahatseedí, bee 'atah, anesthetic (general).

nahaz'á, areas; spaces.

nahaz'áago, since there are spaces.

nahaz'áágóó, where there are spaces.

nahaz'áágóó, łah dah, in other places.

nahaz'áanii, bee, regulations; ordinances; rules; laws.

nahaz'á, bá, there is space for him.

náházbąs, a circular area.

nahdę́ę́', t'ah, in the past; from back.

nahdi, nearby; at a place; aside.

náheeshghał, I am turning over and over.

nahgóó, nearby, to another, or to one side.

nahgóó nini'á, I set it down nearby.

nahgóó tádíiyá, he walked around nearby.

náhidéé'á, I turned it (a stone, etc.) over.

náhidéélmááz, I rolled it over.

náhidéélts'id, it turned over; it capsized.

náhidéshghał, I turned (my body) over.

náhidéshjiish, I turned (body) over.

nahididoolch'ął, it will begin to drip.

náhidiishtah, I sprang up.

náhidiitah, he leaped up.

náhidiitahgo, when he sprang up.

náhidiiyol, bił, they blew away (one after another).

náhidizídígíí, the months; a particular month.

náhidizíid, months passing.

náhidizíid bik'eh, monthly.

náhidizíidgo, when the months pass.

náhidizíidji', until the end of the month.

nahidoonih, bá, to buy for.

náhineests'ee', it is coiled; it is spiralled.

nahji', to a place nearby; to one side.

nahji' 'ahiłhan, to throw it aside.

nahji' hanáádzá, quit (an occupation); stepped aside.

náhodi'áahii, one who usually originates new plans.

nahodit'é, dangerous; doubtful; unsafe; suspicion. **'Atiingóó t'áá sáhí joogáałgo t'áá nahodit'é.** It is unsafe for one to go out on the highway alone.

nahodits'ǫ', a boggy place; bog.

náhodizhdoo'áął, he will select (area); he will choose it (area).

naho'diztseed, they are killed.

náho'dóltah, they were counted (at specified intervals).

náhodoodleeł, will again exist.

náhodoodleełii, bee, that which will renew existence.

nahodoołtįįł nahalin, it looks like it is going to rain.

náhódóót'jjł, baa, will stand trial; will be discussed.

náhódóot'jjłii, baa, defendant (in a trial).

náhojoolni', he delivered a message.

náhoniidoi, the weather is again warm.

náhoniidóohgo, while it was becoming warm weather.

náhoniigah, the weather gets hot every day.

nahonílin, you resemble or seem.

nahoniłne'go, when he went about winning.

náhonoodohgo, when the warm weather was coming back.

náhoo'aahígi, when time permits.

náhoo'aahígi, t'áá bita', when time permits; between tasks.

náhoodleeł, to come back into existence.

náhoojǫǫd, shił, I cheered up again.

náhookǫs, north; Big Dipper.

náhookǫs bóhodiłgizjigo, slightly northward.

náhookǫsdéé', from the north.

náhookǫsjí, north side; northern.

náhookǫsjigo, northern; northward.

nahóółtá, it rained.

náhoot'aahgo, when time permits.

nahootsoii, evening twilight.

nahóóyéí, sweet potato.

nahós'a'déé'go, from the vicinity of.......

nahós'a'di, at the vicinity of ....

nahós'a'dóó, from the vicinity of.........

nahós'a'gi, at the vicinity of.........

nahosdzáán, the earth. (Also: **nahasdzáán.**)

náhozdilkǫǫh, dah, a bare spot of land.

náhozhdii'aahgo, having chosen (an area).

náhwiisdoh, shiih, I composed myself.

nahwiis'náá', bich'į', he had trouble.

na'ididóołkił, he will ask questions.

na'ídíkid, questions; inquisition; inquiry.

ná'iidoodziłígíí, yee, something with which he will get warmed.

na'iidzeeł, dream.

na'iigeeł, to dream.

na'iilghal, to wriggle.

ná'iilkáhígíí, spending the night.

na'iilyéhígíí, wages.

na'ii'ná, movement.

na'iini', barter; commerce; trade.

na'iini' bá haz'ąągi, market.

na'iini' biniiyé, for sale.

na'iiniih, purchase.

na'iiniihdéé', to return from trading.

na'iisgeel, baa, something someone dreamed about.

ná'ildee', they returned (three or more).

na'iłkǫ'igi, concerning your swimming.

nájaa'go, when they were brought back (inanimate objects).

nákááh, just before their return.

nákai, yaa, they (three or more) returned to .... (after an elapse of time).

nák'ee, around the eye.

nák'eedzi', eye drops (zinc).

nák'eedzi' łizhinígíí, argyrol.

nák'eeshchąą', matter which collects in the eye.

nák'eeshto', tear (from the eye).

nák'eesinilí, eye glasses; spectacles.

nákid, gonorrhea.

nákwi, to vomit.

náldzid, wild (untamed); he is afraid.

náldzidgóó, doo, since he is not afraid.

nálwod, he returned running.

nályeedí, t'áadoo, before he returned running.

nályįįh, thawing.

náneeké, we (two) sat down again (in the same place).

naneeshtł'iizh, crooked (unalignment of inanimate objects).

náneeskaadí, slapped bread (owes its name to the manner in which the dough is passed from one hand to the other, then tossed on the griddle to- bake); tortilla.

náneeskáál, they are standing in a circle (vertical objects).

nani'á, a span across.

náni'á, I carried it back.

na'ní'áago, since it spans across.

naní' 'áhígíí, that which spans across.

nanich'įįdii, all right then, have your own way.

nánídaah, he sits down often; it lands (airplane).

nánídaah, dah, it perches.

nánídaahígíí, one who sits down often.

nánídlíní da, t'áadoo, profitless; useless.

ná'ni'ééł, hoł, he returned by boat.

ná'ni'eezhgo, when he arrived back leading.

nanighal, look around. (naashhal, I am looking around).

nanihídíłkid, he is asking you (pl.) questions.

nanihi'niiłtseed, he is going to kill you (many).

nániichaad, to be full of food (a person).

nániikai, we (three or more) returned.

nániit'áázh, we (two) returned.

nánikeeh, dah, they (two) sit.

nánííldzidí, t'áadoo, be not afraid.

na'níle'dii, t'áá, roughly (rude or violent action); haphazard manner.

na'nilkaad, herding.

nánilkaadgo, when they are being herded.

nánilóóz, I led him back.

naniltł'iish, to wobble.

ná'niltsxis, flagellation; to whip.

ná'nilgo, 'atah, when they were put back in the group.

na'nilhod, he limps; he walks lamely.

ná'niligíí, biih, that in which they are usually put.

na'nilkaad, he herds.

na'nilkaadgo, when he herds.

na'nilt'ą'go, he raised many things.

naniltseed, kill them.

naniltseed dooleeł, kill them whenever you see them.

naniná, walk around.

naninóa, t'óó — łeh, you always just loaf.

naninóhi da, t'áadoo baa, loaf around (you do no work).

naninóhi, t'áadoo baa, leave it alone.

náni'ni', (your) desire to go back.

nánisdzá, I returned.

nánisdzáii', when I returned.

nanise', vegetation; plant.

nanise' bich'iyą', fertilizer.

nanise'go, since it grows.

nanise'ígíí, the vegetation.

nanishgo, biká, I am rushing around hunting for it.

nánísh'jjh, I look at it; I am watching it.

nanish'in, I keep it a secret; I concealed it; I keep it hidden.

nanishkaah, I am tracking you.

nánishkai, bił, I came back with them.

nánisht'áázh, bił, I returned with him.

na'nishtin, I teach.

nánisxas, I am scratching it.

na'nit'á, speech.

nanítá, baa, you investigate it.

nanit'áii, orator.

nánit'jjh, it (grain) matures; it ripens.

nanitin, he is being taught.

na'nitin, he teaches; he gives advice or instruction.

nanit'in, he is elusive.

nanit'inee, t'áá, in secret.

na'nitini, teacher.

na'nitinigíí, the teaching.

nanitł'a, it is difficult (mentally).

nanitł'aai, t'áadoo hózhǫ́, without much difficulty.

nanitł'agóó, doo, since it is not difficult.

nanitł'agóó, doo hozhǫ́, not very difficult.

nanitł'aii, a difficult one.

nanitł'a, shił, it is difficult for me.

na'niyeesh, irrigation.

Na'nízhoozhí, Gallup, New Mexico.

nanizhoozhigíí, those that span across.

nanoolzhee', the warp (threads that go lengthwise in weaving).

na'nt'ingo, while he was teaching.

na'ólní, expectation.

naólnínigi, t'áadoo, where it is least expected.

náoltáád, to unroll or unravel.

na'ookǫǫh, to beg; to beseech; supplication.

na'oolne', the intentional dropping of something by someone.

ná'oolyis, to whirl.

ná'ootkǫ́ǫ́ł, he is swimming back.

na'oo'ná', bii', it is occupied again (a house).

ná'oo'oł, bił, he is sailing back.

náoostah, it is run down (a clock); it is unravelled; it became untied.

náootáád, it is uncoiling or unravelling.

násdlíj', to become again.

násdlíj'go, since he or it became again.

násdzid, I am afraid.

násdziid, he became afraid.

násdziidii', because he became afraid.

náshdáάh, biih, I usually go into it.

náshdlíjh, I drink it (customarily).

náshdói, wildcat.

náshdóiłbái, bobcat.

náshdóitsoh, mountain lion; puma; cougar.

náshdóitsoh bitsiiji' daditł'ooígíí, the lion (African).

náshdóitsoh danoodǫ́zigíí, tiger.

náshdóitsoh łikizhí, leopard; jaguar.

náshgάάh, I dry (dehydrate) them.

náshgozh, sausage.

nashił'in, it is barking at me (as a dog).

náshí'ni', t'άά', I wish to go back.

nashíshzhee', I hunted; I went hunting.

náshkwi, I am vomiting.

násidi, further on.

nástasi, ń'oh, foxtail grass.

nástł'ah, corner; nook.

nástłéé', it got wet.

nát'άά', back again.

nát'áahgo, baa, when it is given to him.

nát'áázh, they (two) returned.

nát'áázh, yił, he returned with him.

nát'oh, tobacco.

nát'oh bił da'asdisígíí, cigaret.

nát'oh ntł'izi, chewing tobacco (plug).

nát'ostse', tobacco pipe.

nayésá, he exterminated, destroyed it (animate objects).

nayéskai, they destroyed them (animate objects).

nayídanitaah, they are experimenting with, or trying it out.

nayídéékidgo, when he was questioned.

nayiiłná, it causes it to move.

nayiisnii, he bought it.

nayiisnii, yaa, he bought it from him.

nayiisnii', yá, he bought it for them.

náyiizláá', he gathered them.

náyiiznil, he or she turned them over or around (completely).

nayik'i, concerning it; about it.

nayik'i yádáálti', they discussed it.

nayóli, shit, he suspected me.

náyoogéełgo, while he was carrying or hauling it back.

náyooltááá, she is undoing it (hair braids, etc.); she is unwinding it, or uncoiling it.

náyoottéét, he is carrying it (him) back.

názbqs, circular; round.

názhah, the end is curved.

názhahí, pendant (of silver, used on jewelry).

názhnijaa', he brought them back.

nazh'nitkaadgo, when he herds, or is herding them.

názhniłtj, he brought it back (animate object).

nazhnitá, baa, he is looking it over; he is looking to see how he is getting along.

nazhnitin, he teaches it.

nazhnitinigíí, the fact that he teaches him.

nazh'ntingo, while a person is teaching.

Názlini, Nazlini, Arizona.

názyiz, he made an about-face.

nda, no.

ndaabaah, they make war; they go about raiding.

ndaabaahgo, when they go about raiding.

ndaach'idii, the things that are being handled.

nda'adleehgo, when several events take place.

ndaadleehgo, when they become.

nda'adleehgóó, places where several events take place.

nda'a'eet, bit, they are sailing about.

ndaagéhigíí, naaltsoos, mail services.

nda'ahidzistseed, killing (one another) took place.

nda'ahiltseed, they kill one another.

nda'ahiltseedgo, when they killed one another.

nda'ahintin, they teach one another.

nda'ahintingo, they teach one another.

ndaaht'j, baa, discuss it.

ndaajeeh, baa, they are pursuing them.

ndaajeehgo, when they run about; while they roam.

ndaakaaigíí, those that walk about.

ndaakah, they come back (time and again); they return often.

ndaakaháqgi, the place to which they return often.

ndaakahgo, when they return.

ndaakai, they roam about; they wander about.

ndaakaigo, when they roam about.

ndaakaigo, yaa, when they are doing it.

ndaakaií, t'áadoo koji', without their coming here.

ndaal'a'ígíí, yá, one who gives them orders.

nda'aldeeh, going about.

ndaaldeehę́ę, those that lived.

nda'aldjjhígíí, yee, special privileges allowed.

ndaaldloosh, they go on all fours.

ndaaldlooshígíí, quadrupeds.

ndaaldlooshii, quadrupeds.

ndaaldlooshii bichaan, manure.

ndaaldoígi 'át'éego, they float about (comparatively speaking).

ndaalnish, they are working.

ndaalnishgo, when they work.

ndaalnishígíí, those that work.

ndaalnishígíí, Wáá shindoon yá, federal employees.

ndaalnishii, the workers.

ndaalzheeh, they are hunting.

ndaalzheehgo, while, or when, they hunt.

ndaalzheehígíí, those that hunt.

ndaalzheehii, the hunters.

nda'alzhoodgo, when they are dragging something around.

nda'ałeeh, to put on regularly (as a public performance).

nda'at'eełigíí, sailors.

nda'ałkidgo, when something is caused to move, as a thermometer or movie.

nda'att'a'ágíí, aviators.

ndaané, they are playing.

ndaanéego, when they play.

ndaanée teh, they usually play.

ndaanéhigíí, those who play; team (as football team).

ńdaa'nił, biih, things are put in it.

nda'anishdi, place where people work.

nda'anishidóó, from where they work.

nda'anishígíí, the work.

nda'anishígíí, bee, tools. (Also **bee na'anishi).**

ńdaasdlíí', they changed into.

nda'asdee', they went and returned.

ńdaasdziidii', because they became afraid.

nda'ashch'ąą', there are paintings or decorations.

ndaashch'ąą'go, when they are decorated.

ndaashnish, they worked.

ndaashnishéé, those who work.

ndá'ashoodígíí, those who drag something around.

ndaashzhee', they hunted.

ndaaskáá', they were investigated.

ndaaskai, thev went (in sense of having gone to a place and returned there from).

ndaaskaiigíí, those that went (and returned).

ndaas'nilgo, when they were placed.

ndaat'a', they fly around.

ndaat'a'ígíí, those that fly around.

ndaat'i'góó, to wherever it extends.

ńdaat'jjgo, yaa, when they discuss it.

ńdaat'iinii, yaa, they are discussing the subject.

ńdaat'inígíí, yaa, the subject they are discussing.

nda'eyé, they carry burdens.

nda'eyéhígíí, that (camels, horses, trucks, etc.) which carries burdens.

nda'eyéhígíí, chidí, trucks.

ndaaz, it is heavy.

ndaaz'áhígíí, extend around completely (as foundation to house).

ndaazbaa', yiká, they went after them (with weapons).

ndaazne'ígíí, those who played.

ndaazne', t'óó yee, they wasted it.

ndaazne', yee, they played a game of ....

ndaaznil, they (inanimate objects) lie about in groups.

ndaext'i'ígíí, that which extends down.

nda'eztiingo, since there are roads.

ndabi'diis'nilii, those who were appointed.

ndabidi'niiskaadéé, the ones that were driven there.

ndabidi'ntin, they are being taught.

ndabidi' ntinígíí, the ones that are being taught.

ndabi'ditseedígíí, those that were killed.

ndabi'diztseed, they were killed.

ńdabi'nááł, they observe regularly.

ndabistseed, it killed them.

ndabitiin, their tracks are about.

ndadeeshbéézh, they are scattered about. (Also **ndadeeztąąd).**

ńdadees'nánęędą́ą', at the time they were about to move back.

ndadeeztąąd, they are scattered about. (Also **ndadeeshbéézh).**

ńdadigohgo, when they flow (as washes).

ńdadiibaa', they started raiding (with weapons).

ńdadiilwo'igii, hach'į' dah, those that jumped on him.

ndadii'nił, we shall set them down.

ndadii'nił, 'ahąąh, we shall set them down side by side.

ńdadijahgo, when they run to a point (one after another).

ńdadikah, they usually go.

ńda'dildah, they (people) go.

ńdadinéest'jj'go, when they hid themselves.

ndadiniilnii', bik'i, we have placed our hand on it.

ńda'dini:ka', they drive the herd.

ńdadinilka', they (herds of sheep, cattle, etc.) are driven to a point.

ńda'dinilka'góó, places where the herd is driven.

ńdadoohdleeł, you (pl.) will change back again.

nda'dooldahii, baa, things that are to be done.

nda'doonish, there will be work to do.

ńda'doot'jjł, they will become rich again.

ńdadóot'įįł, yaa, they will discuss it.

ndadzizbaa', biká, they went on the war-path after them.

ndadzizne', there was a game.

ndahaaskai, they arrived one after the other.

ndahaas'nil, they were placed one after another.

ndahaas'nilgo, since they were placed one after another.

ndahaazdéél, yił, they captured them one after another.

ndahaazdláadgo, because they were torn.

ndahaazná, they moved to a point one after another (with their belongings).

ndahaaznáá ńt'éé', they moved (but........).

ndahaaznáné̖e̖dą́ą́', when they migrated.

ndahachííh, t'áá 'ahą́ą́h, a litter (of animals).

ńdahadleehé̖e̖, those that used to grow.

ńdahadleehgo, when they (vegetables, fruit, etc.) grow.

ńdahadleehii, those that grow.

ńdahadleehigíí, those that grow.

ndahaleeh, they become.

ndahalin, they resemble.

ndahalingo, because they resemble.

ndahalinigíí, the ones that resemble; those that seem.

ndahalni'go, when they tell.

ndahalyé, bich'į', they receive (as compensation).

ndahałáago, yiká, they pray for it; they perform a ceremony for it.

ndahałáhigíí, performers (ceremonial).

ńdahałchįįh, they cause trouble; they disturb the peace.

ndahałtingo, when there is rain.

ndahałtinigi 'át'éego, to fall like rain.

ndaha'ná, they stir (animate object).

ndaha'náá ńt'éé', ni', there were many earthquakes.

ndahané̖e̖dą́ą́', t'ah doo, before they arrived at their new homes.

ndahaniih, they are for trade or sale.

ndahaniih, baa, they trade them.

ndahaniihgo, when they are sold.

ndahaniihgóó, to where they are sold; about how they are sold.

ńdaha'níił, 'atah, to be placed back among.

ńdaha'níligíí, 'atah, the ones that are placed back among.

ndahasdzogo, since the boundaries were drawn.

ńdahasdzooigíí, the land that was set aside by boundary.

ńdahast'įįd, baa, they were discussed in a meeting.

ńdahat'inigíí, baa, those things that are under discussion.

ndahaz'á̖, they made plans.

ndahaz'ą́ą́góó, bił dah, in their community.

ndahaz'ą́ą́góó, dah, community.

ndahaz'áonii, 'ąąh dah, the illness.

ndahaz'áné̖e̖gi, bił, in their community.

ndahaz'ánigíí, 'ąąh dah, the sickness.

ndahaz'ánigíí, bąąh dah, the sick.

ndahazni', reports (oral) were made.

ndahazt'i'ii, bá, things subject to spoilage; perishables.

ńdahidii'nił, bąąh dah, things are hung up on it.

ndahidoonih, they will be sold.

ndahidoonihigíí, things to be sold.

ndahidoo'nił, they will be placed.

ndahiilniihgo, when we buy them.

ńdahodiilnih, bił, we will report back to him.

ndahodi'neeskaad, they were driven to a place.

ndaho'ditseed, they are killed (as a penalty).

ńdahodoodleeł, they (plants) will revive.

ndahodoolnih, they will tell their story.

ndahodoołaał, they will perform a ceremony.

ńdahódóot'įįłii, baa, things that are to be discussed.

ndahohkeah, you (three or more) carry some things in a container to a designated place.

ńdahojii'aahgo, bighą́ą́h, because they kept adding to it (land, area).

ndahojiitdlaad, they are plowing.
ndahotniih, you buy or sell them.
ndahotniihgo, when you sell or buy them.
ńdahooldzisígóó, where there are holes (in the ground).
ńdahoolni', yit, they returned and told him.
ńdahoo'naat, they are reviving (animate objects).
ndahwiileeh, to come into being.
ndahwiitdlaadgo, while they were plowing.
ndahwii'náago, bich'į', since they are having a hard time.
ndahwiisdzá, burrows; tunnels; corridors (passage in a building).
ndahwiis'náa'go, bich'į', because they had a hard time.
nda'iditkidii, those who ask questions.
nda'iilé, they pay.
nda'iilyé, pay (money received).
nda'iilyéego, when payment is made.
nda'iilyéhígíí, the wages.
nda'iitchííh, they give birth.
nda'iitniih, they carry on trade.
nda'iiniit, they are preparing food.
nda'iiznánę́ę, bit, those that migrated with them.
nda'iyiilniih, we carry on trade.
nda'iyotniih, you (three or more) trade.
nda'ízhditkidígíí, the questions they asked.
ńda'jidį́į́h, people eat.
ndaji'eesh, to keep (horses).
nda'jiiléego, bik'é, they are paying for it.
ndajiizdélę́ę, bit, those that they captured.
ndajijaah, they carry them around.
ndajikai, they go about.
ndajilzheehgo, when they are hunting.
ńdajithįįhgo, when they thaw them out.
ndajiltseedígíí, the ones that they killed.
ndajistseedígíí, the ones that they had killed.
nda'joosdlíí', 'ách'į', they expected something to happen to themselves.
ńdaneeskáál, stuck along in a line (in a series).
ndaneez'á, rafters.
nda'nibaal, spread between (tightly as the web in a duck's feet or a cloth tacked up).

ndanihíditkid, they are questioning us.
ndanihidi' neestą́ą́', we received directions.
nda'nithęęshgo, because they irrigated.
ndanise', they grow; vegetation.
nda'nise', 'ayóo — léi'gi, where things grow well.
ndanise'ígíí, those that grow.
ndanise'ii, those that grow; plants.
nda'nishinigíí, surveyors.
ńdanit'įhę́ę, things that formerly grew.
nda'ntin, they teach.
nda'ntinígíí 'át'éego, like they teach.
nda'ntinígíí k'ehgo, according to what they teach.
ndashootnish, you (three or more) worked.
ndasiiltseed, we killed them.
ndasooltįįgo, because you have chosen him (as a leader).
ndayiitgéésh, they are cutting it (or them) up.
nda yee', no (very emphatic).
ndayiitnihii, the things they buy.
ndayiitniih, they buy it (or them).
ndayiitniihgo, because they buy them.
ndayiitniihii, those who buy them.
ndayiinitígíí, those that they have chosen (as leaders).
ndayiisnii', they bought it.
ndayii̇zh'eezh, they led them to a point (one after another).
ńdayiizlá'ą́ą, those that they picked.
ńdayiizlá'ígíí, those that they picked.
ndayiiznil, they placed them.
ndayiitchiihgo, when they give them birth.
ńdayókeedgo, because they asked for the return of.
ndayoozlíí', yit, they suspected that they had it. shit nayóó̕lí, he suspects that I have it.
ńdazhdeest'įį', they hid themselves.
ńdazhdikah, they (people) go.
ńdazhdilt'ihgo, when they extend it (in a line).
ńdazhdíneest'į́į', they hid themselves.
ńdazh'dooldįįt, doo bee — da, they will be denied the enjoyment of.
ndazhdoolnish, they will work.

ńdazhdóot'įįł, baa' they will discuss it.

ndazhneezhchą́ą́', they fled (several times) from pursuers.

ndazhnitin, they teach them.

n'deedéelgo, bił, when he was captured.

ndeel'eez, he placed his foot.

ń'dees-bąs, I will drive (back).

n'dees-bąs, to park (a car); I will park (a vehicle).

ndeeshaał, 'a!ą́įį', I shall lead (to a place).

ndeesháát, I shall go (to a place and return).

ńdeeshbah, I shall return (from a raid).

ndeeshbah, to go raiding.

ndeeshch'ąh, I will decorate it; I will design it; I will make a sketch of it.

n'deeshch'ąh, I will paint a picture.

ń'deeshchid, bidaa', he has thick lips.

ń'deeshchid, bidáá', a flange.

ńdeeshdą́ą́ł, I will return.

ńdeeshgizh, gap; pass.

ndeeshłííł da, doo haada, I will do nothing to you.

ndeeshnish, I will work.

ndeestsił, I will kill them.

ńdeet'ą, baa, it (land) was returned to them (or him).

ńdeez'éłí, t'áadoo 'ákǫ́ǫ́, before it floated back.

ńdeezgo', t'ą́ą́', it has started flowing back.

ń'deezh'eezhgo, when he started to lead back.

ńdeezid, a month passed.

ńdeezidę́ę, the month that passed.

ńdeezidę́ę́dą́ą́', táá', three months ago.

ńdeezidgo, at the end of the month.

ńdeezid, hwee, he spent a month.

ńdeezidjį', dįį', for four months.

ndeeztąągdgo, bił, since they were scattered about with them.

ndei'áhígíí, hani', news carrier (oral).

ndeich'ąąh, they decorate it.

ńdeideesxaal, they struck him with a club (one time).

ńdeidiiłtséét, we will see it again.

ńdeididoo'ááł, they will pick it up.

ndeidoołkah, they will investigate it.

ndeidoołtsił, they will kill them.

ndeidoonił, they will appoint them.

ndeidzį́įz, they are dragging it around.

ndeiilnishigíí, bá, our employer.

ńdeiish'nih, I milk them.

ndeiizh'eezhii, those that they led back.

ndeijaahígíí, that which they carry.

ndeiłózígíí, that which they are leading around.

ńdeiichosh, they usually eat it (leafy things).

ndeiłjid, they carry it on their backs.

ndeiłkaah, they are investigating it; they are tracking it.

ndeiłkaahgo, when they track it.

ndeiłkaahígíí, those who track it; those who study it; those who investigate it.

ndeiłtseed, they kill them.

ńdeineest'ą, they raised them.

ndeiniłkaad, they herd them.

ndeinitin, they teach them.

ndeistseed, they killed them.

ndeiyé, they carry it (burden).

ndéízhdíłkidgo, when they asked him.

ndeiznilgo, when they placed them; when they arranged them.

ndi, but; even; though.

ndi, 'áko, even though; even then.

ńdídááh, (you) go back; to walk back and forth (as a sentinel).

ńdideeshjih, I will pick them up.

ńdideeshjoł, I will pick it (loose matter, as wool, weeds, hay, etc.) up later.

ńdideesht'įįł, I will hide.

ńdidoojah, they will leap up.

ńdidínóochxih, it will rust.

ndidoolchį́į́ł, he will sniff around.

ndidoot'ááł, to appropriate.

ndi, doo t'áátá'i, not even one.

ńdiibį́į', I am going swimming; I am going to bathe.

ńdiidzáago, when it reared up.

nidiidzá, dąh, he started back (on foot).

ńdiidzá, yaa, he got busy on it.

ń'dii'ééł, bił dah, he started back (by boat).

ńdiijah, nihich'į' dah, they spring at us.

ńdiijéé', shikéé', they ran after me.

ńdííjih, you must bring them (separable objects) back.

ńdiikai, baa, we started to work on it.

ńdiikai, dah, they started back.

ńdiikai, yaa, they started to work on it.

ndiiltsił, we (two) will kill them.

ndiiltsił, 'ádá, we (two) will kill them for ourselves.

ńdiilwod, he started to run; he leaped up.

ńdiiłṭį, I picked him up; I chose him; I found him.

ńdii'na', he arose; he got up.

ndíínaał, baa, you will do it.

ńdiish'na', I arose.

ndiists'a', I hear you; I understand what you are talking about.

ndiists'a', doo — da, I cannot hear you; cannot understand your language.

ńdiitá, I picked it up.

ńdiit'áázh, we (two) arose.

ńdiit'ash, we (two) will return.

ńdiit'óód, it is tattered, or shabby.

ńdiizą, they (people) started moving simultaneously.

ńditk'as, the weather becomes cold.

ńditk'asgo, when the weather becomes cold.

ńdinésht'ịį, I hid.

ńdinibįįhigíí, dah, those who occupy the seats (as Council Members, or Congress).

ńdiniichxii', it is rusty.

ńdiniilgesh, to stare.

ńdisdzih, I am breathing.

ńdisdzih lágo, t'áá, I was still breathing, to my surprise.

ndishni, I say to you.

ńdisht'įįh, I usually look.

ńdit'aash, shił, you take me back; you escort me.

ndi, t'ah, even yet.

ndiyi'ii, sunflower.

ńdizhdoo'nah, he will arise.

ńdizidigíí, the month is passing.

ńdiziid, the month is passing.

ńdood'óós, he will be led back.

ndoogááł, yich'į', he will walk up to it.

ńdoohah, the years will pass.

ńdoohah, he will run back.

n'doo!yééł, payment will be made.

ndoo'yéełii, that with which payment will be made.

n'doc'oł, shił, I am going boating.

ń'doot'įįlgo, he will again be rich.

ńdóot'ijł, nihá yaa, he will discuss it for us.

ndóstázii, top (toy)

ndzídzá, he returned.

ndzliztą́ągo, while they were sitting.

ndzitbąąsgo, while he was driving it.

ndziskáá', he investigated it; he tracked it.

n'dziskáa'go, because he investigated it.

ndziskai, they made a trip.

ndzisnil, they keep.

nédá, I sat down.

néé'deeshdlííł, I will copy you (what you do); I will do like you.

né'édił, blood (from the nose).

needzíí', game corral.

nee''á, it extends; it reaches.

née'áá', hooshįį, undetermined amount; undetermined number.

nee''á, bi'oh, insufficient.

nee'kááʼ, they (as stakes) are set one after another.

néa'tʼe'oo, bee, equal in amount.

néés'ood, it reached.

neesdon, jelly cake (made of yucca fruit).

ne'esdvánéę, your former wife (ex-wife).

neeshchééł, I am fleeing; I am chasing it.

neeshch'íí', nuts.

neeshch'íí' daalbáhigíí, peanuts.

neeshch'ííts'iil, pine cones; nutshell.

néeshch'il, he has his eyes closed.

né'éshiaa', owl.

né'éshjaayáázh, owlet.

né'éshjaa' yilkee'é, rubber plant.

né'éshtił, snot (mucus from or in the nose).

né'éshto', mucus (watery) from the nose.

neesk'ah, it is fat; obese; corpulent; plump. (See łik'aii).

neesk'ahi, fat one.

neesk'ahígíí, the fat one.

neest'á, it is ripe.

neestł'ah, interfered with; arrested (as, disease); handicapped; mitigated.

ne'etsah, pimples.

neeyá, it matured (an animate object).

neezdá, he sat down.

ncezdáago, when he sat down.

neezdo, it (something) is hot.

neezgai, dah naaltalgo, throbbing pain.

neezgaigo baa 'iit'i', a piercing pain.

neezk'az, it is cold (an object).

neezk'e', it cooled off; it stopped aching or hurting.

neezké, they (two) sat down.

neezná, they are dead; they (two) died.

neeznáá, ten.

necznáá 'asdzohgi, as much as ten inches.

neeznáadi, ten times.

neeznáá nááhaiji', up to ten years.

neeznáá yáál, ten bits ($1.25).

neeznádiin, one hundred.

neeznádiin béeso báąh 'iłįį dooloeł, it will be worth one hundred dollars.

neeznádiin dah hidinishdlo', I weigh one hundred pounds.

neeznádiindi, one hundred times.

neeznádiinigo, t'áá táadi, only three hundred.

neeztį, he lay down.

neheeskai, they arrived (at different intervals).

nehegeeh, it is hauled.

nehegeehgo, when it is hauled.

nehekáahii, those who come in.

nehelceh, they become.

nehelkaałí, tsin bee, adze.

neideesił, I will dream.

néididoo'áál, he will select it (inanimate object).

néididoo'áałgo, when he picks it up.

néidii'ą, he selected it (an inanimate object).

néidiiłtį, he picked it up (animate object).

néidiinil, he picked them up; he selected them.

nédiitá, he picked it up (a stiff, slender inanimate object, as a cane).

neidiyoołnih, he will buy it.

néidoodlįįł, he will drink it again.

neidoołkah, he will investigate it; he will track it.

neiilnishígíí, bá, our (two people) employer.

neii'néego, while we (two) were playing.

neijaah, he carries them; he has them.

néiłkáahgo, naaki, every two days.

neilo', he steers it around.

néiłtsá, I saw him again (after a long time).

néiłtsą́ąshlí, t'áá dó' shí shikék'eh, I saw my own footprints, (could it be that I).

naiłtseedgo, when he killed them.

néinidzáago, when you return.

néinidzáajį', baa, until you come back for it.

néini'eezh, he led them back.

néinighas, he is scratching it (as a dog on a door).

néinikąągo, when he brought them back (in a container, as in a basket, etc.).

neiniłkaadée, those that he was herding.

néiniłtínée, what he brought back (animate object).

neiníshłí, I am expecting it or him.

néinishtah, I read it; I count them.

neiséyeel, I dreamed.

neishoodii, what he, or it, drags around.

neishoodii, 'éé', a priest; minister; clergyman.

neiskáá', he investigated it; he tracked it.

neistsoed, he killed them.

neistseedée, what he had killed.

neiyéhée, one who used to haul it; what he was hauling around; what he used to haul.

néizgiz, to turn; to twist.

néshk'oł, I blinked (my eyes).

ni, you.

ní, he says.

ni', the late .... (preceded by the name of a recently deceased person); earth, ground.

ni'á, it extends (an object as pipe, etc.).

ni'ą, 'ałkéé', it lies in line (inanimate object).

ni'áhąą, that which used to extend (an object as pipe, etc.).

ni'ályaa, arrested (as, disease); made ineffective (disease, etc.).

ni'ánigo, t'áálá'í, singly (inanimate objects).

nibaal, canvas; tarpaulin; tent.

nibaal sinil, camp; tent.

nibaal yadiits'ózigíí, tepee.

nibéédahwiizjjhgo, when information concerning it is acquired.

nibid, your stomach.

ni' bi'nee!'ąąh, surveying.

nibinil'ééł, it (water) carried him.

nich'ah, your hat.

nich'i, breeze; current of air.

nichxǫ́ǫ́'í, it is ugly; it is filthy.

nichxǫ́ǫ́'í, you are ugly.

nid—words containing the nid letter combination may also be found with the omission of the i.

nidáá', squaw dance.

nidaahkai, you (three or more) walk about.

nidá'ák'eh, your cornfield.

nidaalnishgi, where they are working.

nidaashnil, 'ał'ąą, I am sorting them; I am setting them apart.

nidaaz'áa, they lie scattered about (inanimate objects).

nidaazbaa'ii, those who took part in the raid.

nidabidi'neestą́ą́', they were given instructions.

nidabi'ditseedii, those that are killed.

nidadeeshnil, 'ał'ąą, I will sort them; I will set them apart.

nida'deezdíín, the place is well lighted.

nidadigoh, they stumble.

nidaha'áii, governing body.

nidajikahii, those that come.

nida'óltah, they go to school; they read.

nidasénil, 'ał'ąą, I set them apart; I sorted them.

nidasiildzíid, we (three or more) became afraid.

nídeedááh, an invalid.

nideeshghał, I will eat you up.

nideeshkah, I will track it; I will investigate it; I will shoot you (with bow and arrow).

ni'deeshłíít, I will take your picture; I will make a copy of you (your features).

nideidiits'jjhgo, when they hear it.

nideijaah, they carry them around.

nidei'nihii, the ones that are milked.

nídideesh'ááł, naa, I will give it back to you.

nidideeshchii', inflamed again.

nídi'doolyjh, niwoo' bii', your tooth will be filled.

nídidoo'oł, it will dissolve.

nídidooził, a month will pass.

ni'didzih, respiration.

nídii'ééł, it dissolved.

ni'diildee'go, baa, when it (a performance) started.

nidiildloozh, łįį' bił dah, he started back (on horseback).

nídiilkáá', to begin investigation.

ni'diilwod, bił dah, he started back (in an automobile).

nidiilyeed, you run (a command).

nidiishwod, I ran; I jumped to my feet.

ni'diit'a', bił dah, he started back (by airplane).

nídiiyol, bił, the wind blew it away.

nidik'ą', cotton.

nidik'ą' bik'ǫ́ǫ́', cottonseed.

nídikoh, he vomits.

ni'dilkalí, shinny (game), golf, hockey, polo.

nidilt'éego, two of them (persons).

ni'dilt'o, archery.

nídishchíí', pine.

nídishchíí' biya', pine tick.

ni'dit'ááh, the sun travels.

nidiyílii, sunflower.

nídizhdoo'ááł, he will choose (a hard object of similar length and width).

ni'dǫ́ǫ́, from the ground.

nidoochii', pinedrop (plant).

ni'dǫ́ǫ́ deigo, from the ground up.

nídoodleeł, it will again become.

nidoogééł, it will be hauled.

nídooyis, to turn (oneself).

nigeed, tó, I ran a ditch for the water.

nighan, your home, or hogan.

ni'góó, on the ground; on the floor.

ni'góó sitjigo, while he lay on the ground.

nihá, for us or you (as a gift for us).

nihaa, to us; about us. **T'óó nihaa dlo hasin.** We were funny (made people laugh).

nihaa 'áłah náádleeł, they gather at our house often.

nihaa'doonééł, a group of people will move to us.

nihaa doo'nił, they will be given to you.

nihá 'áhodoolníił, it will be built for you.

niha'áłchíní, our children.

nihaa náázhnítaah, hahgo da, come to see us again sometime.

nihaa nídaakahgo, when they come to visit us.

nihaa nináhidoojah, they will return (one by one) running to us.

ni' hadláád, ground lichen.

nihahastói, our elderly men; our leader.

nihá náhásdzogo, since it was marked off for us.

nihe'ashiiké, our boys.

nihe'at'ééké, our girls.

nihee, by means of us; because of us.

nihééhodoozjíł, it will be known about us.

nihee hóló̦, we have.

nihééhósin, he knows us.

niheekaigo, when we (three or more) arrived (one after another).

nihe'ena'í, our (or your) enemies.

niheeshch'iízhgo, since it was sawed up.

niheeshjíí, it was sawed up.

niheeskai, they (three or more) arrived (one after another).

niheestǫ', it was broken up (as a box, etc.).

niheezná, they arrived after migration.

nihénálniih, he remembers us.

nihe'nííł, they are placed.

nihe'níłigíí, the placing of them.

nihí, we do (or are) (in answer to a question); you (pl.) (used for command); ours (in answer to a question); yours (plural).

nihiba', awaiting us.

nihibéeso, our or your (plural) money.

nihich'ą́ąh, something that stands in the way; obstruction.

nihich'į', toward us.

nihich'į' 'anáhóót'i'go, since we have problems.

nihichidí, our car.

nihich'ijí, on the side toward us; on our side.

nihich'iyą' our food.

nihich'į' yideeztsi, he pointed it at us.

nihich'ooní, our associate.

nihidááhgóó, on our way.

nihidááh jígháhí, t'áadoo, before he met us on our way.

nihidááh níyá, he met us on our way.

nihida'alyaa, a picture was taken of us.

nihídadéét'i', we have interest in it.

ni' hidees'náá', the earth quaked, trembled or shook.

ni' hidees'ná'ą̨dą́ą́', at the time of the earthquake.

nihídégoh, bee, I fell to the ground on it (part of body).

nihidiíniid, he said to us; I told you (a command).

nihidine'é, our people.

nihidi'néét'aa', we were deceived.

nihidookah, they will have arrived (one after another).

nihi'doo'niid, we were told (a command).

nihigi 'ádaat'éego, since they are like us.

nihíhigíí, the ones which are ours.

nihíí', ours.

nihiidoołkááł, we will spend the night.

nihiiská, we spent the night.

nihijéí, our hearts.

nihíká, (come) for us.

nihíká 'análwo', he help us.

nihiká 'eelwod, he helped us.

nihik'ehdeesdlį́į́', it overcame us.

nihikéyah, our country; your (pl.) country.

nihikéyahą́ą́, what used to be our land.

nihikéyahgóó, to our country.

nihik'i, upon us.

nihik'iigo', it (water) swept upon us.

nihik'ijį' dah diijéé', they rushed toward us.

nihik'is, our brother (males speaking); our sister (females speaking); our friend.

nihiłą́ąjį', ahead of us.

nihilah, our brother (females speaking); our sister (males speaking).

nihilį́į́', our horse; our pet; our livestock.

nihił, with us.

nihił ch'i'ni'éél, we sailed out.

nihił dah náádiildloozh, it (an animal) again started off with us (riding).

nihił haz'ánigi, in our area; in our community.

nihiłní, he said to us.

nihinaaltsoos, our book; our papers.

nihináář, we are watching (a program); we saw it (an action).

nihinaanish, our work.

nihinahagha', our religion.

nihinahodékaad, a wide open space around us.

nihinant'a'i, our leader; our boss; our superintendent.

nihinázt'i', they surrounded us; they encircled us.

nihi'neelchą́ą́', tsé'naa, they (two) ran across.

nihine'jí, behind us.

nihinii'aa'igi, the fact that he lied to us.

nihi'nitkǫ́ǫ́', he started to swim.

nihinootį́ł, it teaches us; it teaches you (plural).

nihitaadaa'niihigii, your dole.

nihitah, among us; in our body.

nihitahji' bił 'i'iínáago, when they moved with it into our midst.

nihitah yíkai, they (three or more) joined us.

nihits'ąą, moving away from us.

nihits'áá', contrary to our wishes.

nihitsiijį́ł, toward our head.

nihitsiist'a dedétą́, we carry it (a stiff, slender object) on our waist band.

nihitsinaa'eeł, our boat; our ship.

nihizhdookah, they will have arrived.

nihizhi', your (plural) names.

niho'deegį, they (people) were transported (to a point).

nihoneel'ánidi, at the far end (of an area).

nihoni'ą́, yá, he set a period of time for them; he sentenced them.

ni'hoojį́, to become twilight (from sunset to darkness).

nihookáá', on earth.

nihool'á, limit.

nihool'áago, since it is the limit.

nihool'áhigii, the limit.

nihoolzhiish, time is running out.

nihoolzhiizh, a period of time passed.

nihoolzhiizhgo, when a period of time passed.

nihoolzhiizh, nizaadgoo, for a long time (in past sense).

nihooshdlą́ą́, doo — da, I do not believe you (plural).

nihoot'ą́, a time was set.

nihoot'ą́, bee, it was agreed; it became a law.

nihoot'anée, bee, what was agreed upon.

nihoot'áneeal, at the place agreed upon.

nihoot'ánígíí, the agreement; the time which was set.

nihoot'ánígíí, bee, that which was agreed upon.

nihwiishgizhgo, when he cut him to pieces.

niichaad, swelling.

niidee', biih, we fell into it.

ni'idííłííł, you stop (in your vehicle).

ni' 'ídíí, hesitation.

niid'í, we (two) are.

niidoonił, he will place them.

niidzíl'go, because we thought.

ni'l'eoíł, t'áadoo nizaad nihíl, before we had rowed far; before we had sailed far.

niigháhí, t'áadoo ni', before he got down to the ground.

niigo, as he was saying, or demanding.

ni'ilchííh, births.

ni'ilchííh baa 'áháyą́ą́jí, birth control.

ni'ildzííhígíí, the mistakes.

ni'f'il'aa, he stopped (in his vehicle).

níi'il'níil, snuff.

ni'f'iishiaa, I stopped (in my vehicle).

Ni'ílíłhí, Sawmill, Arizona.

ni'ílíłíh, a sawmill.

ni'iijiihgo, when the saw mill was operating.

ni'ilitááh, school ends.

ni'ílívó, wages; compensation.

ni'ilsííh, he makes mistakes.

ni'ilsííhgo, because he makes mistakes.

niik'aaz, it cooled; it (something) became cold.

niik'aazę́edą́ą́, when it cooled off; when it became cold.

niik'aazgo, when it cooled off.

niikai, we arrived.

nii'k'ehę́ę, as was predicted.

niilch'iił, he closed his eyes.

niilch'ííł, you (one) closed your eyes.

niildoíí, bá, it was heated for him.

niilk'aazh, paralysis.

niiltee'go, since he refused to go further.

niiltła, he or it stopped.

niiltłáád, it is stopping.

niiltsooz, it (a flat flexible object) was placed down.

niilwod, tsé'naa, he ran across.

niiłtsǫǫz, it became flat (deflated); it became flabby; it became collapsed (deflated).

niinahjigo, uphill.

Niinahnízaad, Nenahnezad (near Fruitland, New Mexico).

nii'nil, they were appointed.

nii'nilgo, since they were appointed.

nii'niligíí, the fact that they were appointed.

niiniłtsooz, he laid it (a flat flexible object) down.

niiníyí, he hauled it.

nii ńt'éé', he used to say.

nii'oh hidiilchííd, yił, he snatches (steals) them.

niish, you (question); yours (question).

niish nik'ehdi, it does not concern you.

niit'aagóó, along the side of it.

niit'áázh, we (two) arrived.

niit'áazhgo, when we (two) arrived.

niit'óóh, it is about to end (as a performance); it is about to conclude.

niizháásh, to wear away.

niizhniłhaal, bit, he clubbed him to death.

niizį́į', I thought; I began to want.

niizį́į'go, because I thought; since I began to want.

niizį́į́hgo, when he decides.

ni'di'ch'il, thunderstorm.

nij—, words containing the nij letter combination may also be found with the omission of the i.

nijaa', baa, I gave them (separable objects) to him.

ni'il', to, or on, the ground, or floor.

niji'ángo, because he carried it (small hard object) around.

niji'aashgo, while they (two) were walking around.

niilí'ááh, to gather; to pick up (one after another).

niilí'éego, while he was making payments.

niilíílaish hadahachííh, the lightning flashes at night.

niilíílpish, he is working.

ni'ííít'oh, to smoke (a cigarette).

niiísdíį', he became as he was.

niilshnish, he worked.

niiívołnilh, I wish I could buy it.

niiízghal, he looked around.

niká, for (to get) you.

nik'ad 'aadi, now it is your turn.

nik'éédahidoohkah, you will all start home.

nik'éédahizhdoonéét, they will start moving back home.

nik'ééda'ilzná, moving back home has started.

nik'ééda'ilzáádóó, from the time moving back home started.

nikee'na', it or he began to crawl.

nikéyahgóósh, are you going back to your country?

nikidodiibaa', they started going around making war.

nikidodiikai, they started to wander around.

nikida'diłtsi', it (rain) is sprinkling.

nikidahooltjjhgóó, t'ah doo, before the rainy season began.

nikidées'eez, he has his foot placed on the ground.

nik'i'diirǫǫ da, t'áadoo, I did not understand you.

nikihodii'á, a precipice.

nikijikai, they (three or more) begin walking.

nikináádadidoobeh, they will start making war again.

nikináádadiibaa', they began making war again.

niki'nítkǫ́ǫ́', he started to swim.

nikiníyá, I started home.

nik'is, your brother (same sex); your sister (same sex); your friend.

nil— words containing the **nil** letter combination may also be found with the omission of the i.

niláah, go ahead.

niláahdéé', from nearby.

niláahdi, there.

niláahgóó, at a place nearby.

niłch'ił, he blinks his eyes.

niléí (niléí), that one.

niléídi, over there.

nil'í, to see; inspect, or examine.

nilį́, he is; they (two) are. **Naakaii łizhinii niłį́.** He is a negro.

nilį́, you are; it flows (as a river). **Ha'át'íisha' nilį́?** What are you?

nil'íįgo, while it was under observation.

nilį́įgo, since he is.

niljh, (See yiliłh), you taste it.

nilíinii, one who is.

nilínǫǫ, the one who was.

nilínǫǫdą́ą́', when he was.

nilínídi, where it flows.

nil'į́ yát'éahii, one that is attractive; one that is good-looking.

niłk'ah, he becomes fat.

niłk'oł, he blinks his eyes.

niłk'oł, you are blinking your eyes (reflex action).

niłk'ołí, t'áadoo, do not blink your eyes.

niló, hail.

niló naałtin, hailstorm.

niló yázhí, sleet.

nił, with you.

nił 'adeesdǫǫh, you are shot; he shot you.

niłch'i, air; a breeze.

niłch'i bee hane'e, radio.

niłch'i bił 'aa'ada'atsiígíí, pneumothorax.

niłch'i díí'idígíí, carbon dioxide.

niłch'i iłkone, inflammable gas.

Niłch'itsoh, December.

Niłch'its'ósí, November.

niłch'i yá'át'éehii, oxygen.

niłchxon, it has a bad odor; it stinks.

niłdzil, stable; firm; solid; steady; immovable. (See niłt'iz).

niłdzil, bee, it is held firm by it.

niłdzilíǫǫ, yee, with which it was firm.

niłdzilíi, one that is firm; one that is immovable.

niłhin, oily brown; greasy (as wool).

niłhod, (you) rock it (back and forth).

nił hóyéé', 'ayóogo, you are very lazy.

nił neisóíí', I suspect you have it.

niłní, he says to you.

niłt'ees, you broil it, you roast it.

niłtó.i, it (water) is cloudless, or clear.

niłtó.igo, because it (water) is clear.

niłtóó.i, it (a glass) is clear; it is transparent; it is crystalline.

niłtsą́, rain, shower.

niłtsą́ bi'áád, gentle rain.

niłtsá bika', violent rainstorm.

niłtsągo', pine-sawyer or wood-borer.

niłtsątoo', rainwater.

niłts'íí', crystalline; clear (as water).

niłtsǫz, it is flat (deflated).

nímasiitsoh, potatoes.

nímaz, round (spherical).

nimazgo, since it was spherical.

niná, he or I arrived (with all his belongings).

nináá'ákéé', there were some more footprints about.

nináá'ásdee', 'ákǫ́ǫ́, they went there again and returned.

nináá'ázt'i', there is another fence.

ninááda'ahinitingo, since they are again teaching one another.

nináádadeeztqqd, some more were scattered about.

nináádadoolnish, they will work again.

nináádadóot'ííł, yaa, they will discuss it again.

nináádahaas'nánę́ę, those that arrived (with all their belongings) again.

nináádaháaztą́, they are sitting down again.

nináádahaltin, nihee, we are having rain again.

nináádahaltingo, since there are more rains.

nináádahasdlį'igíí, those others that came into existence.

nináádahaz'ą́, they set another date; they set another period of time.

nináádahidoonéét, they will arrive (with their belongings) again.

nináádahózhdééłkid, they asked him more questions.

nináádaneest'ą́, they again grew abundantly.

nináádayidiilkid, we asked him more questions.

nináádéeee', it (liquid) again spread out.

nináádeezidgo, when another month has passed.

nináádeidii'ą́, they lifted it again.

nináádeidoo'nił, they will place them again; they will appoint them again.

nináádídeezííł, the month will pass again.

nináádííjéé', they again leaped up; they again sprang up to their feet.

nináádiilwod, he again sprang up; he again leaped up.

nináádínóot'ííł, they (weeds, etc.) will grow back.

nináádiishwod, I again leaped up

nináádooltsos, hasht'e', it (a flat flexible object) will again be put away for safekeeping.

nináádoo'niligii, the ones who will again be placed.

nináá'doo'oł, shił, I will again go boat riding.

nináá'dooyis, it will again turn around once.

nináago, when they (with their belongings) arrived.

ninááhaasht'eezhgo, ła', when more were lead in.

niná'áhigí 'atch'í', where they (extending objects) run together.

ninááhódóot'ííł, baa, it will again be discussed.

ninááhoot'anígíí, the date which was again set.

nináá'ííyáago, at the next pay day.

ninááijidá, he again walks around.

ninááijiinishgo, when he was working again.

ninaalte', your slave.

ninaalte'ę́ę, one that used to be your slave.

ninaaltsoos, your paper; your book.

nináánááhai, again a year passed.

nináánááhaigo, when a year has again passed.

nináánáikaahgo, when it was being investigated again.

nináánáłtį, he was again appointed.

nináánáłtínígíí, one which was again appointed.

nináánát'aashígíí, yił, one with whom she or he again goes around.

nináánólíkai, we (three or more) are going around.

nináánídeeh, it again came into existence or circulation

nináánídínéesaxs, I will again scratch you up.

nináá'níbezhm ha'naa, he again lead across.

nináánłtseed, you kill them again.

nináánísdzá, I again returned.

ninááshidiníłt'eez, he again placed my foot.

nináázhdóot'ííł, baa, he will again discuss it.

nináázh'nitkaadgo, when he herds again.

ninábi'deeltį, he was reappointed.

ninádaalnish, they work.

ninádaa'neehigíí, the players (in a game).

ninádaas'nilgo, when they were reappointed.

ninádadigoh, it (liquid) spreads.

nináda'doodléél, they will pay back.

ninádahaas'ná, they returned (with all their belongings).

ninádahaazbaa', yaa, they returned to them warring.

ninádahadleeh, they transform.

ninádahaltįįh, it rains.

ninádahaltįįhgo, when it rains.

ninádahanih, they are sold.

nináda'idlé, they will pay back.

nináda'iil'ot, bee, we use it to sail.

nináda'iis'náádóó, from the time when people moved back.

nináda'iis'náago, when people moved back.

nináda'iis'naajį', up to the time when people finished moving back.

nináda'jiidlé, one reimburses.

nináda' jiidléhéę, what they used to pay back.

ninádanilt'įįhgo, since it (crop) was raised.

nináda'niyęsh, people irrigate.

ninádayii'éeshgo, when they lead them back.

ninádayii'nítígíí, what they put back.

ninádayiizh'eezh, they led them back.

ninádayootchxǫǫh, they erase them: they disassemble them; they take it down.

ninádazhnilt'įhéę, what they used to raise.

niná'deet'įįdjį' nídiilyeed, t'áá, run as fast as you can.

niná'deet'įįdjį', t'áá, as hard as possible.

ninádeidii'ą́, they found it (a small hard object) again.

ninádeinilt'įįh, they raise them (crop, etc.).

ninádízi', months go by.

niná'doodléél, he will pay his debt.

niná'doolyéél, bá, he will be reimbursed.

niná'doolyéél, bik'é, payment will be made for it.

ninágéehgo, when it is hauled.

ninágéhigíí, that which is hauled.

nináhá'áahgo, when he sets a date.

nináhá'ááh, yee, he sets a date for it.

nináhaaskai, they returned (one after another).

nináhaas'ná, they moved back (one after another with belongings).

nináhádááh, he returns.

nináhádleeh, it transforms.

nináhádleehí, t'áadoo — da, it does not pay; it is unprofitable.

nináháháah, years go by.

nináháháahgo, when years pass; annually.

nináháháahjį', per year.

nináháhááh, t'áá — bik'eh, every year.

nináháháhígíí, those (particular) years.

nináhákáahgo, as they return.

nináhálzhish, time passes.

nináháltįįh, it rains.

nináháltįįhgo, when it rains.

nináháshįįh, summers go by.

nináhisoohkai, you (pl.) have returned (one after another).

nináhisoohkaigo, when you have returned (one after another).

niná'iis'náago, after people had moved back.

niná'iis'nánigo, t'óó, soon after people had moved back.

niná'ílyáago, when the debt is paid.

ninájiiyeeh, he hauls them back.

ninájijih, hasht'e', he puts them away (for safe keeping).

ninájilzhah, he goes hunting.

ninálts'id, deigo, it fell upright.

nináni'éél, hot, it floated back (to a point) with him.

niná'nilgo, bá, when it (money, etc.) is set aside for them.

ninánii.t'įįhзi, how to raise it (crop, etc.).

nináshiltééh, he puts me.

ninát'áashgo, when it (performance) is put on.

ninátsi'ę́ę, those that are killed.

ninátsi' ńt'ę́ę́', they used to kill.

ninázh'doodléét, bich'į', he will reimburse him.

ni' ndaha'nánigíí, earthquakes.

nínéę, what he used to say.

nineel'á, it extends (to a point).

nineel'áqdi, at the end of its extension.

nineelkɔadgo, 'ahɔa, when they were herded together.

nineet'á, ni'gi, he put his head on the ground.

nineez, it is long; he is tall. **Kǫ' na'ałbąąsii nineez.** The train is long.

ninéí'niłgo, yikáá', when he puts them down on it.

niní'á, I set it down.

niní'áozhgo, when they (two) were tired.

niní'áh, it extends to a point (and stops).

niní'áhígi, yaa, at the lower end of its extension.

ninídéléę, bił, the one that ran him down and caught him.

ninídéléę, yił, the one he ran down and caught; the one whom he raped.

niní'éél, it floated to a point and stopped.

niní'eezh, I led them to a point and stopped.

niniikai, we went to a point and stopped.

nínilgo, 'alta', because they are set alternately.

nínił'į, you (singular) look at it.

ni'nítkǫǫh, you are about to swim (arrive to a point swimming).

ninínáago, when he moved to (a point with belongings and settled down).

nínínáníji, at the place where they moved.

nininil, I put them.

nininil, hasht'e', I put them away (for safekeeping); I put them in readiness.

nininil, ni', I set them down.

ninínítna', bi'oh, it was insufficient.

ninínítna'jį', as long as it lasts.

ninish'náájígo, on your right.

ninishtee', I refused to go further.

ninishtł'ajígo, on your left.

ninít'i', termination.

ninít'i'ígi, at its end.

niniyá, I, or he went to (a point and stopped); I am, or he is tired; I am fatigued.

niníyáago, since I, or he was tired.

ninizhaazhéę, the one which wore out.

ninízinigíí, whatever or whichever you want.

ninohdeeł, bił, you (plural) catch him.

nisdaaz, I am too heavy (for it).

niséghal, I looked around.

nisékwi, I vomited.

niséłhiz, I turned it (a wheel, etc.).

nisétkáá', I tracked it; I investigated.

niséyá, I went and returned.

niséyiz, I turned (standing position) around.

nisézǫǫz, I turned it (as stockings, etc.) inside out.

nishą', what about you? are you?

nishch'ił, I am blinking my eyes.

nishéłgozh, I turned it (intestine, etc.) inside out.

nizhi'deeltį, I was appointed, I was assigned.

nishk'oł, I blink my eyes (reflex action).

nishłį, I am. **Naabeehó nishłį.** I am a Navajo.

nishłį, nił, I am with you.

nish'náájígo, on the right.

nishódahoot'eeh, they are acquired; they are obtained.

nishódajiyoołt'eeh, they acquire it; they obtain it.

nishóhoot'eeh, it is acquired; it is obtained.

nishtł'ajígo, on the left.

nisihwiinídéél, emergency.

nisiidzį, we (three or more) are standing.

nisiikai, we (three or more) went and returned.

nisiildziid, we (two) became afraid.

nisin, I think; I want; I like.

nisin, doo — da, I do not want it; I do not like it.

nisinéę, what I thought; what I wanted.

nisingo, since I thought; since I wanted.

nisíníghal, you looked around.

nisínildziid, you became afraid.

nísísdlį', I again became.........

nísísdzííd, I became afraid.

nisíyá, I went and returned.

nisneez, I am tall.

nisoł, you blow on it

nit— words containing the **nit** letter combination may also be found with the omission of the **i.**

nit'ą́ą, t'ahdii doo — da, it has not ripened.

nitééh, he lies down.

niteeh, you lie down.

niteeh, he started to lie down.

niteel, it is wide; it is broad.

niteelígíí, that which is wide; that which is broad.

nit'inigo, t'áadoo haada, if you behave.

nit'iní, t'áadoo haada, behave yourself.

nitł'iz, it is hard, sturdy, inflexible, stable.

nitsaa, it (inanimate object) is large; it is big; it is huge.

nits'ąą, to avoid you; to shun you.

nits'ą́ą́' dah diishwod, I ran away from vou.

nits'ą́ądóó, from you.

nits'ą́ą́' ná'áshdį́įh dooleeł, I will eat off of you (at your expense).

nitsídaahkees, you (plural) think.

nitsídaakees, they think.

nitsidéesgo', he is kneeling down.

nitsídaikees, we think.

nitsxaaz, it (animate object) is big, strong, large, or big.

niwohádi, further over (or on).

niwohjį' 'ákóó, (you) go away; begone; scram.

niyá, he came.

niyáádą́ą́', if he should come.

niyáago, when he comes.

niyá, 'ákǫ́ǫ́, I went there; he went there.

niyáhą́ądóó, since my arrival.

niyáhágo, t'óó, soon after my arrival.

niyá, kwii, he came here.

niyázhi, your offspring; your progeny.

niyééh, it (animate object) usually matures.

niyi'dę́ę́', from inside of you.

niyih 'anitdóóh, hold your breath.

niyiiłbįįh, he earns them; he wins them.

niyiiłchxǫǫhgo, because he ruins them; because he annoys; because he interrupts.

niyiiniił, ni', he sets them down on the ground (one after another).

niyiiznil, ni', he set them down on the ground (one after another).

níyiz, it is round and slender.

níyol, wind; it is windy.

níyolgo, because it was windy.

níyol tó hayiiłt'oodí, windmill.

niyooch'iid, you are lying (telling an untruth).

niyooch'iid, 'ayóo, you are a liar.

nízaad, it is far.

nízaadę́ę́', from afar.

nízáádę́ę́', haashįį, for quite some tine; from some distant places.

nízaadi, at a far place.

nízaadgóó, afar, for a considerable length of time; into the distance; to a far-away place. **Nízaadgóó niníyáago 'i'íí'ą́.** I (by walking) corered a considerable distance before the sun went down. **Nízaadgóó 'iiniłhaazh.** You slept for quite uwhile.

nízáadi, haashįį, at some distance.

nízaadii, bich'į', the farthest one.

nízaad nihoolzhiizhgo, after a long time.

nízahdę́ę́', haa, from how far?

nízah, haa, how far is it?

nízahįį', haa, to how far?

nízéé', hush your mouth.

nízhdii'ą́, he picked it up; he found it; he selected it (a hard object).

nízhdii'ánigii, that (a hard object) which he has chosen; that (a hard object) which he had found.

nízhdiidzá, baa, he began to work on it; he busied himself on it.

nízhdiijéé', they (three or more) started to run.

nízhdiilwod, he started to run; he ran.

nízhdiinil, he picked them up, found them, chose them.

nizhdilt'é, two people.

nízhdoodą́ą́ł, he will return.

nízhdoogáál, bich'į', he will walk up to it.

nízhi', your name.

nizhi, your voice.

nizhi', your torso.

nizhni'ą, hasht'e', he put it away (for safe-keeping); he put it (in readiness).

nizhnidéél, 'it, he roped.

nizhninil, hasht'e', he put them away (for safekeeping); he put them in order; he put them (in readiness).

nizhniyá, bich'į', he walked up to it.

nizhóní, it, or he is pretty; it is beautiful, clean, good, nice, fine, neat.

nizhónigo, beautifully; nicely; neatly.

nízin, he thinks (something); he wants.

nízingo, because he thought; because he wants.

nízínigo, t'áálá'í, each (animals, people, etc.).; individually (people, animals, etc.).

niznithaal, yił, he clubbed him to death.

nj - words containing the **nj** letter combination may also be found as **nij**.

ńjaa'go, collectively.

nji'aash, bił, he is accompanying him about; he is going around with him.

ńjidzá, he returned; he came back.

njighá, he walks around; he is alive.

njigháágóó, wherever he goes.

njighá, baa, he is working on it.

njiishgizh, he cut it up.

ń'jiizoh, he makes a mark.

njiiztáągo, while they (three or more) were sitting.

ńjildzid, he is afraid.

njiłéego, if one carries (a slender, flexible object).

njiłzheeh, he is hunting; he hunts.

njiłkaah, he is tracking it; he is investigating it.

ńjisdziíd, he became afraid; he got frightened.

ńjisdlįį', he again became ....

njishzhee'ęędą́ą́', the time he went hunting.

njiskai, bee — yęę, that with which they made the trip.

njistseed, he killed them.

ńjit'į, bá baa, he acts on it for them.

ńjit'įįgo, baa, because he bothered it, because he continuously acted on it.

njiyáhą́ądą́ą́', **'ákǫ́ǫ́**, the time he made the trip there; the time he went there.

njizjigo, 'ákǫ́ǫ́, while they were standing nearby.

njiizyínęę, 'ákǫ́ǫ́, what he hauled there and back.

ńjóki'go, when he asks for it.

ń'jóltahgo, when he counts; when he reads; because he goes to school.

ńjookahgo, when they were returning home.

nl - words containing the **nl** letter combination may also be found as **nil**.

ńlááh, go ahead.

ńlááhdę́ę́', from over yonder.

ńláahdi, over there.

ń!áahdi naniná, you go away; stay away from here.

ńláʼáhjí, over yonder.

ńláhgóó, right over there (close by).

ńléí, that one (over there).

ńléidi, over there.

ńléigóó, way over there; there it goes.

ńlį, it flows; you are.

nljigo, since he is; because he was.

ńlį́į́ ńt'éé, it used to flow; you used to be.

nlį́į́ ńt'éé', he was; he used to be.

nlínigíí, the one that is.

ńlínigíí, that which flows.

nohłįįnlí, those of you who are.

neo', storage pit; a cache.

noochał, the swelling is spreading.

noochééł, he is fleeing.

nóóda'í, a Ute; Ute tribe.

noodǫ́ǫ́z, it is striped; it has stripes.

nooji, it is corduroy; it is corrugated.

noolkał, it (a herd of cattle, etc.) is being driven along.

nooltł'iizh, zigzag.

noołch'iił, you (two) close your eyes.

nooshdlą́ą, doo — da, I do not believe you.

noot'įįł, they are growing; he is sneaking along.

noot'įįł, k'ee'ąą, they (people, etc.) are increasing.

noot'ish, a pleat.

nówehédi, farther on.

nt -worda containing the nt letter combination may also be found as nit.

ńt'ą́, it ripens; (plant) matures.

nt'ání, t'áadoo 'ałtso, before they are all
ripe.

ńt'ę́ę́', it was; it used to be.

ńt'ę́'ę́ę, the one that was.

nteel, it is wide. Bich'ah nteel. He has a
wide-brim hat.

nteelgo, because it was wide.

nteeligíí, the one which is wide.

ńt'ę́'igíí, the one which was.

ńt'i', it extends along (as wire).

nt'jjhgo, when it ripens.

nt'iz, it (an object) it hard.

ntsaaígíí, that which is large; the big one.

ntsaaígíí, miil, one million.

ntsáhákees, the thinking.

ntsáhákeesgo, when one thinks.

ntsáhákeesgo, baa, when one gives it a
thought.

ntsáháskézí, t'áadoo hazhó'ó baa, without
careful thought about it; without giving
it careful consideration.

ntsékees, he is thinking; he thinks.

ntsékeesgo, when he is thinking; while he
thinks.

ntsékeesga, yaa, when he thinks about it.

ntsékeesigi 'át'eégo, like the way he thinks.

ntsékeesigi, yaa — 'át'éego, like he thinks
(of it).

ntsékeesii, one who can think.

ntsékees, yaa, he is thinking about it.

ntsékos, yaa, he thinks about it.

ntséskees, I am thinking.

ntséskees, baa, I am thinking about it.

ntsézkééz, yaa, he thought about it; he
gave it a thought.

ntsídaahkees, you (plural) think.

ntsídaahkeesgo, since you (plural) think.

ntsídaahkeesi, t'áadoo łahgo 'át'éego, you
(plural) do not think otherwise.

ntsídaakees, they are thinking; they think.

ntsídaakeesgo, when they are thinking;
when they think.

ntsídaakeesigíí, yaa, what they thinking
about.

ntsídaazkééz, yaa, they thought about it;
they gave it a thought.

ńtsídaadiikééz, they started to think.

ńtsídadiikéę́, yaa, they started to think
about it.

ntsídadiniilgo', we (three or more) knelt
down.

ntsídadzikees, they think; they are thinking.

ntsídadzikeesgo, according to what they
think.

ntsídadzikeesigíí, baa, about which they
are thinking.

ntsídajikees, baa, they are thinking about
it.

ntsídajikeesgo, baa, when they think about
it.

nitsídéesgo, he is kneeling down.

ntsídéesgo'go, while he was kneeling down.

ntsídeiikeesgo, baa, when we think about
it.

ntsídeikeesii, our thinking.

ntsídideeshgoh, I will kneel down.

ńtsídiikééz, he, or I began to think.

ntsídinigeeh, you kneel down.

ntsídinigo', he knelt down.

ntsídzíkeesgo, when one thinks.

ntsíjízkééz, he thought; he pondered.

ntsíjízkééz, haa'i lá doo — da, he thouht
and thought.

ńtsínáádiikééz, baa, I again began to think
about it.

ntsísékééz, I thought and thought; I
pondered.

ntsísékééz, baa, I thought about it; I gave
it a thought; I pondered over it.

ntsizhdinigo', he knelt down.

ntsxaazii, a big one (animate object).

– O –

'ódleeh, to trap.

'ohónéedzá, ideal place.

'óhoneestą́ą́', trial (a try).

'ólta', school; reading (noun).

'ólta'ádi, at the school.

'ólta'ági, at the school.

'ólta' binant'a'í, director of schools; school superintendent; school principal.

'ólta'di, at school.

'ólta' dóó 'ak'e'elchi, reading and writing.

'ólta'gi, at school,

'ólta'go, when, or while the school was, or is in session.

'ólta'góó, to school.

'ólta' hótsaaigíí, a boarding school.

'ólta'ídi, at school.

'ólta'ídóó, from the school.

'ólta'ígíí, the school.

'ólta'jj', as far as the school.

'ólta'ji, in school.

'ólta'í, t'áadoo, no school session.

'ólta' yinant'a'í niliinii, he who is the superintendent, or school principal.

'ólta'go, while he was in school.

'ood, eagle trap.

'oodlá, he gives credence to it; he believes; he is a believer in Christ.

'oodlą́ą́', he drank; he got drunk.

'oodláanii, believer.

'oodzíí', mistakes; failure; a miss (failure).

'óola, gold; the hour; o'clock.

'ooljéé', moon.

'ooljéé' 'ałníí' bééłhéél, half-moon (first quarter).

'ooljéé' bee 'adinídinígíí, moonlight.

'ooljéé' biná'ástłéé', halo (around the moon).

'ooljéé' chahalheeł náádzá, new moon.

'ooljéé' daaztsą́, eclipse of the moon.

'ooljéé' dah yiitą́, crescent moon.

'ooljéé' haniíbą́ą́z, full moon.

'ooljéé' łahgo 'ánáá'nííł, phases of the moon.

'oolkił, díkwíígóó, what time is it?

'oolkiłgo, díkwíígóó, at what time (hour)?

'óolyé, it means. Ha'át'íí 'óolyé? What does it mean?

'óolyé, ha'át'íí, what is meant by.

'oolyeedí, t'áadoo niká — da, There is no one here that might help you.

'óólzin, kept (maintained; maintenance.

'oołch'jjd, 'ayóo, he is a faultfinder.

'oołdjjł, t'ah ndi, still fighting to remain alive; still alive; he is still living (as said of a real old person).

'oołkǫ́ǫ́ł, he is swimming along.

'ooł' oł, hoł, he is rowing along.

'oonéełgo, when they (people) were moving along (with their belongings).

'oonishgi, at the place of work.

'ó'oolkąąh, advertisement.

'o'oolwod, nihiká, we received (charitable) aid; we got help.

'oo'oł, shił, I am sailing along.

'oosdląąd, he became a believer.

'ooshdlą́, I believe it; I believe it is true; I am a believer.

'ooshdlą́ą́ da, t'ahdii doo, I still do not believe.

'ooshgéézh, gristle; cartilage.

'ooshgéézh bee ts'in 'áhéshjéé' gónaa k'é'éłtǫ', epiphyseal fracture.

'ooshk'iizh nít'i'í, traces (of a harness).

'óoshne'gi, t'áadoo—da, I cannot foresee any danger; I was helpless.

'oot'į, vision.

'ootsą, pregnancy.

'oozbá, to win.

'oozhé, hunting (noun).

'ouu', yes.

- S -

sá, old age.

saad, word; language; speech.

saad 'ahídeit'ááh, they are fussing, or arguing.

saadigii, the words.

saad náánáłahdéé' saadii bee háádílnééh, translation.

saadtah, an argument

sáunii, womenfolks.

sahdii, hogan uprights; tent poles.

sahdii, t'áá, separately; to one side.

sáhí, t'áá, alone, by oneself.

sání, aged, old one.

sánígo since it was old.

sédá, I am sitting.

sédáhígi, where I am sitting.

sédis, I rolled it (as paper, etc.) up.

sédiz, I spun it (wool).

sees, wart, callous.

seesyį, it was killed.

seesyínígíí, one that was killed.

séghas, I scratched it.

ségis, I washed it.

séí, sand.

Séí Bee Hooghan, San Felipe Pueblo (New Mexico).

Séé Bídaagai, Seba Dalkai (Arizona).

séígo', scorpion (Also **dzidiłháshii**).

séí hooyolí, sand drifts.

sé'įįd, it turns my stomach.

sélįh, I tasted it.

sélįį', I became; I have become.

séloh, I roped it.

séłgan, I dried them (food).

séłhį, I killed it.

séłkah, I shot it (with bow and arrow).

séłmas, I swung it.

séłt'ę́, I roasted it.

séłt'i', bizéé', I put a band around its neck.

séłtłah, I greased, oiled, or waxed it.

séshish, I poked it.

sésiih, I missed it (failed to hit it).

sésoł, I blew it out.

sétał, I kicked it.

sétį, I am lying down.

sétįįgo, while I am lying down.

sétł'ǫ́, I wove it.

séts'ih, I pinched it.

séts'ǫs, I kissed him.

sézhash, I tied a knot in it.

sézį, I am standing.

shą', what about (me, etc.)?

shá, for me; sun.

shaa, to, or about me.

shą́ą́', sunshine.

shąąh, on me.

shą́ą́jį'. in the sunshine.

sha'áłchíní, my children; my family.

shaa nikaah, hand it (something in a container, as a bowl of soup, etc.) to me.

shááłis, over me.

Shą́ą́'tóhí, Shonto, Arizona.

shaazh, knot.

shá bitł'ájiiłchii', halo (around the sun).

shá bitł'óól, sunbeam; sunrays.

shádi'ááh, south.

sádi'áahjigo, southward.

shádi'ááh biyaadę́ę́' naagháii, southerner.

shádi'ááh biyaadi, in the far south.

shádi'ááhjí, on the south.

shadi'ááhjígo, on the south side.

sha'díínił, you must lend them to me.

shahani', my story; my statement (as in court).

sha hodoochįįł, I will be angry.

shánah, vigorous; energetic; healthy.

sándíín, sunlight, or sunshine.

sha'niltsóód, give me some (food).

shash, bear.

Shash Bitoo, Bear Springs (near Ft. Wingate, New Mexico). Fort Wingate, New Mexico.

sha'shin, possibly; might; perhaps; maybe.

shash ligaii, polar bear.

shashtsoh, grizzly bear.

shash yáázh, bear cub.

she'abani, my buckskin.

she'aghaa', my wool.

she'atsį', my meat.

shébizh, I braided it.

shee 'ádin, I have none.

shéédidoochił, I will be set free; I will be released.

she'ena'í, my enemy, or enemies.

shélwod, he caught up with me (by running).

shélbéézh, I boiled it.Gohwééh shélbéézh. I made some coffee.

shéłch'il, I scorched it.

shi, I, me, mine.

shį, summer.

shiba', wait for me; go ahead (until).

shibeechaha'ohí, my umbrella.

shibee'eldǫǫh, my gun.

shibéeso, my money.

shibéézh, my knife, metal, iron, or flint; boiled.

shibid, my stomach, or belly.

shich'ah, my hat, or cap; helmet.

shich'é'é, my daughter (woman speaking).

shich'į', toward me.

shich'į' dah ndeesnii', he waved his hand at me.

shidááh díínááł, meet me (at a point on my way).

shidá'ák'ehgi, at my farm; at my cornpatch.

shi'diił'ąą da, doo, I am not worring about it.

shidííniid, he said to me.

shidine'é, my people; my tribe.

shidi' niilyįįgóó, to where I will be killed.

shídin, t'áá, without me.

shidiyiiłhééł, you might, or will kill me.

shidiyoołhééł, he might (or will) kill me.

shi'dizhchį, I was born.

shidó', I also; I too; me too.

shi'doochééł, I will be (as in the distribution of something which becomes exhausted before one can receive his share) left out.

shighan, my house, or my home.

shighandi, at my home, or house.

shigi'át'é, he is like me.

shigod, my knees.

shigodist'áni, my knee cap.

shigodta gónaa, around my knees.

shihodééłni, 'ayóo, I am highly susceptible; I am allergic.

shíhólníih, shi, I am in charge.

shii', in me; inside of me.

shįį, may; probably; possibly; perhaps; maybe.

shíí', mine.

shiid, be quiet (to call one's attention without being overheard).

shįįdą́ą́', last summer.

shiidą́ą́'dii, t'áá, for a long time.

shįį, díkwíí, several.

shįį, díkwíidi, several times.

shįįgo, during the summer.

shiijéé', we (three, or more) are lying down.

shiiłkaah, I am staying all night.

shiiłtsá, he saw me.

shíínááł, I watched (a performance); I saw it (an act, etc.) all.

shíínílghal, you ate me up.

shííni'ni, you want me (to —); you think (I —).

shiish shik'ehdii, it is not my concern.

shiiská, I stayed all night; I camped all night.

shiisxį, he killed me.

shiitéézh, we (two) are lying down.

shijéé', they are lying down; they are recumbent.

shiijįzh, it (as fender on a car) is crushed, or dented; it is smashed.

shijéí, my heart.

shijjzhgo k'é'éłtǫ', compression fracture.

shijoost'e'go, when he acquired it.

shik'a', my arrow (bik'a', his arrow).

shiká, for, or after me.

shikadantáhąą, those who were searching for me.

shiké'achogii, my overshoes.

shikéé', behind me; my tracks.

shikéé'jígo, in my rear.

shikee', my feet; my shoes; my foot.

shikéédę́ę́', behind me; in my rear; after me.

shik'ehodeesdlį́į́', I was overpowered; I was conquered; I was defeated; I lost.

shikék'eh, my footprints.

shikéyah, my land; my country.

'ikéyahą́ągóó, toward, or to my former land.

shikéychdi, in my country.

shik'i, upon, on top of me.

shik'iidoołdas, it will crash down on me.

shik'i'iidoolchííł, I will have a nightmare.

shik'ináádiilkǫ, it (water) again covered me.

shik'ináánéigeeh, k'adę́ę, it (water) is again about to cover me.

shik'ináánéigo', it (water) again covered me.

shikingóó, to my house.

shik'i'oolchííł lágo, I hope I do not have a nightmare.

shikǫ', my fire.

shíla', my hands.

shíla' yiisíí, my hand is asleep.

shílázhoozh, my fingers.

shilghał, you eat me up.

shił, with me; in my company.

shił 'ayói 'áhoot'é, I am very partial to it.

shił bééhodoozjíł, I will know about it.

shił bééhózin, I know it; I am informed of it.

shił hodiik'ąąd, I became lonesome; I am homesick.

shił honeeni, I have, or am having fun; I enjoy.........

shił honeesgaigo, since it was nurting me.

shił hóyéé', I am lazy.

shił hóyéé', bik'ee, I am scared of it.

shiłní, he says to me.

shimósí, my cat.

shina'adlo', I am tricky.

shinááhai, I spent............years.

shinááhaigo, since I spent.... ....years.

shinaaí, my older brother.

shinaalte', my slave; my servant.

shináát, in my presence; I am watching (a performance).

shinaanishigíí, the work I do.

shináxt'i', they surrounded me; they have encircled me.

shíni', my mind; my wish.

shiniijj', in, or on my face.

shi'niiłhí, it (disease, etc.) began to kill me.

shí niinii, claimant (at law).

shi'niitsá, I became ill.

shinił'į́, he is looking at me.

shí'níłkǫ́ǫ́', he caught up with me (by swimming).

shíni' náhásdlį́į́', I regained consciousness.

shinínił'į́, you (singular) look at me.

shinísá, he caught up with me (walking).

shinishtł'ajígo, on my left.

shishah, it hooked me.

shishhash, it bit me.

shishish, it stung me.

shisił, he grabbed me.

shistłee', stockings; my socks.

shitah hoditłid, I am shaking (all over); I am shaky.

shitł'izi, my goats.

shitsj', my flesh.

shitsi', my (man speaking) daughter.

shitsídii, my bird.

shitsii', my hair.

shiwos, my shoulder.

shiyáázh, my (a woman speaking) son.

shiya hodíníłhiz, you frightened me; you scared me.

shiye', my (man speaking) son; my (male speaking) nephew (brother's son).

shiyéél, my pack; my load; my packages (as when shopping).

shiyih, my breath.

shiyol, my breath.

shiyol t'áá' 'íínisin, I am holding my breath.

shizhah, it is bent (curved in the middle).

shizhé'é, my father; my uncle (father's brother).

shiztsah, he caught me (with his teeth).

sho, frost.

shódaoozt'e', they were acquired.

shódayoost'e', they acquired them.

shódayoost'e'go, when they acquired it.

shódayoost'e'góó, doo, if they did not acquire it.

shoh, oh, yes (as one says when recalling something).

shóideesht'eeł, I will acquire it.

shóidoot'eeł', it will be acquired.

shóidoot'eełgo, when it is acquired.

shóisélt'e', I acquired it.

shoo, I see (oh, yes).

shọọdí, t'áá, please.

shó'oozt'e', acquisition.

shóozt'e', it has been acquired.

shóozt'e'ę́ę, that which was acquired.

shóozt'e'go, after it was, or is acquired.

si'á, it lies (a single round, or bulky object, as a house, book, mountain, hat, etc.); it sets.

si'á, bił yaa, it is covered by it (as a box is put over raked up leaves to keep them from blowing away).

si'áá, t'áá—ńt'éé', all of it (the whole thing).

si'áné̜egi, where it (a boulder, etc.) used to lie.

si'ánídóó, from where it (a house, etc.) is sitting.

si'ánígíí, that (a house, etc.) which it sitting.

sid, scar.

sidá, he sits (as is said of a baby); he is sitting.

sidáago, while he was sitting.

sidá, dah,· he is perching.

sidáhą́ągóó. where he was siting.

sidáhí, 'awéé' yá, baby-sitter.

sidá, hooghandi, he is at home.

sidá, t'óó, he just sits around.

sido, it is hot; it (object) it warm.

sidogo, t'ahdii, while it (object) was still hot; while it (object) was still warm.

sido, tó, hot water.

sidziil, I am strong; my strength.

sigan, dry; dried (up); dessicated; withered.

sigházla, cigar.

siidzį we (two) are standing.

siii, steam; vapor.

sii! bitoo', distilled water.

siką́, it sets (in a vessel, or container).

sikaad, it (a tree, brush etc.) is standing; it (a rug, blanket, etc.) is spread out.

sik'az, it (an object) is cold.

sik'ází, it (an object) is cool.

sikéh:ę, those (two) that were sitting.

sikéhígíí, those (two) who are sitting.

sik'is, my friend; my sibling (of the same sex).

silá, it lies (a rope, etc.).

siláago binant'a'í, chief of police; army officer.

siláagodę́ę́', from the army; from the armed services.

siláhí, doo—da, there is nothing.

siláoltsoosí, branch of the army.

siláoo, soldier; armed forces; police; law and order forces; policemen; policeman; sheriff.

silį́į́', it, or he became.........

silį́į́'go, since it became.

siłhé, you kill him.

siltsooz, it lies ,a sheet of paper, etc.).

siltsoozgo, while it (a sheet of paper, etc.) was lying.

sindáo, one penny; one cent.

sínídá, you (singular) sit down (a command).

sinil, lying (several inaminate objects); there are appointed ones.

siniłgo, because they were lying (several inanimate objects).

siniligíí, appointed ones.

sinilhí, you killed it.

sinítí, you are lying down; you lie down (a command).

sis, belt, sash; girdle.

sis bighánt'i'í, belt loops.

sisíí', it is piquant, cooling, sour.

sis lichí'i, a sash (woven belt).

sitá, it lies (a single slender stiff object, as a pencil, a pole, etc.).

sitą́ągi, where it (a slender, stiff object) lies.

sitą́ą́góó, t'ááłáhádi tsin, one mile away.

sitánígíí, that (a stiff, slender object) which lies. ,

sit'é, it is cooked (roasting);; it is done (roasting); it is roasted.

sití, he is lying down.

sitíjgo, while he was lying down.

sitíinii, one who is lying down.

Sitíinii, Wáashindoondi, President of the United States.

sitłéé', it (mushy matter as cement, etc.) lies.

sits'áhoniyéé', bąą, I protect myself with it; I am feared because of it.

sitsásk'eh, my bed; my place; the imprint of my body.

sits'il, it shattered; it (as a vase, etc.) is broken.

sitsilí, my younger brother.

sizí, he is standing.

sizíígi, where he is standing.

sizíigo, while he is standing.

siziiz, my belt.

sizílí, it is lukewarm; it is tepid.

sizínę́ę, the one who was standing.

sizínę́ę, where he stood.

sizínigíí, the one who is standing.

sizínigíí, t'ááłá'í, per animal.

sǫ', stars.

sodadeelzin, we prayed; we said a prayer.

sodadiilzingo, when we pray; while we were praying.

sodadilzin, they pray; they are praying.

sodahodizingi, where the people pray.

sodeezin, I said a prayer.

sodizin, a prayer.

sohdool'jił, doo yee——da, he thinks it is too much for him.

sohodizingo, during prayer.

sohodoozin, a prayer was said; there was a prayer.

sonáádadoolzingo, after they again prayed.

Soodził, Mount Taylor.

sǫ'tsoh, evening and morning star.

– T –

t'ą́ą́', back (as move back), backward.

t'áá, just (a particularizing element not readily translatable).

táá', three.

t'áá 'ązdi, back there

t'áá 'aaníí, really; truly; actually; so.

t'áá 'aaníí 'ádíshní, I mean what I said.

t'áá 'aaníí 'át'éii, the real thing; the truth.

t'áá 'ádaat'éegi, every detail.

t'áá 'ádabidii'nínígi 'ádaat'é, they mind us.

t'áá 'ádzaagóó, just aimlessly; just for fun.

t'áá'ágis, to wash; dipping (as dipping sheep in an insecticidal solution).

t'áá 'ádą́ą́dígo, since it was nearby.

t'áá 'ahąąh, simultaneously; at the came time; close together.

t'áá 'aháąh, frequently; often.

t'áá 'aháni, near; close.

t'áá 'ahánídę́ę́', from nearby.

t'áá 'ahánídi, at nearby

t'áá 'ahánígi, nearby; near; adjacent.

t'áá 'ahánígóó, nearby.

t'áá 'ahéédahalníísh, they work all week.

t'áá 'ahinoolingo, since they (two) are identical; since they (two) look alike.

t'áá 'ąjiltso, all of them (people).

t'áá 'áko, all right; that is O.K. (to agree to something); it is satisfactory.

t'áá 'ákódí, that is all.

t'áá 'ákódigo, since that was all.

t'áá 'ákogi na'alkid, it is normal; he has a temperature.

t'áá 'ákónáánádzaa, recur.

t'áá 'ákónáánát'é, it is again the same.

t'áá 'ákónéehee 'át'éii, necessary

t'áá 'ákóniltsóhí, that is all of it (as a story); that is the size of it.

t'áá 'ákǫ́ǫ́, still there; nearby.

t'áá 'ákót'éego, in the same way; if he is the same.

t'áá 'ákwíí, it is the same (in number); each; every.

t'áá 'ákwii, there; at the same place.

t'áá 'ákwíí jį́, each day; every day.

t'áá 'áłah, both; both of them.

t'áá 'áłajį', always; all the time; frequently.

t'áá 'áłch'įįdígo, just a little bit; just a few.

t'áá 'ałch'ishdę́ę́', from both sides

t'áá 'ałch'ishjí, on both sides.

t'áá 'áłts'íísígo, just a small piece.

t'áá 'ałtso, all of it (or them).

t'áá 'ałtsogo, everywhere.

t'áá 'ałtsogóó, everywhere; in all direction.

t'áá 'ałtsoni, everything.

t'áá 'ałtsoni naalkaah bá haz'ą́ą́ góne', hospital laboratory.

t'áá 'anáágo', it fell back; it again flowed back.

t'áá' 'ánát'é, hem; cuff.

t'áá 'ániidígo, recently; a short while ago.

t'áá 'ániit'é, all of us.

t'áá 'ánółtso, all of you.

t'áá 'át'é, all of it; all of them.

t'áá 'át'ego, the total; the whole.

t'áá 'ayáhágo, very little; not much.

t'áá 'áyídigi, nearby; close by.

t'áá 'áyídigóó, nearby.

t'áá bééhodoozįįł, it must be solved; it must be explained.

t'áá béeso, cash; in cash.

t'áá bi, of his own accord; of his own free will; he himself; his own. Díí t'áá bi bikin. This is his own house.

t'áá bí bikéyah, it is his own land.

t'áá bí bini' bik'ehgo, of his own free will.

t'áá bí bini' bik'ehgo chooz'įįdii, a volunteer.

t'áá bí bóhólníih, he himself is the authority; he, or she has the final say.

t'áá bidaneel'ánígíí, those that are of the same size.

t'áá bidziilgo, since he is stronger.

t'áá bighą́ąhjį', it was followed by (event).

t'áá bíhólníhigíí, anything.

t'áá bíhólníhigíí woodlá̧, gullibility.

t'áá bíhólníhigíí yoodlá̧, gullible.

T'áá Bíích'įįdii, Aneth, Utah.

t'áá biji, in his own way; in accord with his own customs.

t'áá bilgo, only with.

t'áá bini'dii, automatically, uncontrolled, unchecked, unattended, uninhabited, unsettled. (Also t'áá bini'idii).

t'áá bi'oh, there is a deficiency.

t'áá bita'ági na'adá, homelessness

t'áá bíyó, rather, slightly, somewhat.

t'áá bizáákớ, not cautious (at the risk of ones life); intrepidly.

t'áá bízhání, only.

t'áá bóhólníihgi, any place; any time; outdoors.

T'á̧ąchil, April.

t'áá dadoohts'a', you have heard about it.

t'áá dahojíyánígíí, the adults (people).

t'áá danitsaa, they are quite large.

tąądee, slowly; gradually.

táádę́ę́', from three places; from three sides; from three directions.

táadi, three times; thrice.

tá'ádígis, to wash (ones self).

t'áá dikwíí, just a few; only a few.

t'áá dilkǫǫhgo, unsaddled, bareback.

táadi mííl, three thousand.

táadi mííl ntsaaigíí, three million.

t'áá diné, Navajo(s).

táadi neeznádíingi 'ánéelą́ą́', there are three hundred.

t'áadoo, do not; did not; without.

t'áadoo 'ádíníní, stop talking; do not say that; hush; be quiet.

t'áadoo 'ájiidzaai da, nothing happened to him.

t'áadoo 'ánít'íní, do not do that (a warning given to a person who is annoying one).

t'áadoo bahat'aadí, obviously; clearly; evidently.

t'áadoo bee choosh'íní da, I am useless.

t'áadoo biniiyéhé da, it is useless , fruitless, futile, profitless, unserviceable, vain, worthless.

t'áadoo haadzíí' da, he said nothing.

t'áadoo hodíína'í, done, or occurring in a short time, soon, quickly, soon after. or in a speedy manner.

t'áado hodina'í, right away; quickly; very soon.

t'áadoo hooyání, suddenly; unexpectedly; without warning.

t'áá doo 'iiníxin da, he just does not want to.

t'áadoo kót'é 'ilíní, unexpectedly; suddenly; without warning; all of a sudden.

t'áadoo le'é, things; something; anything.

t'áadoo le'é, 'ádaal'jigi, a factory.

t'áadoo le'é 'alch'į' be'estł'óonii, bundle.

t'áadoo le'égóó, about anything; about something.

t'áadoo le'é leeyi' dahólóonii, mineral; mineral resources.

t'áadoo naha'nání, motionless.

t'áadoo nahí'nání, keep still; do not move.

t'áadoo nákáhí, before they returned.

t'áadoo shaa nánít'íní, do not bother me; leave me alone.

t'áadoo shich'ą́ą́h sínízíní, do not stand in my way.

t'áadoo yee choo'íní da, valueless (as land), it is useless; he, or it is worthless.

t'áado yígháhí, before he comes; before he came.

t'áadoo yináldzidí da, he is brave; he is bold.

t'áágééd, without.

t'áágééd, bi'éé', he is naked.

tá'ágíí, number three.

táa'go, three of them.

táágóó, three directions; three ways.

taah, into the water.

t'áá haa'í, da, anywhere; any place; any time; some other time; somewhere.

t'áá hahí, soon; in the near future.

t'áá háiida, anyone; someone; whosoever.

t'áá hazhó'ó, rather; somewhat; considerable.

taah dadziz'á, they put it in the water.

taah doot'ááł, it will be put into the water.

taah heełtł'íid, we threw them into the water.

taah jíí'á, he put it in the water.

taah hoyíiłhan, I, or he threw him into the water.

t'áá hó, himself (he himself).

t'áá hó 'ák'ina'adzil, self-sufficiency.

t'áá hooghan haz'ánigi, right around home.

t'áá hooshch'į', suddenly; all at once.

t'áá hótsaago, since the place was larger.

taah yi'á, I put it in the water.

taah yiyíinil, he put them in the water.

t'áá 'iidą́ą́', already; even now.

t'áá 'iishjání, evidently; plainly; unmistakable; visible; conspicuous.

t'áá 'iiyisíí, very; extremely; really.

t'áá 'iiyisíí yá'át'ééh, excellent.

t'áá 'íł hasih, encouragement.

t'ą́ąjigo, backward.

t'áá jiik'é, free of charge; gratis.

t'áákáágóó, outdoors; outside (in the open).

t'áá k'éhózdon, short cut; straight across.

t'áá kojį', just to here.

t'áá kónighánigo, at short intervals; often; frequently.

t'áá kóódigo, slowly.

t'áá łą́ą́góó, in many ways; in many places; many things (as he talked about many things).

t'áá ła'ąjí, in a single day; per day.

t'áá ła'atł'éé', in a single night; over night.

t'áá łá'hádęę', from one direction; from the same place; from one side.

t'áá łáhádi, once (without repetition); one time.

t'áá łáhádi 'adées'eez, one foot (measurement).

t'áálahádi dah 'adiyédlo'go 'áadi hastą́'áadahdi 'ałts'á náánáádzogo t'áałá'í si'ánígíí, one ounce (weight).

t'ááłáhádi mííl, one thousand.

t'ááłáhádi neeznádiin nináháhááhdi, a century.

t'áá łáhádóó, from the same place.

t'áá łáhági, in the same place.

t'ááłáhági 'ádaat'éhigii, those that are of one kind.

t'ááłáhági 'át'éego, constantly; continuously; in just one way.

t'ááłáhá góne', in one place; in the same room.

t'ááłáhágóó, all at one place.

t'áá łáhájigo, all in one direction.

t'áálá'í, one.

t'áálá'í béeso, one dollar.

t'áálá'í dootł'izh, one dime.

t'áá łá'í dzizinígíí, each (person); individually (person).

t'áálá'í hooghanígíí, a family; each hogan.

t'áálá'í ní'ánigo, individually (inanimate object); each one (inaninate object); one by one (inanimate object).

t'áálá'í nitínígo, one by one (animate object); individually (inanimate object).

t'áálá'í nizínígo, individually (animal).

t'áálá'í' sizinígíí, individual (animal).

t'áá łánígo, a little more (in quantity).

t'áá łanináánályaa, relapsed.

t'áá łichí'í, naked; nude; unclothed.

t'áá łichíí, it is raw (uncooked).

t'áá łichíí'go, because it is raw (uncooked).

t'áá naakihigo, just two of them; just two.

t'áá náás daazlíj'íí, the older ones.

táá' naaznili, chapter officers (in Navajo tribal goverment).

t'áá ni', on foot.

tá'ánidadigis góne', in their washrooms.

t'áá nihí, you yourself; you yourselves.

t'áá niik'é, gratis; free of charge.

t'áá niłtééł ńt'éé', everywhere; all over the place.

t''áá nináháhááh bik'eh, annually; each year.

t'"'áá nízaadi, at a distance.

t'áá 'o'oogalíí', everywhere one looks.........

t'áá sahdii, alone; apart; separate; different.

t'áá sáhí, alone; solely; singly; by oneself.

táásógiz, I washed it; I scrubbed it.

t'áá shighangi, right at my house.

t'áá shihí, I myself.

t'áá shíí, perhaps; probably.

t'áá shíí 'áko, oh, well (resignation).

t'áá shiidą́ą́'dii, for a long time.

t'áá shǫǫdí, please.

taaskaal, oatmeal.

t'áá tági, only three (as when asked how many).

t'áá t'ééh, uncooked; raw; not done.

t'áá t''éehgo, since it was not done; because it was uncooked.

t'áá tidílyaa gónaa k'é'éltǫ', direct fracture.

t'áá tł'éé', through the night.

táá'ts'áadah, thirteen.

táá'ts'áadah jí, thirteen days.

t'áá tsjjłgo, faster.

T'ą́ą́tsoh, May (month).

t'áá tsxjjłgo, faster.

t'áá yéego, harder (as pull harder); more severely.

t'áá yiit'ashgo, while we (two) were still walking.

t'áá yikéé' góne', immediately after it.

t'áá yíl''áá ńt'éé', all of them (population); the whole population.

t'áá yílá bee 'ályaa, handmade.

tábąąh, shore, beach.

tábąąhgi, at the shore; at the beach.

tábąąhgóó, along the shore; along the beach.

tábąąhjį'', to the shore; to the beach.

tábąąh mą'ii, muskrat.

tábąąsdísí, snipe.

tábąąstíín, otter.

táchééh, sweathouse.

tádadinééh, they migrate.

tádeidi'aah, they carry it (a bulky, hard object) around.

tádeididzíisgo, when they dragged it around; when they pulled it around.

tádeidigéeshgo, when they shear them.

tádeidíí'eezh, they led them around.

tádídíin, corn pollen.

tádídíin dootł'izh, wild purple larkspur.

tádidookah, they will go around (as inspectors, visitors, etc.).

tádigéésh, it is being shorn.

tádigéeshgo, while they were shearing it.

tádigéshigíí, the one which is being shorn.

tádii'áázh, they (two) walked around; they (two) toured.

tá'dii'eezh, he led (his army) around.

tádiigeeh, we (two) carry it (a burden) around.

tádiin, thirty.

tádiindi, thirty times.

tádiindi mííl, thirty thousand.

tádiin dóó ba'aan tseebíí, thirty eight.

tádiiyá, I traveled.

tádijeeh, they roam.

tá'dínéehgo, when they migrate.

tá'dínéhigíí, their migration.

tádisháah, I am wandering around.

tági jí, for three days.

Tági jí Nda'anish, Wednesday.

t'ahádóó, later on.

t'aháloo, .wait.

táhánii', alkali.

t'ah 'áníid nagháhéędą́ą́', when he was young.

t'ah biláhági 'át'éego, because it was surpassed.

t'ah bítséedi, previous to it; earlier.

t'ahdii, still (adjective), yet; even yet; still.

t'ahdoo, not yet.

t'ah kodą́ą́', beforehand.

t'ah nááśidi, farther away; further on.

t'ah nahdę́ę́', awhile back; in the past.

t'ah ndi, still (time).

tahoniigááh łichii'go naałniihigii, scarlet fever.

tahoniigááh ntsaaigíí, influenza (flu).

tá'í, triplets.

tájiłt'éego, three of them (people).

táláwosh, soap; yucca suds; foam.

tált'é, threesome; trio; three of them (people).

tátchaa' (or chátchaa'), brown prionid beetle.

tátkáá', on the surface of the water.

tátkáá, dijádii, water-strider.

tátkáa'gi, on the surface of the water.

táttł'ááh, the bottom of the water.

táttł'ááh ha'alééh, blue heron.

táttł'ááh yí'éél, it sank; it went to the bottom.

tánáádoodzá, he again traveled; he again went around.

taná'nítka', he brings his herd to the water.

tanáoskai, they (people) dispersed; they adjourned.

ta'neesk'ání, muskmelon; cantaloupe.

ta'neesk'ání 'átts'óózígíí, cucumber.

ta'neets'éhii, cocklebur.

tánídeidi'ish, they take them around (tour).

tániil'éí, dragon fly.

taos'nii', dough.

táshchozhii, swallow (brid).

tátł'id, watermoss; algae.

táyi', in the water.

táyi'déé', out of the water.

táyi'ji', into the water.

tázhdíghááhgóó, wherever he wanders; everywhere he goes.

tázhii, turkey.

tééh', valley.

t'ééhjiyáán, watermelon.

tééh łįį', zebra.

té'é'į, poverty.

tééłhalchi'i, robin.

teeł, cat-tail.

t'eesh, charcoal.

t'éí, only.

t'éiyá, only.

tééłii, burro; donkey; ass.

tééłii yázhí, a young burro.

tį', let's go.

tidááchįįd, beyond human aid; mortally injured.

tidáálnáanii, the casualties.

tidáálná, they were injured.

tidáálnáhéę, those who were injured.

tidáálnánígíí, the injured ones; the wounded.

tidadiilyaa, they were injured.

ti'dahooníih, they are suffering; they are having a hard time.

ti'dahooznii', they suffered.

ti'dahwiizhdoonih, they will suffer; they will be punished.

tidiilyaa, he was wounded; or injured.

ti'dílyaa, wound; injury.

ti'hoo'níih, suffering.

ti'hwiisénii', I suffered; I underwent hardship.

ti'hwiizhdoonih, he will suffer; he will he punished.

t'įįhdigo, a little bit; somewhat.

t'įįhí ba'ánigo, a little more than it; a few more than it.

t'iis, cottonwood.

t'iisbái, aspen.

T'iis 'Íí'áhí, Pine Springs, Arizona.

T'iis Názhąs, Teec Nos Pos, Arizona; Fort Summer, New Mexico.

T'iis Nitsaa Ch'éélį, Bluewater, New Mexico.

T'iistoh, Puertocito, New Mexico.

T'iistoh Sikaad, Burnham, New Mexico.

T'iists'óóz Nídeeshgizh, Crownpoint, New Mexico.

T'iis Yaakin, Holbrook, Arizona.

T'iis Yáázh Łání, Valley Store, via Chinle, Arizona.

tin, ice.

tin 'atk'i dilkǫǫh, glacier.

tin bee naajaahí, ice tongs.

tiniléí, gila monster.

tł'aai, a left-handed person.

tł'aaji'éé', trousers; pants; slacks.

tł'aakał, skirts; dresses.

tłah, salve; ointment.

tł'éé'', night.

tł'éédą́ą́', last night.

tł'ée'go, during the, or at night.

tł'eestsooz, kotex; breech-cloth.

tł'éhonaa'éí, moon.

tł'é'iigáhí, evening primrose.

tł'é'iiłnii', mid-night.
tł'ézhii, bee.
tł''id, flatulent expulsion.
tł'iish, snake.
tł'iish 'ánínígíí, rattle snake.
tł'ízí, goat.
tł'ízí chǫǫh, billygoat (also, tł'ízíkǫ').
tłízí da'ałchíní, mountain goat.
tł'ízíkǫ', billygoat.
tł'ízí'ílí, angora goat.
tł'ízí yázhí, kid.
tł'oh, grass; hay; straw.
tł'ohazihii, mormon tea (plant).
tł'oh bee hilghaałí, scythe.
tł'oh bee naaljoołí, pitch forks.
tł'oh bee yilzhéhí, mowing machine; grass shears; scythe.
tł'ohchin, onion.
Tł'ohchini, Ramah, New Mexico
tł'oh naadą́ą́', wheat
tł'oh naadą́ą́' biya', chinch bug.
tł'oh nástasí, foxtail grass; grama grass
tł'oh waa'í, alfalta.
tł'oh yishbizh, burlap; gunnysack.
tł'óó', outdoors.
tł'óó'dę́ę́', from the outside.
tł'óo'di, (at) the outside; outdoors.
tł'óo'góó, outdoors; toward; outside.
tł'óół, rop; cord; twine; lariat; string.
tł'óółts'ósí, cord; string.
tó, water.
Tó Bééhwiisgání, Pinedate, New Mexico
tó bee naakáhí, bucket; pail.
tó biishgháán, waves (on water).
tó biisxį́, he drowned.
tó dilchxoshí, soda pop.
tódiłhił, whiskey.
Tódiłhił Biih yilį́, Snowflake, Arizona.
Tó Díneeshzhee', Kayenta, Arizona.
tó dóó níyol 'ooghashigii, erosion.
tó hą́ą́, what used to be water.
Tóhaach'į', Tohatchi, New Mexico.
Tóháálį, Toadlena, New Mexico.
tó hahadleeh, well (water).
Tó Hahadleeh, Indian Wells, Arizona.
Tó Hajiileehé, Canoncito, New Mexico.

Tó Hajilohnii, Santo Domingo Tribe.
tó hayiiłt'oodí, pump (water).
Tó Hwiisxíní, White Horse Lake, New Mexico.
tó'iiłtą́, water blister.
tók'eh hashchiin, reservoir.
tókǫ'í, petroleum.
Tó Łání, Tolani Lakes, Arizona.
tó łichxi'í, soda pop; wine.
tó łikaní, soda pop; wine.
tó łigání halchiní, perfume.
tó náádadiidáhigíí, waves (as of sea, or ocean).
Tó Naneesdizí, Tuba City, Arizona.
Tó Nehelį́įh, Tonalea, Arizona.
tó nílínígíí, stream; brook; river.
Tóníłts'ílí, Crystal, New Mexico.
Tónitsaa, Tunicha Lake.
tónteel, ocean; sea, lake.
tónteel bibąąhgi, seashore.
tónteeldi, on the ocean.
tónteelgóó, to the ocean.
tónteel tsá'naadi, abroad; overseas.
tónteel wónaanídi, over-seas.
t'óó, merely; just for fun.
t'óó 'aa'ádeet'aah, surrender.
t'óó'ádíni, you are just kidding.
t'óó'ádishni, I am just joking.
t'óó'hayói, there are many; there are lots of them; there is much; numerous.
t'óó'ąhayóidi, many times.
t'óó'ahayóigo, a lot of them; in many places.
t'óó'ahojíyóí, there are many people.
t'óó'áni, he says it without meaning it; he is just kidding.
t'óó'átsééd, temporary; temporarily.
t'óó'átsééd, hooghan, camp.
t'óó baa hasti', risky; hazard.
t'óó baa'ih, dirty; filthy; ugly; no good.
t'óó báhodoonih, he, or it, is a nuisance; it is annoying.
t'óó bahoo'ih, the place is unsanitary; the place is disagreeable.
t'óó béédoochid, he was merely released.

t'óó bík'ijigóó, wishy-washy (giving lip service, assenting just because others do without serious intentions).

t'óó bił daahaadago, because they were confused.

t'óó ch'idaast'ánigo, briefly.

t'óó dahwéédzíí', they merel cussed them out.

t'óó dzólníigóó, just any way; aimlessly.

tóógóó, to the waterhole.

tooh, river; lake.

toohjj', up to the river.

toohjj' nidiigaii, snowy egret.

toohjj' noołnahii, blue heron.

tooh nílíní, river.

t'óó 'ił 'át'į, imagination.

t'óó kónígháníjį', temporarily; just for a little while.

t'óó kónízáháji', just for a little while; temporarily.

t'óó nahalin, it merely seems.

t'óó náhodi'naahgo, every once in a while.

t'óó nichxǫ'í, it is filthy ,ugly, no good.

t'óó níhéśdzíí', he merely cussed us out.

tó shąąh hazlįį', I am sweating; I am perspiriing.

tóshchíín, cornmeal gruel.

tóshjeeh, water-bottle (wicker); water-barrel (with staves and hoops); keg.

Tóta', Farmington, New Mexico.

tótł'iish, water snake.

Tówoł, Taos, New Mexico.

Tó Wołnii, Taos Indians.

tó yigeed, canal; ditch (for water).

tózháán, thin (as a batter); mushy.

tózis, bottle; tumblers; jars (glass).

ts'aa', a basket (wicker).

ts''aa' 'ádeił'íní, basket makers.

tsá'ászi', yucca; soapweed.

tsá'ászi' nteeli, broad !eafed (latil) yucca.

tsá'ászi'ts'óóz, narrow leafed (amote) yucca.

ts'ah, sagebrush; sage.

tsah, awl; needle.

tsąhodiniihtsoh, typhoid fever.

tsąhodiniihtsoh naałniih, typhoid.

tsahts'ósí, needle.

tsa'ii, female (animal).

ts'ání, pinon jay.

tsásk'eh, a bed.

tsásk'ed bikáá' dah naazyinigíí, mattress.

tsé, rock; stone; boulder.

tsé'áán, rock cave.

tsé'ak'i ya'ii'áhii, sphinx caterpillar.

Tsé 'Ałnáozt'i'í, Sanostee, New Mexico.

tsé 'ást'éí, piki (Indian paper. cornbread); hotcakes; flapjacks; griddel cakes.

tsé 'ást'éí łigaaigíí, white piki.

tsé 'áwózí, flint (rocks).

tsé bee 'ak'aashí, grindstone; whetstone.

tsé bilátahjį' dahees'óozgo daastł'inii, pyraminds.

Tsé Bit'a'í, Shiprock Pinnacle, New Mexico.

Tséch'ízhí, Rough Rock, Arizona.

tsédaashch'íní, upper millstone; mano (of the metate).

tsédaashjéé', millstone (lower); metate.

tsédei (tséde), lying on one's back (in a supine position).

tsé dík'ǫ́ǫ́zh, alum.

tseebídiin, eighty.

tseebíí, eight.

tseebíidi míil, eight thousand.

tseebíijj, eight days.

tseebííts'áadah, eighteen.

tsé'édǫ́ǫ́ii, a fly (insect).

tsee'é, skillet; frying pan.

tseek'inásténii, squirrel.

tsé'ésdaazii, mountain mahogany.

tsé'ést'éí, pancake; hotcake; paper bread.

tséghádi'nídinii, rock crystal.

Tségháhoodzání, Window Rock, Arizona.

tsehégod, a stump (tree).

tséhigíí, the rocks.

Tséhootsooí, Fort Defiance, Arizona.

Tsé 'Íí'áhí, Standing Rock, New Mexico.

tsékáá'jį', to the top of the rock.

tsék'ina'azólii, rock lizard.

tsék'iz, rock crevice.

tsékooh, rock canyon; gorge.

Tse Łichíí' Dah Azkání, Red Rock, Arizona.

tsé'naa, across.

tsé'naa na'nízhoozh, bridge.

Tsé Náhádzoh, Twin Lakes, New Mexico.

Tsé Naní'áhí, Rainbow Natural Bridge, Utah.

Tsé Náshchii', Hunter's Point, Arizona.

tsé nástánii, petrified wood.

tsé nei'áhí, scarabee. (Also tsé yoo'áłí, or chąąneiłhizii).

tsé nidaaz, iron ore.

tsénił, ax; stone ax.

tsénil yázhí, hatchet; tomhawk.

Tsé Nitsaa Deez'áhí, Rock Point, Arizona.

tsé noolch'óshii, rock wren.

tsé sikaad, pavement.

tésǫ', glass; mica; window; pane; window.

tsésǫ'déé', through the window.

tsésǫ naat'oodí, celluloid; film.

tséstíin, a chronic physical condition.

tsétah, a rocky place.

tsétah dibé, bighorn; mountain sheep.

tsétahgo, because the place was rocky.

tsétahgóó, amongst the rocks.

tsétah tł'izí, rocky mountain goat.

tsét'ees, griddle stone.

tsétł'ééł, stone flint (igniter).

tsétsoh, boulder.

Tsétsohk'id, Mishongnovi (Second Mesa, Arizona).

tsé'yaa, face down.

Tsé Yaaniichii', Rehoboth, New Mexico.

tsé yázhí, pebbles.

Tséyi', Canyon de Chelly.

tsé yoo'áłí, scarabee (Also chąąneiłhizii, or tsé nei'áhí).

tsézéí, gravel.

Tsézhįįh Deezlį, Black Rock, New Mexico (near zuni).

tsézhin (chézhin), lava; traprock.

Tsézhin Deez'áhí, St. Johns, Arizona.

tsibąąs, hoop (wooden).

ts'idá, really; verily; exactly; precisely.

ts'idá 'áłtsé, the original; the very first one; the very first thing.

tsí'deesyiz, astonishment.

tsi'deeyá, he got drunk; he became delirious.

tsídeezkééz, yaa, he started thinking about it.

tsídékééz, I began to think.

tsídídééh, purple four-O'clock.

tsídii, bird.

tsídii bichaan, guano.

tsídii bidaa', beak (bird).

tsídii bit'oh, nest (bird).

tsídiiłtsooí, yellow warbler.

tsídíkos, yąąh, he begins to think about it.

tsidił, stick dice.

tsidiłdǫǫhii, screech owl.

tsigháą'di, in a tree top.

tsihał, wooden club.

tsi'"hidikááh, they get drunk.

tsíhodeeskééz, it caused him to realize.

Ts"íhootso, St. Michaels, Arizona.

ts'iid, t'áá, it is better.

tsii'détáán, spear.

tsiighá yilzhééh bá hooghan, a barbar shop.

tsiighá yishéhé, a barber.

ts'íih niidóóh, fever.

tsiih yít'óód, abrasion.

ts'i'ii, gnat.

ts'i'ii danineezí, mosquito.

ts'iilzéí, trash; rubbish.

tsįįł, rapidly,

tsįįłgo, quickly; fast; rapidly; swiftly.

tsįįkaałii, woodpecker.

tsiináxt'i'í, headband.

tsiis'áál, pillow.

tsiisch'ilí, curly hair.

tsiishgaii, pygmy nuthatch.

tsiitah'aba', dandruff.

tsiitł'óół, hair cord (for tying up the hair).

tsiits'iin diniih 'azee', aspirin.

tsiis'in, skull.

ts'iiyahwozhii, meadow lark.

ts'iizis, headbasket (used for carrying things).

tsiízis, scalp

Tsiizizii, Leupp, Arizona.

tsilghááh, waterdog; salamander; mud puppy.

tsįłígo, t'áá, hurriedly.

tsilkéi, young men; adolescents (male).

tsilt'ádineez'ééł, It ran aground.

tsilts'áhájeehgo, when they run ashore.

tsilts'áná'níłkǫ́ǫ́', he swam back to shore.

tsilts'ání'ááxh, they (two) went ashore.

tsilts'áníjéé', they ran ashore.

tsilts'ázhníjaa', he took them ashore.

ts'in, bone.

tsin, wood, tree timber.

tsinaabąąs, wagon.

tsinaabąąs bee bínídiidlohí bá naní'áhí, brake bar.

tsinaabąąs bíishghą́ą́n, coupling pole (of a wagon).

tsinaabąąs bijáád, wagon wheel.

tsinaabąąs bijáád béésh bináz'áhígíí, tire rim (wagon wheel).

tsinaabąąs bijáád binaneeskáligíí, spokes (of a wagon wheel).

tsinaabąąs bijáád bita' naní'áhí, axle tree (of wagon).

tsinaabąąs bijáád bitsiits'iin, hub (of wagon wheel).

tsinaabąąs bijáád tsin bináz'áhígíí, felloes (of a wagon wheel).

tsinaabąąs bik'ésti'í, wagon cover.

tsinaabąąs bits'a', wagon box.

tsinaabąąs bítsą́ą́', wagon bows.

tsinaabąąs bits'a' bá ni'áhí, bolster (of a wagon)

tsinaabąąs bits'a' bá ni'áhí bił 'ii'áhígíí, king bolt (of a wagon).

tsinaabąąs dijadí, buggy.

tsinaabąąs yázhí bijáád naakiigíí, cart.

tsinaa'eeł, ship; boat; canoe; vessel; raft.

tsinaa'eeł bee da'ahijigánígíí, battleship.

tsinaa'eeł táłtł'áahdi ndaakaaígíí, submarine.

tsinaalk'į, boomerang.

tsinaalzhoodí, sled; sleigh.

ts'inádzid, he awakened.

ts'in 'aháálkid, dislocation (of the bone).

ts'in 'aháálto' loose fracture.

ts'in 'ahiihyííjzh, impacted fracture.

tsin 'anáhálghą́hí, javelin.

tsin bahásht'óózh, bark. (Also 'azhííh).

tsin bee bigháda'a'nilí, brace and bit.

tsin bee diilkǫǫhí, wood plane.

tsin bee hahalzhíshí, wood chisel.

tsin bee na'adáhí, crutches.

tsin bee nihech'iishí, saw (tool).

tsin bee nihijíhí, wood saw.

tsin bee yigołí, wood rasp.

ts'in bik'é'sti' gónaa k'é'éłtǫ', intra-capsular fracture.

tsin bineest'ą', fruit.

tsin bisgą', snag; dead tree.

tsin bits'áoz'a', bough.

tsindáo, penny; one cent.

ts'in di'įdí siljį'go k'é'éłtǫ', senile fracture.

ts'in díízáíí, multiple fracture.

tsin dit'inii, rock squirrel.

ts'in doo bik'é'ásti' gónaa k'é'éłtǫ', extra-capsular fracture.

ts'inę́ę, the bones.

ts'in hasht'e' ninálkeed, setting a bone.

tsindi'ni', bull-roarer.

tsin 'ii'áii, a tree.

ts'in k'égiz, spiral fracture.

ts'in k'idi'nidééł dóó binaatidílyaa, compound fracture.

tsinlátah 'ayánii, giraffe.

tsin naalzhoodí, sled.

tsin na'ayq'ii, wood louse; termites.

tsin niheeshjíí', lumber; hoards.

ts'in niheestǫ', multiple fracture.

ts'in ni't'eezdił, greenstick fracture.

tsin sitą́, mile; yard (measurement).

tsintah, forest.

tsintahgi, in the forest.

tsin tóshjeeh, wooden barrel.

tsints'ósí, sticks (objects).

tsis'ná, bee, honey bee.

tsis'ná bighan, beehive.

tsis'ná bijeeh, beeswax.

tsis'ná bitł'izh, honey.

tsis'náłtsooí, wasp.

tsis'nátsoh, bumble-bee.

tsisteeł, turtle.

tsístíín, chronic.

tsístł'aakahgo, when they are cornered; when they get stumped.

tsitł'éłí, matches (articles for starting a fire).

tsi't'oolyiz, shock.

tsits'aa', wooden box.

tsits'aa' bee yóó' 'ádaho'dilne'ígíí, coffin, casket.

tsits'aa' naadlo'í, suitcase; valise.

tsits'aa' ntsaaígíí, trunk (used for packing articles); footlocker.

tsízdookos, bąqh, he will think about it.

ts'ǫ'asánii, tadpole.

........tsoh, big; large.

tsosts'id, seven.

tsosts'id dootł'izh, seventy cents.

tsosts'idgo, seven of them.

tsosts'idi, seven times.

tsosts'idiin, seventy.

tsosts'idi neeznádiin, seven hundred.

tsosts'id ts'áadah, seventeen.

tsxįįłgo, hurry up.

- W -

waa', beeweed.

Wááshindoon, Washington, D. C.; the Federal Government.

Wááshindoondi 'atah bee haz'áanii 'íít'íní-gíí, congressman.

Wááshindoondi beehaz'áanii 'ádeit'jjgo dah naháaztánigíí, Congress.

Wááshindoon yá ndaalnishigíí, Federal employees.

Wááshindoon yá nda'atkaahigíí, Federal Bureau of Investigation.

wódah, up.

wódahdéé', from above.

wódahgo, up higher.

wókeed, petition.

wóláchíí', red ant.

wólázihní, black ant.

wólta'go, when it is being counted.

wolyé, he, she, is called; it means; his name is.

wolyéego, since it is called.

wolyéii, that which is called.

wónaanídee', from the other side.

wónaanídi, the other side.

wónaanígóó, toward the other side.

wónáásdóó, finally; after that; later on; and then.

wóne é, inside, in the interior, of an enclosure.

wóniidi, the area between the fire and the back wall of the hogan; rear part of a room.

woodlánigíí, belief.

wóóh, yoo hoo!

woolk'ááh, tinder box.

wóóneeshc'jjdii, seventeen year cicada.

wóóshiyishí, measuring worm.

wóósits'ílí, bedbug.

woosye', he was named.

wóózhch'jjd, March.

wóshch'ishidi, come closer; farther this way.

woshdéé', from there to here; this way; here ....here (as in calling to another player to throw the ball to one).

wóshdéé'go, this way (direction).

wótsiní, pyorrhea.

wóyah, low.

wóyahgo dit na"atkid, low blood pressure.

– Y –

yá, for him; sky.

ya', shall I? isn't it?

yaa, he (gave it, etc.) to him; he (talked, etc.) about it; down; downward.

yaa', louse; tick; mite.

yaa 'ádahalyáanii, those over which they are in charge.

yaa 'áhályą́ągo, since he is charge of it; since he is looking after it.

yaa 'ahééh daniizį́į', they are thankful for it.

yá'qqsh, heaven; celestial space; region beyond the sky.

yaa bił hózhǫ́, he is happy about it he is pleased about it.

yáádaa'á, piles of.........

yáádaa'áa łeh, there are usually piles of.....

yaa daadlee', they are generous · ·· ·· ·· ·· ··

yá'ą́łaashǫ́ǫ' doo da, they are evil, they are wicked.

yá'áłaat'ééh, they are good; they are well; they are getting along fine.

yá'áłaat'ééh, bił, they like it; they are satisfied with it.

yá'ádaat'éeh, da, doo bił, they dislike it. they do not approve of it.

yá'ádaat'ééhgóó, doo bił, because they dislike it; because they do not approve of it.

yá'áłaat'ééhii, those that are good.

yá'ádaat'ééhii, doo, those that are worthless; the evil ones.

yaa dahalni', they are telling about it.

yaa dahalni'ii, whatever they are talking about.

yaa dahani'go, when they tell about it.

yaa dahaniih, they praise it.

yá'édahoot'ééh, nice, clean places.

yá'édahoot'éehgo, because they are nice places.

yaa dajoobe they treat him well; show him mercy

yaa deinít'į, they are discussing it.

yeego, downward

yąqh, alongside it.

yáah, wow (amazement)!

yąqh 'áda'iilaago, after they treated it (with something).

yáah what (did you say)?

yaa halni he tells about it.

yaa nalni go, when he tells bout it.

yaʕ halni'igii, what he tells about.

yǫ ą dah neeshjįįd, he grabbed it (before it got away).

yáhiideeshchah, I will jump up.

ʕá'áhoot'ééh, it is a good place; the weather is good.

yá'áhoot'ééhgóó, doo, if the weather is bad; if the place is bad.

yaa jooba', he is kind to it.

yáál, bit (12 ½ cents).

yaaltáalgo, when he took off (running).

yá 'ałnii', the zenith.

yááłti', he talked; he made a speech.

yááłti'go, when he made a speech.

yaa nádáahgo, when he visits him.

yaa ndaas'na', they ambushed them; they sneaked up on them.

yaa ńdaast'jįd, they discussed it.

yaa ńdaat'jįgo, while they were discussing it.

yaa ńdaat'inígíí, whatever they are discussing.

yaa nichį́', to value it highly, cherish it; to be stingy with it.

Yaa Niilk'id, Gap, Arizona (sometimes called **Tsinaabąąs Habitiin**).

yaa'nił'ééI, he rowed to it.

yaa nínáádaast'įįd, they again discussed it.

yá'ánisht'ééh, I am well.

yá'át'ééh, greetings; hello; fine; suitable; pretty; he is well; he is good; must (when used as good for an action) as, The applicant must speak English. **Naanish yó keedii Bilagáana yidiits'a'go yá'át'ééh.** (Lit. work one who asks English he understand must.).

yá'át'éehgo, if he is well.

yá'át'ééh, bił, he likes it.

yá'át'éehgo nísékeesii, one that thinks well.

yá''át'ééh náádleeł, he is recuperating.

yá'át'ééh náádleełii, convalescent (person).

yá'át'ééh ná'oodleeł, convalescence.

yá'át'ééh násdlį́į', he recovered (from illness, or injury), he got well.

yá'át'ééh ndoohdleeł, you (two) will get well.

yá'át'ééh ni'doodleeł, to get well.

yaareeł, sheepskin (for bedding).

yá áti', speech.

yaa tiih yikaigo, when they ganged up on them.

yáátis, over it (up).

yáá tsik'eh, really (to express incredulity of a tale, or statement that appears to be a gross exaggeration of the truth)!

yáázh, little; small; young (as **béégashii yáázh**, a calf.

yádaałti', they are talking.

yádaałti'go, when they talk.

yádaałti', yee, they speak it.

yadadiitł'inę́ę, those that were piled up (systematically).

yá dadilwoshgo, while they were cheering for him.

yádajiłti', baa, they are talking abut it.

yádajiłti'go, while they were talking.

yá deiiłkango, because they kept pepping them up.

yadiizíní, tin can.

yá dithił, blue sky.

yah, inside.

yah 'adahakááh, they go in (one after another).

yah 'adeesbąs, I will drive it in (as to drive a car into a garage).

yah 'anáálwod, he ran back inside.

yáhásin, embarrassment; bashfulness; shame.

yah 'íí'áázh, they (two) walked in; they (two) entered (as into a house).

yah 'i'iiniiłii, policeman; sheriff.

yáhóółchįįd, he made it, or him angry.

Ya'iishjááshchilí, June.

Ya'iishjáástsoh, July.

yajiiłtáál, he took off (running).

yájiłti'go, when he was talking.

yáłti', he is talking; he talks.

yáłti'go, while he was talking.

yanáá'á, pile (a heap).

yá naał'a'go, while he (as a servant) was serving him.

yanáałdááz, it splashed up into the air.

yá naaziinii, their representatives.

Ya'niilzhiin, Torreon, New Mexico.

yánílti', speak up.

yá'níłtsood, he shared with him (as food).

ya'ooz.ii', he put his trust in him.

yas, snow.

yas bił 'ahaniheeyołígii, snowdrift.

yáshti', I am talking.

Yas Niłt'ees, January. (Also **Zas Niłt'ees**).

yátashki', bastard.

yáti', speech.

yáti'ii, baa, what is being talked about.

yayiitsih, he raised it up (slender stiff object.)

yázhí, little; small; young (as **télii yázhí**, young burro).

yee, with; by means of.

yéé', terror; fright; horror.

yę́ę, aforementioned; the one already referred to.

yee' ák'idadéekáah, they support themselves by it.
yéedą́ą́', at a time in the past; ago; since.
yéédaaldzid, they fear it.
yéédaaldzidí, t'áadoo—da, they are brave.
yéédaalniih, they remember it.
yéédaasdziid, they became scared of it; they became afraid of it.
yééda'deeztą́, they came to understand it; they invented it.
yééda''deeztą́ą́go, when they invented it.
yééda'diitjihii, what they have invented.
yéédahoosjįd, they recognized it, or him.
yéédahósin!'' they know it, or him; they are familiar with it.
yéédahósinii, doo, something with which they are unfamiliar; something they do not know.
yeeda'iidlaa, they copied it.
yéédeidiiłt'ihgo, because they tie it to it.
yéédi'nítą́, he invented it; he guessed it.
yéego, diligently; hard; seriously.
yéego 'áhoodzaa, to get worse.
yee hadadít'éii, what they wear.
yééji', it was named.
yéélta', they were counted; it was read.
yee ndaanéhigii, that which they are playing (music, etc).
yee ńdadiineehgo, when they start playing it (music, etc.).
yee ńdahonilnééh, they win with it.
yee 'oo''į, he sees with it.
yee yich'į' haadzii', he mentioned it to him.
yee yinééł'įį'go, after he looked at him with it.
yéigo, hard. (Also yéego).
yé'ii, the gods.
ye'iił'įih, he copies it.
Ye'iineezii, Shalako (of Zuni Indian).
yé'iitsoh, a giant.
yélyeed, he is catching up (running) to it.
yénáálnii', he recalled it; he remembered it
yi'ash, yił, he is walking with him.

yibqqhgóó, along its edge.
yibéezhgo, while it was boiling.
yibizh, he is braiding it. Bitsii' yibizh. She is braiding her hair
yicha, he is crying.
yichago, while he was crying.
yich'į', toward him.
yichííhii, bá, their offspring.
yich'iji, on his side (as team, etc.).
yich'iji siijj', he took sides with him.
yíchxǫ', it is spoiled; it (as a dance, etc.) was interruupted. It went out of order; it is ruined.
yiłchxǫ', I ruined it.
yidą́, it is being eaten; it is edible.
yidáąh yílwod, he ran out to meet him.
yida'asnii'go, since they notified them.
yidá lanooiní, they want it (badly).
yida leeschid, they put their thumb prints on it; they touched it (one after another).
yida'dooliił, they will copy it; they will adapt themselves to it.
yidchooł'ą́'qq, what they had learned.
yidchooł'ą́ą́', they learned it; they studied it.
yidchooł'ą́ą'go, when they learned it.
yidchooł'aah, they are studying it; they are learning it.
yidchooł'aahii, what they are learning; what they are studying.
yiadhooł'aahí, t'áadoo, before they learned it.
yid hooł'ą́'igíí, what they learned.
yida'iiłt'o'go, since they suckle them.
yidaneedlį, they are interested in it.
yidanéédlįįd, they became interested in it
yida'niiyą́ą́', they began to eat it.
yidaniłdzil, they can stand it; they resist it
yide'ádzaa, they (livestock) became too much for it (land).
yídéelni'go, yíchą́, since he craved it.
yidéeltǫ', slippery (as a bar of soap).
yidéeshbeeł, I will pick them (berries, etc)

yideeshchih, I will dye it red.
yideeshch'it, I will curl it.
yideests'ǫ́ǫd, he pulled on it.
yideez, it was signed.
yideezgoh, it collided with it.
yideeztsi, he pointed it.
yidii'eezh, dah, he led them off.
yidiijaa', dad, he carried them off.
yidiit'a', dah, he sent him off (as on an errand, etc.).
yidiitkǫǫh, he is getting it smooth.
yidiiltaa', he shattered it.
yidiittła, he set it afire.
yidiilts'a'go, since he is making noise with it.
yidiiniid, she said to him.
yidiizts'ą́ą́', he heard it (a noise, etc.); he came to understand it.
yidin danlį, they crave it; they need it; they lack it; they coved it.
yidin danliinii, those things that they crave, lack, or need.
yidini'ánígíí, yaa, that which he turned over to them.
yidiniil'ą́, he put his head against it.
yidinlį, he craves it; he needs it.
yidinóot'įįł, he will see it.
yidisin, he, or she observes.
yidloh, he is smiling; he is laughing; he is giggling.
yidoo'aał, it (event) will be put on.
yidoochih, it will become red.
yidooghas, it will scratch it; it will claw it.
yidooyįįłii, that which he will eat.
yidoolch'it, it will become curly; it (shirt, etc.) will become wrinkled.
yi'dooliił, he will copy it; he will adapt himself to it.
yidooliił, doo haada—da, he will do nothing to it; he will not hurt him.
yidóoltah, they will be counted; it will be read.
yidoot'aał, he will send him (as on an errand).
yidootchxǫǫłigíí, that which will ruin.

yi'doołnih, yee, he will notify him of it.
yidoonih, he will hear about it.
yidoonił, haa, he will give them to him.
yidooyįįł, he will eat it.
yidzíí'', they remained, are left.
yidzíí', t'áá díkwíí, few are left.
yidzíí', 'áłch'įįdi, there is a little bit left.
yidziih, it remains, is remaining, or is left.
  Shibéégashii 'ashdladiin ńt'éé', k'ad 'éí naadiin yidziih. I had fifty head of cattle, now I only have 20 left.
yidziihígíí, remainder.
yigáát, he is walking.
yigáałgo, while he was walking.
yigháád, he is shaking it.
yigháahgo, yiih, as he was walking into it.
yiháázh, he nibbles it.
yigíí, that which is; the one............
yih, oops (as when one nearly drops something)!
yihah, a year is going by.
yihahą́ą́dą́ą́', during the course of a (past) year.
yihę́ę́s, an itching of the skin.
yihoot'ą́ą́', he learned it.
yihoot'ąą go, when he learns it.
yii', in it.
yiideestsxis, he banged it against it.
yiih, into it.
yiih yi'na', he crawled into it.
yiih yiyiijaa', he put them (separable objects) into it.
yi'iilaa, he copied it.
yi'iilaago, because he copied it.
yi'iit'įįh, he copies it.
yiijéé', biih, we ran into it.
yii'jį', to a point in it.
yiijįį', it turned black; it became black.
yiilgááh, to whiten.
yiiljh, you taste it.
yiiltsą́, we (two) saw it; it was seen.
yiiltsánígíí, what we (two) saw; what was seen.
yiiltsxóóh, to dye yellow.

yiiłch'iil, I curled it. Shitsii' yiiłch'iil. I curled my hair.

yiiłkah, you shoot it (with bow and arrow).

yiiłtsą́, I saw it.

yiiłtsą́nę́ę, what I saw.

yiiłtsání, t'áadoo—da, I saw nothing.

yiishchįįh, I know how to do it; I am good at it.

yiishgááh, to get white.

y'ishłihgóó, t'ah doo, before I tasted it.

yiishnih, I am milking her (a cow).

yiisíí', it became numb.

yiitsxóóh, to turn yellow.

yiízhniiłdon, he fired at it; he took a shot at it.

yiizį', or he, stood up; it (a car, etc.) stopped.

yiiznil, yaa, he gave them (one after another).

yijah, they are running.

yikáá', upon it.

yikáá'dóó, from upon it.

yikáá'góó, above it.

yikáa'jį', to a point upon it.

yiká'anájahgo, because they help him.

yiká 'análwo', he helps him.

yiká 'análwo'go, because he helps him.

yilk'ąąs, he is straightening it (staff slender object) out.

yik'aash, he is grinding it; he is sharpening it.

yikáá' yoozohgo, he is putting them down in writing.

yikahígíí, those that are walking.

yikai, they arrived; they (people) came.

yikáisdáhí, milky way, (See Łee'áán yilzhódí).

yikai, yił, they arrived with him.

yiká nda'ałkid, they are scheming around for it.

yik'é, for it (in payment).

yik'ee, because; on account of.

yikéé', after it (pursuing).

yikéédę́ę́', behind it; following it.

yik'ehnáádadeesdlįį'go, after they again defeated them.

yikék'eh, in place of it; in its footprint.

yikék'e nájah, they readily accept his way.

yik'élwod, he came upon it.

yik'é ndaalnishígíí, what they work for.

yik'é nda'azłáago, since they paid for it.

yik'i, upon it.

yik'i bił ch'i'iłwodgo, when he ran over it (with his car).

yik'i da'di'dootįįł, they will understand it.

yik'i da'diitánę́ę, those that came to understand it.

yik'i dahineezhchą́ą́', they abandoned it (by fleeing); they ran away and left it.

yik'i dahoneeskaad, they were driven off of it.

yik'i dées'eez, he has his foot on it.

yik'i deiłgish, they cut it (skin, etc.) off of it.

yik'ídeisas, they sprinkled it with it.

yik'i'diitįįhgo, when he understands it.

yikiin, on their sustenance.

yik'i haajeeh, they run around on it; they are trampling it.

yik'i naakai, they are walking on it.

yik'i naháaztánígíí, what they are sitting on.

yik'inéijah, they attack them.

yik'iniyá, he came upon it; he found it.

yil'á, they are scattered.

yilqqd, it became much, many; it increased.

yiláah, beyond it.

yiłą́ąjį', ahead of it.

yil'áá ńt'éé', all of them (animate objects).

yilák'edoolnii', he shook hands with him.

yilch'ozh, boil; furuncle.

yildééh, to wipe off.

yildin da, doo, he is despised.

yildloozh, it came (animal).

yildzis, furrow; groove.

yileeh, he will become.

yileehę́ędą́ą́', t'ah doo, before he became.....

yileehgo, while he was becoming.

yilį, biih, it is flowing into it.

yilk'id, ridge.

yilk'ool, ripples; waves (as of a pond).

yilk'ooligii, wave.

yilt'ę, there are............of them (people).

yilt'éego, since there are............or them.

yiltsooz, it (a flat flexible object) was brought (to a point).

yilwod, yiih, he ran into it (went inside); he went aboard (train, etc.).

yilwoł, he is running.

yilyá, baa, it (a slender flexible object) was given to him.

yilzą, it (a hide) was cured.

yilzhóli, fluffy; soft.

yilzólii, bijéí, his, or its lungs.

yił, with (See bił).

yiłąąd, I made many.

yił 'ahijoodłáhąą, one whom he used to dislike.

yił 'ahinoolin, he looks like him.

yił 'áłah dadooleeł, they will hold a meeting with them.

yiłch'al, he is lapping it.

yił chxǫ', I ruined it.

yił yidiniiyood, he drove it off with it (as a packhorse with a load).

yił hodoolnih, he will tell him of it.

yiłkaahi, t'áadoo, before dawn.

yiłmaz, he is shaking it (his head); he is whirling it around.

yił nákai, they (three, or more) returned with him.

yił nákaigo, after they returned with him.

yił nát'áázh, he returned with him.

yił ndaazne', they played a game with them.

yiłne', bitsiits'iin, he is nodding his head.

yiłní, he says to him.

yił siké, he is sitting with him.

yiłtsei, it is dry.

yił yíkai, he came with them; they arrived with him.

yi'na', he crawled.

yináádááł, he is walking around it.

yinááda'niidą́ą́', they again start eating it.

yinaagi, around it; in the vicinity of it.

yinaalnish, he works on it.

yinaalnishgo, when he works on it.

yinabiniłtiingo, when he teaches him.

yi'nah, he is crawling.

yinahjį', against it.

yinahódídéołkił, he will ask him about it.

yináká, through it.

yináldzid, he is afraid of them; he fears them.

yináldzidge, because he was afraid of it.

yinaa'niłtin, he teaches it.

yinant'a'í, their chief; their boss.

yiná'oołzhish, he is dancing around it.

yinás'na', he crawled around it.

yi'na'', yiih, he crawled into it.

yináyóóki', he asks him for it.

yindaalnish, they are working on it.

yindaha'áá lá, they are planning on it.

yinda'idiłkid, they are asking about it.

yinda'niłtinigíí, what they teach.

yíndiłkoh, he vomits it out.

yíneedlį, he is interested in it; he is enthusiastic about it.

yinééł, they are moving along (with their household goods, etc.).

yinéełgo, while they were moving along.

yinééł'íí', he looked at it; he examined it.

yineez'įį'go, because he stole it.

yine'go'ąą, over behind it.

yine'jį', to a point behind it.

yiní'át'éegi, know for sure; assure beyond question.

yinichjih, you know how.

yinida'ilzhiish, they are dancing around it.

yinidayóókeed, they are asking him for its return.

yínii', I head about it; I guess it (as in a moccasin game).

yiniihí, t'áadoo, without his knowing it.

yini'įįh, he is stealing it; he steals them.

yiniiłdea, I took a shot at it; I fired at it.

yíniił na'adá, to worry, or get worried; melancholy.

yiniinaa, on account of it; because of it. (Also biniinaa).

yiniiyé, for that purpose; for that reason.

yi'nil, baa, they were given to him.

yi'nílę́ę, haa, what was given him.

yinílyé, you are called; your name is.........

yinít'į́, he is looking at it; he is examining it.

yiniłtsá, you saw it; you have seen it.

yiniłtsą́ągo, if you see it.

yinináádaha'á, they are again making plans for it.

yínínii', you heard about it.

yinínił, yaa, he gave them to them.

yiníshbaal, I am holding it up (as a curtain).

yínishtą', I am holding on to it.

yinishyé, I am called; my name is.........

yinit'į́, haa, he bothers him; he talks about him.

yinízin, he wants it.

yinízinii, one who wants it.

yi'ołgóó, doo, because it was not floating along.

yisbąs, I am driving it (a car, wagon).

yisdá, safety; into a safe place.

yisdáákai, they escaped to safety; they survived.

yisdá 'á'níił, salvation.

yisdááyá, he, or I survived.

yisdá bidi'doot'ish, they will be led to safety.

yisdádíínáát, you will survive; you will be saved.

yisdádoo'niłígíí, the fact that they will be saved.

yisdáhaaskai, they escaped to safety.

yisdah hóyéé', ill-ventilated.

yisdah jizlį́į́', to be out of breath; to be puffing; to be panting.

yisdah nízin, he is out of breath; he is breathing hard.

yisdá'li'níłgi, salvation.

yisdá 'iiniiłii, saviour.

yisdáiłtį, I saved him; I rescued him.

yisdá nihidooniłígíí, one who will save us.

yisdáshiiłtį, he saved me; he recused me.

yisdáyííłtínę́ę, the one that he had saved; the one he rescued.

yisdáyíinil, he saved them; he rescued them.

yisdił, concussion, jar.

yisdiz, it is twisted; I am spinning it.

yisénah, baa, I forgot about it.

yishá, I am eating it; I eat them.

yisháą da, doo, I do not eat them; I do not like it (food).

yishínéé̱ł' I am moving (with belongings).

yisháát, I am walking.

yishbéézh, I am boiling it.

yishbizh, it is braided; I am braiding it.

yishcháá', he smelled it; he scented it.

yishch'il, it is curly; it (shirt, etc.) is wrinkled.

yishdlá, I am drinking it.

yishdleeshgo, while I was painting it; while I was coating it (with wax, paint, etc.).

yishdloh, I am laughing; I am smiling.

yishgal, I ate it up (meat).

yishgał, I am eating it (meat).

yishgish, incision.

yishhizh, I am harvesting it (corn).

yishideestsxis, he threw me against it.

yish'į́, I see it.

yish'įį łeh, I usually see him.

yish'nah, I am crawling; I am creeping.

yishnéé̱ł, I am moving (with belongings).

yisht'į́, I am rich (or wealthy) in it; I am visible.

yisht'íinii, my wealth.

yishtłizh, it is brown.

yishzhoh, it is damp.

yiską́ągo, tomorrow.

Yiská Damjjgo, Saturday.

yiskah, he shot it (with bow and arrow).

yiskándą́á', naaki, two days ago.

yisk'is, to crack (a very fine, barely visible crack as those in turquoise).

yisnááh, captive.

yisnil, he keeps them.

yisoł, he is blowing on it.

yistoł, shiné'édił, I have a nosebleed.

yist'éí, luch; subsistence.

yist'įįd, he got rich in it.

yistin, it is frozen; it is cold. **Shíla' yistin.** My hands are cold.

yistłé, stockings; socks.

yistłeel'óól, garter.

yistł'in, pile (a heap).

yistł'ónígíí, textile.

yistseel, I am chopping it.

yítaa, amongst them.

yíta'gi, at a place, or a point between them.

yit'ah, it is flying (bird, airplane, etc.).

yitahakááh, they join them.

yitahgóó, out amongst them.

yitah tádookai, they went around amongst them.

yit'į, it is visible; he is rich in it.

yit'įįgo, since it is visible; since he is rich in it.

yítł'is, it became hard (as concrete, etc).

yitłish, he is falling.

yitłishgo, while he was falling.

yitł'ó, she is weaving it.

yit'ood, to wipe off.

yits'ą́ądóó, from it.

yits'ąąįį', away from him.

yits'á'ńdei'nitgo, when they separate them from them.

yits'áníyá, he went away from it.

yits'áyiiniitgo, while he was separating them from them.

yitsee', its tail (or their tails).

yits'éininil, he separated them from it.

yiwozh, to be ticklish.

yiyii'aal, he chewed it.

yiyíįh, to melt.

yiyiinil, yiIh, he put them into it.

yiyíiyį, yiih, he put it (a pack, etc.) into it.

yiyiizhgizh, he cut them (ropes, etc.) off.

yiyoł, approaching sandstorm; approaching wind.

yíyooyił, he is pushing it along.

yizák'iidiinii', he strangled him.

yizdlad, it cracked.

yízeez, I singed it.

yízhchį, he or, it was born.

yizhchįįdą́ą́', at the time of its birth.

yízhi, name.

yízhǫǫd, tamed.

yizts'ǫs, he sucked it (once); he kissed it.

yódí, valued possessions; wealth.

yókeedgo, since he was asking for it.

yóó 'ahoolzhóód, the storm is passed; it (weather) cleared up.

yoo', beads, necklace; bells.

yóó 'anájah, bee, he usually chases them away.

yóó 'anídeeshwoł, I will escape; I will run away.

yóó bee bighá da'diltsasí, bead drill.

yooch'íid, a lie; a falsehood.

yooch'iid "át'é, it is a lie.

yooch'iid yinił'a', you have lied.

yoo' diits'a'í, bell.

yoodlą́ą́', he drank it.

yóó'eelwod, he ran away; he escaped.

yoo'į, he sees it.

yóó 'iiyá, I am lost; he is lost.

yooldéél, he ate them (separable objects, as sugar cubes, etc.).

yoo' nitchíní, button.

yoo' nitchini bá bigháhoodzánigíí, button hole.

yoo' nímazí, (silver) bead.

yoosbą́, he earned it; he won it.

yooshnééh, bee, do not let me forget it.

yoostsah, ring (for ringer).

yoostsah bináá', ring set.

Yootó, Santa Fe, New Mexico.

yooyéelgo, while he was hauling it along.

yooyéłę́ę, what he was hauling along.

yeoznah, yaa he forgot about it.

yówehdi, farther on.

– Z –

zahelánii, mocking bird.

zas, snow. (Also yas).

zéédevldoi, neckerchief.

zéédééltsoozí, scarf; neckerchief.

zéédéet'i'i, neckie.

zéé'iilwo'ii, foxtail grass.

zénézt'i'i, shirt collar; necktie.

www.ingramcontent.com/pod-product-compliance
Lightning Source LLC
Jackson TN
JSHW011403130125
77033JS00023B/821